~~SLOW~~
~~DOWN~~
~~PILGRIM~~

— CAMINO DE SANTIAGO —

PART ONE
SAINT-JEAN-PIED-DE-PORT
TO BURGOS

~~PAUL MIDDLETON~~

Copyright© Paul M Ltd 2024
This book is sold subject to the condition that it shall not, by way of trade or otherwise, be lent, resold, hired out, or otherwise circulated without the publisher's prior consent in any form of binding or cover than that in which it is published and without a similar condition including this condition being imposed on the subsequent publisher.
The moral right of Paul Middleton has been asserted.

ISBN: 9798326139672

'Save a seat for me at God's Bar, mate.'

This journey of a million steps wouldn't have been possible without the support of:
→ Rosie Mills → Terry Bush → Martha Le Poidevin → Joss Gillespie
→ Kezia Richmond → Carly Lazarus-Dittrich → Judith & Dani
→ Emma McDonald → Sophie Elder → Lovisa Holst
→ Chris Lonie → Lucinda Meade → Neil French.

I have tried to recreate events, locales and conversations from my memories of them. In order to maintain their anonymity in some instances I have changed the names of individuals and places. I may have changed some identifying characteristics and details such as physical properties, occupations and places of residence.

Saint-Jean-Pied-de-Port – Burgos

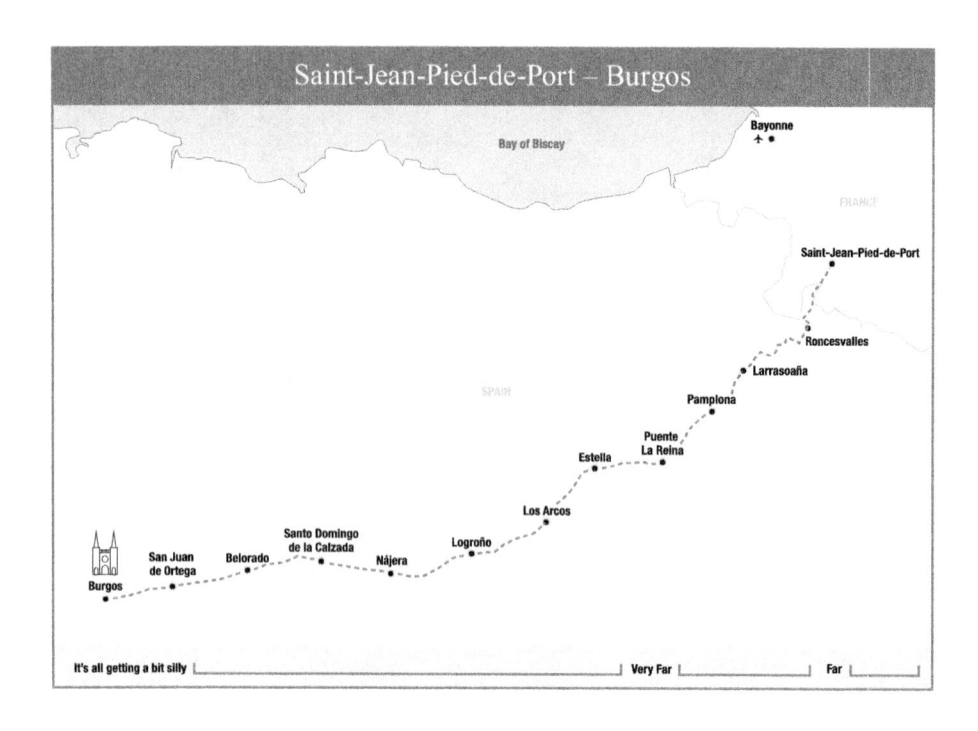

Bayonne

Bay of Biscay

FRANCE

Saint-Jean-Pied-de-Port

Roncesvalles

Larrasoaña

SPAIN

Pamplona

Puente La Reina

Estella

Los Arcos

Logroño

Nájera

Santo Domingo de la Calzada

Belorado

San Juan de Ortega

Burgos

It's all getting a bit silly   Very Far   Far

CONTENTS

Ghosts..06

Chapter 1 – Highway to Hell..09

Chapter 2 – Last Supper..16

Chapter 3 – Fellowship..24

Chapter 4 – Sleeping Giant...35

Chapter 5 – Honeymoon...53

Chapter 6 – Poohsticks..68

Chapter 7 – Dream to Me..83

Chapter 8 – Spirit...95

Chapter 9 – Slow Down Pilgrim...109

Chapter 10 – Detox...124

Chapter 11 – It's time...139

Chapter 12 – First Date..157

Chapter 13 – Big Toe 'Tone'..177

Chapter 14 – Eye Spy...192

Chapter 15 – 72 Beds..193

Chapter 16 – 7 Caminos...208

~~GHOSTS~~

September 2012, Finisterre, Galicia

"Can anyone else see them, or is it just me?"

All around me, newly arrived day-trippers shuffled about, like emperor penguins, with their heads hunched, beaks chattering and feet waddling from side-to-side. The relief on their faces was plain for all to see. They'd finally arrived at the 'End of the World': the lighthouse at Finisterre. The rock-bound peninsula situated on one of the most westerly points on Galicia, Spain.

But their journey there, hugging the treacherous 'Coast of Death' (the graveyard of too many a ship and sailor) had left them in a perilous position.

To pee or not to pee? That was the question.

Whatever decision they chose would decide their fate. If they prioritised pee before purchase, they risked missing out on the 'deals of the day' amongst the tourist tat of the market stalls. Yet, if they prioritised tat before tinkling, they risked something even bigger. Personally, I wasn't one for playing Russian Roulette with my bladder – but that's just me.

Thankfully, the vast majority of tourists opted for the safety and sanctuary of the khazi. However, there were a few rogue hustlers prepared to risk it all in the market's mosh pit. They headed there eagerly with their elbows out, shoulders wide, and hands nervously fingering the zip on their bum bags.

While all these shenanigans were going on, my eyes were drawn elsewhere – to the horizon. Out of the corner of my eye, I saw two flickers of movement. What was it? I raised my hand towards my forehead, in the vain hope that it would help me see through the piercing brightness of the sun and the shimmering heat haze.

Then slowly, the blurred shapes took form. I could see two figures, walking in single file, about five hundred metres out. They appeared locked in a battle of wills against a fierce headwind. A wind that seemed hell-bent on throwing them off the tightrope-thin path, and onto the razor-sharp rocks below. But neither walker seemed fazed. They simply tightened the shoulder straps on their packs, leaned into the wind and ploughed on.

Who were these two? What were they doing here? And why were they carrying the world and its wife on their backs? I didn't know. But there was something about this image that stirred a memory from deep within my soul.

Suddenly, I was transported back in time to Snowdonia National Park. I was a scrawny, bowl-headed, buck-toothed seventeen-year-old again, taking part in the Gold Duke of Edinburgh. I could see myself and my best mate George, hanging off the back of the pack that included Higgs, Pepe, Big Steve and Buddha. George and I were fucked.

Fucked from a sleepless night spent shivering inside a Force Ten tent, while Wales unleashed a biblical rainstorm that would make Moses twitchy. Fucked from a route that ragged us for eight hours over some of Wales' fearsome ridges. And fucked from a whole day living off cold rations and Farley's Rusks. It was deemed too wet, too wild, and too windy to light our Trangia cooking stoves – or put a brew on.

But that night, as we crawled broken and piss-wet through into our damp sleeping bags, I could sense pride and exhilaration deep within us all. None of us had ever felt so uncomfortable, so vulnerable and so far out of our depth – but we were loving it.

Which was exactly the same look the couple trudging towards me wore. Yes, their faces had been baked hard by the sun. Yes, their bodies were creaking under the immense weight of their packs. Yes, their feet appeared battered and broken by blisters. But there was a steeliness and an unshakeable pride in their eyes. They knew the pain of today's blisters would soon become tomorrow's badges of honour. Forever weaved into the very fabric of the epic journey they had undertaken.

The couple were just across the car park from me now. Eighty metres and closing. What intrigued me most though, was the fact that only I seemed able to see them. Which was the reason why I had called out, "Can anyone else see them, or is it just me?"

The simple answer was no. No one else could. While the day-trippers appeared lost in a world of two-for-one offers, shells and snow globes. I was caught between two worlds. The real world, and the 'other world' the walkers inhabited.

The female walker was quick to seize on my perplexed gaze as she headed towards me. It was as she drew near, I started to notice her rag-tag look, her walking stick, fashioned from a bit of dead wood and the wincing in her face. It was then that she smiled, winked and whispered "Buen Camino".

"Buen Camino?" I muttered in reply.

What the hell did that mean? Well, I knew 'buen' meant good. But what was a 'Camino'? As she passed by, I turned, curious to see where they were headed. Other than the nineteenth century, white-washed granite lighthouse, the hermitage of Saint Guillerme and the rocks overlooking the Atlantic – there didn't appear much else there.

It was then that I noticed a three-foot high, stone granite marker. It lay halfway between the market stalls and the lighthouse to the left of the path. It was there they stopped dead in their tracks. For almost a minute they stood in awed silence, as if having seen a ghost. What was the significance of the marker? Why were they drawn to it?

"Yaaaaaaaaaaaaaaaaaaaaaaaaaaaaaaaay!"

Suddenly, out of nowhere, there came this howl of raw human emotion. One that was filled with pride, relief and exhaustion – then came the tears.

For several minutes I lingered nearby. Pretending, but failing miserably, to look out across the abyss that Galicia offered. I was too intrigued to go anywhere else. After several minutes, the two walkers shuffled off arm-in-arm along the concrete. That was when I swooped in.

The granite marker stone that they'd stared at was shaped like a regular pedestrian cone, just bigger. Set into it were two key features. Near the top, was a blue and yellow coloured tile. The blue of the tile formed the background, whilst the yellow fanned out in a rather crude-looking shell shape. Halfway down the marker, I could see a four-inch long, pencil-thin brass plaque. Engraved on it in black was 'Km 0,000'.

So, if this was the end, where the hell was the beginning?

By now the couple were long gone. Yet I had so many questions. As I slowly wandered back, down the road into Finisterre, I couldn't shake off what I'd seen. I'd just seen *two ghosts*. Why was I the only one who saw them? Why me? And what was with the whole, 'Buen Camino' thing?

I'd initially come to Spain to capture a glimpse of my heroes in the Vuelta a España. Yet something in the faces of those two ghosts told me my life was about to be nudged in a whole new direction.

Km 0,000 wasn't the end of my journey. It would be the very beginning.

CHAPTER 1: HIGHWAY TO HELL

January 2015, The Shire (Home)
"I think your mate's been killed in Afghanistan."

It was just after midnight when the Grim Reaper appeared in my bedroom. Armed as ever with his trusty scythe. At the time I, much like my Samsung phone, had been sleeping soundly.

Beep, beep, beep, beep.

My first thought when my phone started beeping was to chuckle. Typically, any incoming text at this ungodly hour would be nonsensical gibberish. Gibberish littered with profanities, pettiness, and inappropriate gags. Or better still, as was in this instance, 'The Misadventures of the Intrepid Mr. Lynch,' who would undoubtedly be in one of three precarious situations:

1. Outside one of the late-night chippies along Castle Foregate, Shrewsbury. Moaning about how hard our BTEC course was in '91, how hard it is to lose weight while fighting off the ravenous hoards daring to steal his stunning doner kebab, chips, salad and – you guessed it – his Diet Coke.

2. Talking conspiracy theories to the great unwashed of the 'Shire.'

3. Face-planted into the cleavage of a large-breasted, equally inebriated bint in one of the late-night bars that remind me of Mos Eisley from Star Wars.

Whilst I always appreciated updates of his deviant behaviour, what I wasn't quite prepared for were the words, 'I think your mate's been killed'. These words seemed to flash like a beacon at me from my phone screen.

I slowly wriggled my way up to sitting, while scraping the crusty eye bogies from my pillow-indented face. As I did, I had one thought: if I wriggled and shook my phone hard enough, would it be possible to make the words I'd read slip off their text line? Thus, plunging them into the ether – lost forever? Sadly, this wasn't the case. If anything, the words just glared harder at me, as I read and re-read each one in shocked disbelief. By the tenth time of reading, I could feel my mind start to whir and get antsy.

"Hang on a feckin' minute. It's Friday. It's midnight, and the source of this rather dubious info, 'The Intrepid Mr. Lynch', would be cabbaged and dad dancing." I muttered to myself.

He was, if nothing else, utterly predictable. So why was I getting wound up by his vague, and as yet, unsubstantiated nonsense? I didn't know. But what intrigued me was how this info had got inside his wispy-haired, Mekon-shaped dome in the first place?

The only logical explanation I could think of after him having supped eight pints of cider would be that perhaps he'd got himself into a muddle. My guess was he'd taken one half-baked story, added another and mixed them with a little dash of lime and soda. And hey presto – madness.

But what really gripped my shitter was: what was I supposed to do with this info? I had a location, yes – Afghanistan. But I had no name, no regiment and no source. In short, I was fecked.

I certainly wasn't about to start pinging messages to mates to ask if I could have their car, bike or their holiday homes. If they had somehow found themselves well, kinda, maybe... a little bit dead (which was the standard joke).

The only thing I could do was dismiss it for what it was. The ramblings of a madman. Who, at this hour, would be bouncing along the pavement caked in dinner medals and kebab juice. With that thought squared away in my mind, I put my phone down in the hope that I'd finally be able to get some shut-eye.

But who was I kidding? I could feel thoughts start to slam hard against my brain's tired and empty domed walls.

What if The Intrepid Mr. Lynch is right?

Seriously! Surely to feck, my conscience wasn't going to entertain this. But with each passing second, the 'what if' seeds of doubt started to germinate and grow.

"Oh! For fuck's sake!" I muttered.

Reluctantly, I reached across and turned on my bedside light. I then quickly grabbed a pen and paper and began to write a list of all the military lads I knew who were overseas.

The list didn't take long. When it was done, I stared down at six names. Of those, two had been pinged dad-dancing in Birmingham. While they'd undoubtedly be hanging by morning, they'd survive. Three others, if I trusted their social media feed (or more importantly – them), were safely at home.

Which left only one person unaccounted for – Mitch.

The last time I'd spoken to him, he was sipping on cocktails in some swanky, Cambodian bar (which sounded surreal). I'd known Mitch for twenty years. We'd met, much like George, Higgs, Pepe, Big Steve and Buddha, during our time in the Air Cadets. Long before Mitch tootled off to join the RAF, quit the RAF, before re-joining the RAF and quitting again.

Upon leaving, he'd somehow *smeagoled* his way (his words) into a job with an American munitions company. It was a role he was born to do. Mainly because it involved blowing shit up. The shit being war remnants that had been left behind and posed a threat to the local civilian population.

Was he still in Cambodia? Or had he moved on? It was hard to tell. The only thing I knew for sure was his family's home was closer to Afghanistan than Cambodia was. Therefore, if he was in either of those places, he'd be the best part of four thousand miles from harm's way. A distance, and odds, that I was very happy with.

If you're worried Numbnuts, why not text the lad?

Came the ever-familiar, almost rational sound of my conscience.

Text Mitch, and say what? Are you still shit with a sand wedge? I muttered.

I got halfway through a text before I binned it off. Something wasn't sitting well with me. But what was it?

I knew 'The Intrepid Mr. Lynch' knew Mitch. They'd met twice before. The first time during one of his infamous homecoming piss-ups in Shrewsbury. The second, more comical occasion, was when I was getting frogmarched out of a local late-night bar, by two burly bouncers on the suspicion of, wait for it – drug dealing.

What was comical about the situation was everyone knew who the dealers were. Me not being one of them. While I resisted telling the bouncers the truth of why I'd spent thirty minutes locked in a toilet cubicle (with an unexpected bout of diarrhoea), Mitch stood casually at the bar, sipping his Guinness and chuckling wildly.

So 'The Intrepid Mr. Lynch' knew Mitch. But Mitch, to Shire folk was, much like me – an outsider. Which begs the question: how, having not seen Mitch in two years, did 'The Intrepid Mr. Lynch' conjure up his name? Also, who the hell could he have bumped into in a rural farming community, who was a) military and b) knew Mitch?

The next morning, I woke up exhausted and irritable. I opted to bypass my immediate need of conducting a Spanish Inquisition. Instead, I opted to ping Jim a message. Jim was a top lad, well respected and known for both his level-headedness and savage wit.

He was also well connected within the golf club where Mitch's family played. He, like me, was highly sceptical of what I'd been told. But due to the sensitivity of it, he said he'd keep an ear out – and let me know.

The next two weeks crawled by cruelly. There was no word from anyone. No social media updates. No chatter in texts. Nor any updates in the local press. With each passing day, the silence grew and grew – to the point that it had become deafening. What I'd originally dismissed as madness left me raw, empty and filled with dread. Until finally, I snapped.

"Fuck this! I've had enough of dancing around this bullshit."

With that, I pulled out my mobile, scrolled through the numbers until Mitch's contact details came up, then hit CALL.

"Come on...come on, for feck's sake", I began strumming my fingers impatiently on the desk.

"Why! Why is it taking so feckin' long to connect, you useless bag of wank? Honest to..." By now, my patience had run out.

The only explanation I could think of was that Mitch was out in the arse end of nowhere practising his golf shots. Or in some club, taking selfies with his latest all-singing-all-dancing mega-pixel mobile. A mobile that would simultaneously allow him to play Tetris and record videos in high definition. But failed to do the job it was intended for – to make and receive calls.

Beep, beep, beep, beep.

Finally, it started to ring. All I needed now was for Mitch to put down his sand wedge, stop blowing kisses at camels and pick up. And I knew as soon as he did, I'd have to hang up. Or I'd be hit with a torrent of sarcastic abuse. But even that was better than the numbed silence.

"Hi, this is Mitch. I'm a bit busy at the moment..."

I'd been fooled by this gag before. He'd typically wait, just long enough for me to get flustered before unleashing a tirade of one-liners. But not today.

"Mitch, it's Monkey. Put down your sand wedge for a second and stop, for feck's sake, blowing kisses at the frisky camels. You know how horny it makes them? Let me know when you are back in the Shire – as it's my round." I said enthusiastically.

When I'd finally hung up, I felt a weight had been lifted. I was relieved that no part of my tone came across as alarmist or concerned. I knew if he picked up on even the slightest whiff of that he'd tear strips off me. Most likely something along the lines of, "It's about fucking time you bought me a Guinness, student boy."

God, I'd have loved to have heard him say that. Or hear his infectious cackle that always used to set me off. But no, not that day.

Then one Saturday, just as I was finishing a Pilates class, the call came in. As soon as I saw the caller ID, Magic (my pet name for my mum), my stomach dropped. Nervously, I fumbled with my phone as my sweaty forefinger hit the receive button.

For a second there was nothing, just static. There was none of the usual, warm bubbly greeting I'd come to expect from my mum. Nor was there an enthusiastic,

"Hi Babs," (her pet name for me) delivered in a soft, southern Irish accent.

"Magic, are you alright honey?" I asked.

My words seemed to hang in the air for an age before shattering on the wooden floor at my feet. Shit, this was bad – really bad.

"Babs, there's been an accident..."

I could feel her voice crack and tremble as she delivered these words. This must be horrifying, especially as she had known Mitch for twenty years too.

I could feel my chest begin to tighten and my lungs started to scramble for air. I wanted to reply, but the words got choked in my throat.

"It's Mitch. There's been an accident in Herat..."

Her voice tailed off as she tried to compose herself. At this point I'd already started crying. This was feckin' awful.

"...I'm so sorry. Mitch... Mitch has been killed."

Instantly, I could feel bile start to travel up and down my windpipe, much like the high striker game you'd see in the old circus.

Her words were met with a wall of numbed silence. Suddenly, everything around me started to fall away, the walls, the floor, the lighting. I was now standing alone, in a darkened and eerie landscape. All around me was death, and the only source of comfort came from Magic's soft, thoughtful voice.

I tried to keep up with her conversation, but my mind had gone. All I heard were the words: *Herat... Afghanistan... explosion.* What more did I need to know?

My mind's way of dealing with the pain of his loss was to fill my head with images of our youth. From our first meeting at the Air Cadets when he joined aged thirteen, to him and Hatters turning up for a DofE expedition with a rucksack full of lager, the sound of his cackle then panic at almost setting his tent alight with a stray match, the time I drove him back to his parents' house in pitch darkness (I hadn't quite worked out to dip the headlights on my Mark 2 Escort). Or Mitch's all-time classic, the day he called to ask me if I fancied going to Paris for a cup of tea, courtesy of Eurostar.

I left the Pilates class numb, confused and utterly convinced that both Magic and 'The Intrepid Mr. Lynch' had got it wrong. After all, this was Mitch we were talking about, not some regular Joe. Mitch was like Harry Houdini. His ability to get out of the tightest of scraps and come up smelling of roses was legendary.

Dark days soon followed. The next thing I recall was pulling up in my car, as the coffin bearers were wheeling his coffin into church. Even then, none of it seemed real.

Upon seeing the coffin my mind flashed back to a scene from one of my favourite movies, *Steptoe & Son Rides Again*. In it, old man Steptoe fakes his own death. All in an attempt to get Frankie Barrow, a loan shark, off his back and cash in on a life insurance policy.

All was going exactly to plan, until they lowered old man Steptoe's coffin into the ground. It was then he lost it and began screaming like a banshee to let him out. The effect of which caused many relatives and well-wishers to faint.

Why had that sprung to mind? And why now? It wasn't a time for laughter. Or maybe I was just hoping that Mitch had one final gag up his sleeve. Sadly, this idea, like many in the previous week, would go unanswered.

Then during the service, I started to hear the faintest sounds of whispering. At first, I thought it was simply feedback from someone's hearing aid. Was I losing the plot? What was making the sound? The whisper felt as though it was moving its way through the church pews, as if seeking someone out. Somehow, I knew it was headed my way, the effect of which sparked a memory.

It was the memory of the couple walking in Finisterre. And the moment when the girl turned to me, smiled and said *"Buen Camino"*.

Did Mitch have anything to do with this? But how could he? Or was this simply my mind seeking a safe haven, away from the deafening silence? Soon after the ceremony, I bumped into two familiar faces from the DofE days – Hatters and Buddha. As we stood reminiscing, one thought kept reappearing.

We all missed the freedom, camaraderie and adventures of those wild days in Wales.

That thought stuck with me as I headed home. That and the sound of "Buen Camino" ringing in my ears. By now I'd learnt that it meant 'good Camino'. Much like how I'd learnt that the word Camino was associated with pilgrimage – or a long walk.

I'd read that one of the most famous pilgrim routes belonged to the Camino Francés, which formed a seven-hundred-and-ninety-nine-kilometre walk, from Saint-Jean-Pied-de-Port in the foothills of the Pyrenees to the cathedral at Santiago de Compostela or Finisterre – Km 0,000.

As I closed my eyes that night, choking back the tears, I couldn't shake the images of the young couple. It felt as though they'd handed me an invisible torch. One that at first, I didn't want to accept or bear. Now I could feel myself reach and grab for it. I couldn't think of a more fitting way to say goodbye to Mitch.

And this time around I wouldn't be asking him to carry a Bergen, a Force Ten tent or to live off AB biscuits or Farley's Rusks. All I'd ask was he took a seat at God's Bar, grab himself a Guinness and sit back and watch the show.

This Camino would be in memory of Mitch. It would also be my chance to raise funds for Help For Heroes, a charity set up to support service personnel injured in service.

Mitch's legacy would forever be the thousands of lives he'd undoubtedly helped save through his work in Cambodia, Afghanistan and around the globe.

A new path had been laid for me. As if to signify this, Mitch's encore of 'Highway to Hell' came blasting out of the church speakers.

~~CHAPTER 2: LAST SUPPER~~

29th August 2016, Holmewood Gardens, Brixton
I woke at 6 am from slumber like a bear wakes from hibernation. Slowly, thoughtfully, but with a hunger that could embarrass a street urchin.

As I lay in bed, I quickly ran through my pre-morning checks:
- Head - Check
- Arms - Check
- Legs - Check.

Everything seemed attached. Granted, that was no guarantee that everything worked. But it was as good a place to start. With that in mind, I waddled off down the corridor towards the bathroom, looking like a baby chimp with a full nappy.

"Wakey, wakey."

I blasted the cold water from the shower head against my naked body.

"Holy-Mary-Mother-of-God! A-r-r-g-h!"

Within seconds, my teeth and body shook wildly. I hated cold showers. No, it was worse than that, I loathed them. But I'd learnt over the years that waterboarding myself awake was the quickest way to get my brain sparking. Once washed, I wandered back to my room. As I did, an old, military mantra kept repeating itself.

Prior Preparation and Planning Prevents Piss Poor Performance.

The 7 Ps as they are known, are the backbone to success. While they can't prevent me from being mugged by a gang of marauding field mice, trampled by a herd of line-dancing cattle, or yodelled to death by a group of close harmony Austrian ramblers, they would, at least, minimise the number of, 'Oh, for fuck's sake' moments on my Camino.

First off, kit check. Traditionally, my kit got squared away two to three days prior to departure (and this trip was no exception). Then, on the day of travel (today), I'd pull everything out from my Osprey pack, and start again. I began by laying everything out on the bed. I did this in the order of feet first, then slowly worked upwards.

That gave me one last chance to prevent any 'Oh, for fuck's sake,' prior to the off.

On the bed before me I could see:
- 1 pair of Meindl walking shoes (plus spare laces)
- 1 pair of New Balance trainers
- 3 pairs of Smartwool walking socks
- 3 pairs of boxer shorts
- 2 pairs of Rab traverse walking shorts
- 2 pairs of Rab base layer tops
- 1 Help For Heroes t-shirt
- 1 Rab fleece
- 1 set of waterproofs
- 1 travel towel
- 1 sunscreen bottle
- 1 wash kit
- 1 telephone charger
- 2 Sigg traveller 0.6L water bottles
- 1 Petzl head torch
- 1 washing line
- 3 sets of 3M ear plugs
- 1 Twat hat
- 1 pack of Maynards wine gums

Emergency kit
- 1 compass/whistle
- Emergency rations - 2 Wayfayrer all day breakfast camping meals

Travel documents/others
- 1 passport
- 1 travel insurance printout
- 2 plane tickets
- 1 Pilgrim Passport
- Michelin Guide to Camino de Santiago.

I knew just looking at my kit, there wasn't much fat in my pack. There were no iPads, no overdue library books, no hair straighteners or jazz mags. To the point that it wasn't looking overly full.

But try telling that to my conscience. It was only too keen to plant seeds of doubt and stir up old insecurities of expeditions from days gone by.

Are three pairs of socks enough? What if it rains? What if you can't get to dry them in time? Remember the time you got trench foot? You don't want that again surely? If you recall, it took six months to regain any sensation in your big toes. What about a sleeping bag? Roncesvalles is three-thousand-two-hundred feet above sea level, so at night it's gonna get cold. How about taking an extra fleece, just in case? You know, you'll kick yourself if you don't. And what's with the emergency rations? They made sense on the DofE expeditions, where you're only allowed to eat what you carry. But you don't have to do that. Plus, you do know Spain has shops?

My conscience's chit-chat always had a way of stirring my inner madness. But this time I was saved by the most unlikely of sources. None other than Baloo from *The Jungle Book*. While my conscience was arguing the pros and cons of food vs fleece, Baloo was starting to dance around inside my head, singing the 'Bare Necessities.' He made a good point.

With no more gear allowed in my pack, by order of Baloo, I simply stuffed, zipped and clipped my pack shut. With the packing done, all that was left was to give my housemate Annie a hug goodbye.

Once that was done, I popped the lock and walked down the hallway towards the front door. With each step, I could feel my brain struggling to contain the wealth of emotions. I was energised, excited, relieved, nervous and just a tad anxious. But overriding all these emotions was the sense that finally, I was going home.

As I turned the latch to leave, I stopped and looked down at my feet. They were both half-in and half-out of the flat. It was then that it hit me, this was real. This was really happening. After months of thinking, dreaming and imagining it – *I was going on Camino*. And my very next step would be my first on it. A step I was more than happy to take.

I stopped outside Holmewood Gardens for a few seconds to take it all in. The beauty of the morning with its watery sun, the cheep of parakeets and the chuckle of a child walking with her dad. All I needed now was my trusty steed, known locally as the 35 bus, to appear and take me away from it all.

At the bus stop the usual argy-bargy was going on. I could feel the nervous energy of those around me as the bus drew near, and their demeanour darkened. Those already on board glared through the bus window at us in disdain. As we slowly boarded, we were welcomed with death stares, bags on vacant seats and uncompromising feet. Feet that planted defiantly and refused to budge.

Further down the bus, an old granny clung to a bus pole, like an out-of-work pole dancer. Her seat had been cruelly stolen by some young, scruffy, weed-smelling scrote in tracksuit bottoms who sat transfixed, staring into his phone's abyss, while homophobic drill rap rang out from its speakers.

I was about to escape this toxic, self-absorbed world of me-me-me, of greed, envy, poor manners and shit clothes. And I for one, couldn't be happier.

As I stepped from the bus pressure cooker at Clapham Junction, I smiled and said my thanks to the female driver. Her eyes seemed to say, "Why can't more people be like that?" This was followed milliseconds later by a commuter repeatedly bashing the bell and shouting, "Get off the bus you fat wanker. I haven't got all day."

Off I went into Clapham Junction train station, chuckling. I was now in search of a platform, peace of mind and my getaway vehicle – which was slowly starting to rev up on platform thirteen. Once inside, I sought out the emptiest carriage I could find. Then I propped my head against the window and duly – fell asleep.

I was woken some time later by the dulcet tones of the train announcer, who sounded remarkably like Boysie from *Only Fools and Horses*.

"Good afternoon, ladies and gentlemen. We'll shortly be arriving at Gatwick Airport."

Cushty. Within seconds of walking into the departure lounge I was hit by dot matrix flight screens displaying the immortal words: Delayed. Delayed. Delayed.

"Oh, for fuck's sake", I muttered.

There's one thing you could always count on when being English. No matter how much you plan, our transport network – whether rail, road or plane – will always find new and innovative ways to send your day sideways. Guaranteed.

Don't panic. Don't panic.

Instead of flapping, I did the next best thing – the maths. I knew roughly how long it would take to board, taxi, fly, disembark, reclaim my bag and grab a taxi. Therefore, I figured I had roughly one hour's wiggle room to play with. Anything close to, or over, that and I would miss my connecting train from Bayonne into Saint-Jean-Pied-de-Port.

But if Lady Luck was on my side, and I had a fair wind behind me, then I still had an outsider's chance of making it to Saint-Jean-Pied-de-Port by 6:30 pm. That would give more than enough time to drop my kit off, bag some scran and get my gob around a large glass of red. That was by no means ideal preparation for the next day's twenty-seven-kilometre schlep up and over the Col de Lepoeder. But it could definitely be a whole lot worse.

With the maths done, my mind started to calm. Then I had to remind myself that I was at the airport – I loved airports. There was always some drama going on, guaranteed. Whether that was families squabbling, kids kicking off or the amateur dramatics of people rocking up late, in floods of tears.

While I had one eye on the drama, I also had one eye in the sky, as allegedly the new Monarch Airlines digital display ads that I'd worked on were up. This would be my first chance to see them out in the wild. And much like an expectant father, I wanted the masses to stop, admire and validate how frighteningly smart I was (which in itself was laughable).

And there it was. A four-metre digital screen in the main hall, just by the escalators, leading up into the food court. The ad featured Rebekah, one of Monarch's most glamourous air hostesses attempting to recreate Bob Dylan's famous '*Subterranean Homesick Blues*' video. In it, she drops individual cards displaying holiday destinations, while above her head was the headline 'Where next?'

"You see that ad? I did that. Aren't I clever?" I muttered sarcastically to myself.

I stood around for a few minutes, my eyes flicking up towards the ad, all in the hope that others might join in and acknowledge my genius. But the truth of the matter was no one gave a shit. People in airports are more interested in checking out other people's partners, scratching their balls or mining for gold in the mine shafts of their nostrils while thinking about where they might head for their Last Supper.

I couldn't quite grasp the logic of promoting people's next holiday, prior to them taking their current one. But all the airlines were at it, offering last-minute flights or one-way deals. Which was perfect if you were a suicide bomber or someone looking for a cheap getaway to Dignitas. Why pay more?

With my self-gratification satisfied, I headed off to check-in.

"Good morning, sir, anything to declare?" said a sprightly, well-dressed chap.

Well, I wouldn't be declaring that last sentence. Within seconds, the cracks in my smile soon started to disappear, as I was given the heartbreaking news. My bag was oversized. Talk about bag-shaming me. It wasn't my pack's fault. It tried its best. It exercised, it got outdoors, it ate healthy and avoided sugars and fatty food (unlike the rest of the UK).

As the father to this 'fatty' I was ordered to do the walk of shame as I shuffled off to the oversized baggage area. Behind me, I could hear unforgiving sniggers of fellow travellers. I simply patted my pack on the head and told it everything was going to be alright.

My pack let out a somewhat depressed sigh as it hit the scales in the oversized baggage area. Nine point six kilograms. It was all my fault. I'd overfed it. Therefore, I took full responsibility for it. With my bag dropped off it was time to do the security dance.

Empty your pockets. Remove your shoes. Lose your belt. I pre-warned the bored, sour-faced-looking guard that this wasn't the best idea. My shorts were a little on the large side and losing the belt could affect my modesty.

"Feet apart. Arms out to the sides" came his blunt reply.

No sooner did my arms come up than my shorts came down. Fantastic. What a way to kick-start my holiday. Everyone in the queue started to snigger. While I stood there in my M&S parrot boxers, holding onto my shorts.

"Sir, would you mind going through the body scanner?"

That was a rhetorical question, right? What were the options? If it was simply a choice between the scanner and the glove – I was all about the scanner.

I stepped into the scanner, turning first one way, then the other. Is this what it felt like being a rotisserie chicken? I was desperate to ask what they were looking for. Or what was the dodgiest thing they'd ever come across? But on second thoughts, it seemed best not to poke the bear.

"Why me though?"

Why was it that every time I flew, I got stopped? Without fail. Was it because I liked to travel alone? Was it because I once owned a copy of U2's 'The Joshua Tree' album? That in itself was reason enough to not allow me on the plane. Or was it because I was half Irish? Surely not, it wasn't the eighties.

Far from upsetting me, all the horse-arsing around only fuelled my desire for mischief. With that in mind, I headed off to the departure lounge.

I spied with my little eye something beginning with... 'C'. Chicken shagger. 'W'. Wife swapper. 'H'. Hamster smuggler. These weren't the typical antics you'd expect from a forty-two-year-old, but it passed the time.

After fifteen minutes, I was bored. Plus, I was becoming aware that stomach numbers two and three had started to growl.

"Righto, lads. Last Supper time. Now, where's it going to be?"

The Last Supper was created by me as a way to offset my irrational fear of flying. The idea behind it was very simple. If the plane I was about to board ditched into the drink, what meal would I like inside me before I entered Dante's Inferno? While the idea of dying didn't bother me – the idea of dying hungry did.

Choices...choices...choices. I knew – Nando's. What with their long wooden tables, healthy-ish food and great views across the airfield. What more could I ask for? Surely even JC and his disciples would approve of this.

I was shown to a seat on a single table, overlooking the runway. Not that I minded, though it did leave me feeling like a travel leper. But at least I got seated five minutes before the large groups of people started amassing.

I didn't bother with the menu. I knew I wanted a half chicken, medium spice with creamy mash and coleslaw. With that ordered, I settled down on their plush, red leather seats and waited excitedly to be served.

"Waaaaaaaaaaaaaaaaaaaaahhhhhhhhhhhhhhhhh!"

All hell broke loose. On the table opposite there was a newborn baby wailing like a banshee. Not that I cared. I was still in south London mode, so I kept my head down, avoiding the risk of eye contact.

"Waaaaaaaaaaaaaaaaaaaaahhhhhhhhhhhhhhhhh!"

This stopped me seeing the child but did nothing for the high-pitched shrieking. One minute turned to two. Two minutes of shrieking turned to three. I wasn't far behind the baby at that point. My stomachs were empty, and I was about to start wailing too.

"Waaaaaaaaaaaaaaaaaaaaahhhhhhhhhhhhhhhhh!"

God love her. Whoever was trying to sort this baby out deserved a medal. Not only had the mum not reacted, but her voice also carried with it the sound of an angel.

"Here you go, half a chicken with creamy mash and coleslaw. Is there anything else I can get for you?" said the smiling waiter.

His eyes acknowledged mine, and he quickly retreated. Far and away from the fallout zone of the squawking.

"Don't be a dick, Monkey! Help the lady out."

That was the voice of Mitch inside my head. He was right, I couldn't avoid the situation any longer. But my timing couldn't have been worse. As I looked up, I came face-to-face with the sight of a mum, holding her baby out at arm's length. She was doing this as the little fella had only gone and shat through his nappy. There was shit everywhere. Over the mum's shirt, jeans, the floor and the inside of the baby buggy.

Before I'd even had time to think, I was up and headed her way (backed up by a flurry of Nando's staff). I came with the only two things I could find: a handful of napkins and my somewhat quirky sense of humour.

"Jesus, what did the little fella order?" I said while wearing the biggest grin my face could muster. As strategic approaches go, I'd gone for shit or bust.

"Home-made juice," she replied with a flicker of a smile.

"Thank God! My chicken over there was starting to get nervous," I chuckled.

My approach, far from heightening the situation, made things marginally better. With that, I handed over the armload of napkins I'd come over with.

"Good lad, Monkey!" came the sound of Mitch's voice inside my head.

By now, my appetite had gone. As I headed out of Nando's I knew one thing was for certain – as Last Suppers went, this had been memorable. It was then that the plane was called. Next stop, Biarritz.

~~CHAPTER 3: FELLOWSHIP~~

29th August, Biarritz Airport
Squeaky-bum time.
My Easysweat flight touched down on the beachfront runway at Biarritz, forty-five minutes behind schedule. This left me little over thirty minutes to disembark, dance through immigration and hot foot it to Bayonne train station – roughly 10km away.

In fact, with so much time to spare, surely, I could have squeezed in a look at the Rocher de la Vierge? Grabbed a brew at the Miremont Tearooms? Better still, sauntered down to La Grande Plage Beach and pummelled a few 'Frenchies' at boules?

Thankfully, Biarritz airport resembled little more than a shack, so recovering my pack was quick and easy. Though it did seem somewhat cruel to tear my pack away from the baggage carousel, where it seemed to be enjoying competing in some bizarre version of the Bag Grand Prix.

While my pack was having fun, I had bigger concerns. A quick gawp at the travel information noticeboard told me everything I needed to know. If I spoke French that was. Sadly, I didn't. Undeterred, I headed outside to explore what possible transport options there might be – high-speed donkey, car jackin' or a taxi.

While the idea of tearing up the road, strapped to a high-speed donkey with smoke billowing from its jacksie sounded fun, I did have some concerns about last-minute availability and issuing instructions. Also, how would I have paid?

Car jackin' seemed viable, though a high-risk one. Especially as the French weren't shy, unlike the English, of lobbing someone in gaol for a stretch. Where the idea of two inmates per cell was considered almost, well, novel. So, taxi it was.

As I stepped out into the furnace of the day, I could feel my skin starting to melt. It may only have been 2 pm, but the temperature had already hit 27C.

Over to my right, I saw a taxi rank, full of cream-coloured Beamers. I stood anxiously, hopping from one foot to another. Yet somehow, I barely seemed to notice the seventies Mafia-looking staff car as it rolled towards me. Its passenger door stopped ominously in line with my feet.

Sitting behind the wheel was an impeccably dressed, sixty-year-old 'Don'. Dressed in a khaki suit, with Ray-Ban Aviator sunglasses and tan leather gloves. Before I even had time to resist, he was out of his car, interlinking his arm in mine and walking me towards the boot. Once there, he popped the lock, leaving me to stare into its deep, empty recess.

"*Dépêchez-vous, dépêchez-vous,*" he yelled at me.

WTF did that mean? In my flustered state, I pointed first at my pack, then myself. Which one of us did he want to put into the boot? Noticing my reluctance, the driver simply made a grab for my pack and slung it in.

Righto, Monkey! Just tell the nice hitman where you want to go, came the waspish sound of my conscience.

Fat chance of that. The only French I knew were the words to 'Joe Le Taxi' by Vanessa Paradis. Which I guessed wasn't what he wanted to hear right then. In the absence of French, I did the thing that came most naturally to me – mimicry. I started by making choo-choo noises, then began to pump my arms frantically, as if they were train pistons. Suddenly the tables were turned. Now it was the turn of the 'Don' to look petrified. I noticed the slow shuffling of his feet as he retreated towards the safety of his car.

"Dépêchez-vous! Dépêchez-vous!" I screamed at him.

If only I knew what dépêchez-vous meant. Either way, it had the desired effect. He jumped into the driver's seat and began to nervously fumble with his keys in his pocket. Once they were found, he tried but repeatedly failed to start the car (hitman my arse). On the third attempt, the engine fired into life.

With that, we set off at a hair-raising pace, down the back streets, along darkened alleys and out across open waste land. Were we really heading to Bayonne train station? Or was he secretly scoping out where to dump my body?

All the while the car was bucking like a bronco and my eyes glared hard at the minute hand of my G-SHOCK watch. Shit, it was going to be close. Was I going to make it? If I did, job done. If I didn't, what then? What was my backup plan? With time on the wane and me needing serious help, I called for back-up. Back-up in this instance, came from the most unlikely of sources.

"Hi God, remember me? I'm guessing not. Look, I'm short of time, so I'll get to the point. I need your help. Would it be possible for you to make my train a) a tad late b) a little bit dilapidated? But not too much. Cheers. I mean – Amen."

Now with the big 'G' on the case, I felt like I could relax – a tad. I knew she wouldn't let me down. After all, I was out here on pilgrimage. So, in many respects, I was working for her. I was hoping that was worth a few brownie points.

Ten nail-biting minutes later, I arrived at Bayonne train station, under a screech of brakes and the stench of freshly burnt tyre rubber. I rushed out, popped the boot, grabbed my gear, stuffed a wad of Euros into the driver's leathered palm, then proceeded to race into the air-conditioned, blissfully cool terminal.

I was met by a doddering couple of head-scratching old duffers, who were fannying about trying to work out the ticket machine. Oh, for fuck's sake, it really wasn't that hard. It was a simple process: where did you want to go? When? Did you want to go one way or both? Then pay – simples.

After five anxious minutes of waiting, I bashed in my destination then, hey presto – a ticket. With the ticket in hand, I clocked the platform and legged it. Once there, I collapsed into a sweaty mess. Finally, after a day of comedy madness, I could relax.

But even that proved to be hard work. Made harder still, by the fact the sun was melting the stones on the platform. It was hot, and this Shire Hobbit (by 'Shire' I mean Shropshire) was too hot. By our nature, us Shire Hobbits weren't great in fierce heat. We much preferred cooler climes with overcast skies. Fierce heat tended to addle our brains and burn our feetsies.

None of which boded well, as an unannounced warm front was just about to hit southwestern France and Spain. One which was expected to push the temperature needle from 26C up towards the mid-thirties. But that was tomorrow's problem. For now, all I needed to focus on was making myself at home, until the choo-choo train came.

The train platform was almost entirely deserted. All except for one hulking, man-mountain of a unit, pacing backwards and forwards sixty metres away. Whoever, or more importantly, whatever manner of beast he was, one thing was for certain – he looked menacing. And judging by the size of his bulging pack, it was clear why he was here. He was hunting Orcs.

I'd heard rumours from Shire Hobbits about this before I'd left. Allegedly, some Orcs may well have survived the fall of Mordor. If that was true, they would invariably be small in number. Therefore, they'd most likely stick close to the western shores of France. There they could take advantage of the forests, using them for refuge. While at night, they could use the cover of darkness to move quickly up and down the River Nive.

But it was clear whatever manner of Orc he'd been hunting had eluded him. Did his lack of hunting trophies mean he might turn his attention elsewhere? If so, would that put Shire Hobbits at the top, middle or bottom of his menu?

By then his pacing had begun to unnerve me. So much so, that I started to pack away what would have been second breakfast before re-clipping my pack and readying myself – to RUN. This was made more urgent by the last click of the strap on my pack that went off like a gunshot. Bollocks. That sound to a trained hunter was all he would need. He stopped pacing then slowly turned. He then shouldered his pack and began to charge down the platform towards me. Shit!

"Hi, I'm Dan."

Suddenly the air around me turned cold, as his humongous silhouette towered over me. I tried to look up, but I was blinded by the sun sitting behind his right shoulder. Then slowly, out of nowhere, this giant, broad-knuckled man paw came my way. My hand lifted itself limply in defeat. Seconds later, my hand disappeared within his. Would I ever get to see it again?

Well, don't just sit there you muppet. Tell the big guy your name! And whatever you do, DON'T make him angry, came the ever-cautious words of my conscience.

"Hi, I'm Paul," I said nervously.

As he stepped out of the light, I got a proper look at him. Sweet Jesus of Nazareth, he was enormous. He was easily six foot three possibly six foot four and could easily tip the scales at two hundred and thirty pounds. Any thoughts I had of escape quickly evaporated as I noticed that he'd blocked off all escape routes. In which case, my next best course of action would be to befriend him.

Within the opening few gambits of our conversation it seemed I might have misread the situation – go figure. It turned out that Dan was very much a man of the woods. But he was definitely not here hunting Orc. Which was as much a relief to me as I expected it would be to the entire Orc nation.

It appeared as though Dan, like me, had other things on his mind. He too was heading towards Saint-Jean-Pied-de-Port to begin his pilgrimage.

His epic, twenty-four-hour schlep started in downtown Santa Barbara. Then onto Paris, where he caught a night train down to Biarritz. Then a cab over to this station. His was a proper case of planes, trains, and automobiles – all without a dot of sleep. I was so engrossed in listening to his tale of getting here, that I'd barely noticed the platform slowly starting to fill up.

But as the minutes ticked by, the noise and number of newbie pilgrims started to grow. So too did the ever-familiar sounds of squeaks from new rucksacks, the crisp packet rustle of new walking gear and the clickety-click of walking poles. But it wasn't these things that struck me the most, it was the smell. Everyone smelt fresh. Almost as if they'd polished themselves up, ready for an adventure. They knew as well as I did that this wouldn't last. I could see it in the anxious looks of a few faces. They knew it would be a long, long time before they smelt this fresh again.

In and amongst the noise, anxious looks, and mash-up of global accents I could sense something else brewing. What was it? It took me a few minutes of being bounced between new faces before I registered what it was. It was shock. The shock was caused by the fact that something they'd read about, even dreamt about for months (or years) had become real. Maybe a little too real.

With so much going on, it came as no surprise that everyone failed to notice the sight of three hundred tonnes of steel, as our train rolled down the tracks towards us. Once it pulled up alongside, there was a giant hiss prior to it opening its giant, metal jaws.

One by one we stepped inside the belly of the beast. It was molten hot. A result, no doubt, caused by the fact that the air-conditioning unit was kaput, knackered, up the swanny – take your pick. But on the plus side, it did have seats. So at least we could sit comfortably in our discomfort, as our bodies slowly sous vide themselves.

All around me, I could see the first threads of friendship being spun. Though tired, I knew these opening moments of 'hi's, hugs and high-fives were vital. It would be these that bonded us all together, as from that day onwards we were all part of one, newly-formed travelling family.

All the while the chit-chat was going on, I couldn't help but notice the nervous second glances, as people subconsciously eyed each other up. I'd clocked it mainly because I was doing the same.

My mind was simply full of questions: what footwear were people wearing? Were people wearing full boots, half boots or cross-trainers? Likewise, who was wearing shorts? How many were wearing trousers? I also began to wonder what else they had packed. Did people have fleeces, base layers, Merino wool tops and sleeping bags? What had they struggled to choose between? More importantly, what had they chosen to leave behind – and why? Each question simply fuelled another. But the biggest question I had was: how big were people's packs? Mine was forty-eight litres. How many had larger? How many had smaller packs and why?

Looking around, it was clear to see a pattern among the racing snakes. They were easy to spot as their faces tended to look tough, like old leather. While their faces and frowns had been sculpted by life's winds and changing seasons. Typically, they were smaller and leaner, much like their packs.

Thankfully, the pre-Camino nerves, excitement and camaraderie were enough to keep one subject at bay. One that I was keen not to be drawn in on – religion.

With the train chugging south, following the source of the River Nive, I could feel my mind starting to slow, relax and wander. This trip reminded me of so many of my DofE days. Back to a time when life was simpler, humbler and happier.

"UUUUUUURRRGHHHH!"

Suddenly, there came a screech of brakes, as the train crunched to a halt. The effect of which caused packs to scurry and scatter all along the carriage floor. Shit! That didn't sound clever. Suddenly, eyes began to dart from face to face, all looking for signs of reassurance. Our Camino now was officially on pause. Everyone sat gingerly on the edge of their seats, nervously waiting to see what would happen next.

"Zere 'as been a landslide furzer up ze track. Zerefore zis train will now complete its journey at Cambo-les-Bains train station, where a mini-bus replacement service will take you onto Saint-Jean-Pied-de-Port." At that point, I wasn't sure who was more annoyed – me or the apologetic, French train conductor.

"A landslide. A feckin' landslide. You couldn't make this shit up," I chuckled.

At Cambo-les-Bains we got herded into one of six cream, eight-seater mini-buses. Was it me, or was it odd how everyone just jumped aboard, without any questions being asked? Or perhaps this was just one part of my London paranoia that I needed to work on.

With no roof-rack to speak of, it became a case of packs on laps. As we headed off into the balmy French afternoon. It soon became obvious we were no longer alone. With each mile, the mountains started to close in around us, until we were surrounded. I could see the fear in people's eyes. These mountains were beasts.

How could you possibly believe that doing two to three laps of Richmond Park would ever prepare you to take on any of this?

I knew my conscience was trying to rattle my cage. What it was saying just didn't faze me. While I hadn't gone crazy training for this, I'd worn my boots in and did Pilates five times a week to strengthen my core. I'd also done ten to twelve fifteen milers around Richmond Park. So, was I worried? Not particularly.

While the wheels of the bus turned, Dan and I were lost in our chit-chat. I learned that he was a retired cop, now a bar owner, a keen surfer and a veteran walker, having completed the infamous Pacific Crest Trail. A four-thousand-kilometre schlep through the Sierra and Cascades mountains.

The more he spoke, the more I realised we had in common. While I hadn't served, many of my family had. Also, my best-mate-cum-little-brother George had done a few tours of Northern Ireland with the Rock Apes before switching to join the police.

While Dan was keen to talk about the wonder of life in downtown Santa Barbara, what I really wanted to find out was what had brought him on Camino? And why now?

These questions were met with a thoughtful and composed silence. He then leaned closer, keen that others didn't hear. I knew, even before he spoke, what was coming. I knew because I recognised that hollow look of sorrow in his eyes. He didn't have to say. I knew he'd lost someone very dear to him (and I was right.) He'd lost someone whom his heart yearned for and would trade in everything he had just to see them again. As he spoke, I could feel my eyes starting to well up.

This loss was the catalyst for his Camino. This, along with the fact that he was also approaching sixty years of age. A time in life when he felt that he'd like to take some time out to reset and wonder before going on again.

For the next hour I simply listened, fascinated by his story. There was something so familiar about Dan. In many ways, he reminded me of the lads back home: George, Higgs, Buddha, the 'Intrepid Mr. Lynch' – and Mitch. All those lads were refreshingly honest and bullshit free. Without a second's hesitation, all of them would rip into me mercilessly about any aspect of my life: my dodgy fashion, limp, love of shite music or the girls I'd dated. But in the same breath, they'd be there at a drop of a hat, if I, or anyone in my family, ever needed them. Friendships like those were golden.

Through the midst of our conversation my mind started to drift. Was this the effect of jet lag, or the meandering of the road as it followed the River Nive south, past Alzuya, Apeztéguia, Louhossoa, Gahardou, Eyharce and Itzalguy?

I looked at the timeless hamlets. They represented a beauty and simplicity of life, from a time gone by. But with each hamlet and each sign, my heart jumped a little more. I knew it couldn't be long before we saw a sign saying 'Saint-Jean-Pied-de-Port.'

Then, as if to answer my prayer, I heard a cry from the front of the minibus. It was a cry that ricocheted down the bus, as people began to point to the right-hand side of the road. There were the immortal words I'd been waiting so long to see – Saint-Jean-Pied-de-Port.

Within seconds, the once-weary travellers were up and awake and starting to whoop, cheer and high-five. After what seemed like an eternity, we were there. Moments later, the mini-bus pulled in and came to a halt at Gare de Saint-Jean-Pied-de-Port. I clocked the time – it was 7:30 pm.

The bus descended into an eerie silence. It was so silent that I could hear the thump of people's hearts. Their faces were in a state of shock. All eyes were fixed, surveying our new surroundings. This was it. This was the moment we'd all been waiting for. Once we stepped outside of this bus – it was officially on.

"Off we pop then," I uttered joyfully.

One by one, people edged their way out of the door. Once out, they stood mesmerised. Their hearts were stolen by the beauty of the surroundings, while their nostrils became overwhelmed by the stinging purity of mountain air. For the next while, it would be bye-bye toxic London air – hello giddy, intoxicating mountain air.

While everyone began to fiddle nervously with their kit, I stood open-mouthed. I was in awe at the beauty of the Gare de Saint-Jean-Pied-de-Port. It had a magnificent, white-washed facade, along with red tiles, window frames, shutters and door. It was hard to believe that this tiny, timeless platform welcomed in more than three hundred thousand pilgrims a year – sometimes even more.

"This, my son, is going to be something very, very special," I muttered to Dan.

The road in front of us was full of stiff-walking and weary pilgrims. Many of whom had trotted on ahead in the hope of securing a bed in any of the gites, albergues or nearby hotels that made Saint-Jean-Pied-de-Port their home.

Thankfully, I didn't need to worry, as I'd booked my accommodation months ago. Was that the right thing to do? Was that the pilgrim way? Or was I meant to let go of the reins of certainty and trust my life to a higher power? My response to that? Well, it hadn't exactly worked out for Mary and Joseph in biblical times, so why should it work now? That's why I was sticking to the 7 Ps. After a long day hauling ass in the baking heat, the last thing I needed to be worrying about was bedroom bingo.

The joy of this meant that I could relax and savour these early moments as I sauntered up the sprawling Avenue Renaud. An avenue lined with enormous two-to-three-storey, white-washed stone houses. All of which were decked out in red roof tiles, red window frames, red gates and red balconies. The effect of such uniformity gave even more prominence to the trees, hedgerows and mouth-watering pastel-coloured sky.

Approximately two-thirds of my way up Avenue Renaud, my eyes were drawn to an uncharacteristic-looking sandstone building. As I edged closer towards it, I could see a wooden rectangular plaque embossed with a silhouette of a person walking. Alongside it was a blue square with a golden yellow arrow. I could feel my heart suddenly leap into my mouth. This was it. I'd just seen my very first Camino symbol.

Buen Camino.

Once again, I was reminded of the couple I saw in Finisterre, all those years ago. I wondered if they knew or had any idea of the power of that saying? Or how it had redirected my life?

I found my accommodation, not more than a few minutes' wander from the intersection of Avenue Renaud and Place Charles de Gaulle. With that sorted, I turned and wished Dan good luck. He was off in search of a nearby albergue (which was essentially a hostel open exclusively to pilgrims).

"Fancy a beer later?" Dan asked.

"It would be rude not to," I replied.

This to me was perfect prep for tomorrow. I also knew that, based on the time, most albergues, municipals or gites (all forms of pilgrim accommodation) shut their doors for the night at around 10:30 pm. That meant we only had time for one or two beers.

With the beer booked in, I checked in dumped my pack and showered before sorting my kit for tomorrow. Once done, and with me smelling minty fresh, I tootled down Place Charles de Gaulle, past the minimalist-looking, glass-fronted Office de Tourisme.

This would be the first place of call for any new pilgrim arriving at Saint Jean. There, pilgrims (including me) could pick up their Pilgrim Credencial (as it was more commonly known). Opposite this building, stood the elegant and rather opulent-looking Hotel de Ville, known locally as Herriko Etxea.

I stopped when I hit the bridge overlooking the River Nive. I just needed a few minutes to myself to appreciate the calm and listen to the soft trickle of the stream beneath me. Over to my left, I could see another stone bridge, covered in moss and lit thoughtfully by some well-placed streetlights.

Once over the bridge, the world started up again and I was hit by the sight of restaurants and noisy locals quaffing wine, laughing and filling their gullets. Upon seeing their dishes my stomachs let out a huge roar of disapproval. Not at the food, which looked spectacular, but more at the fact that they, stomachs one, two and three hadn't eaten in hours. And judging by how full the restaurants were, there was little chance of being fed before morning.

With no sign of Dan at the first restaurant, I continued down towards Cafe de la Paix – there he was. He was sitting at a low, circular table. Beside him was a lean, wiry-looking fella in his mid-fifties, who looked remarkably like Uncle Travelling Matt from *Fraggle Rock*.

Before I had the chance to introduce myself or sit down, Uncle Travelling Matt pointed towards the new, frosty beer on the table. A beer that was obviously looking for an owner. He didn't need to ask twice. I swooped down upon it with the speed of a vulture that had just been invited to an all-you-can-eat zebra buffet.

"Cheers!" rang out around the table.

The first sip tasted heavenly. So much so that everyone stopped and savoured it before launching into their introductions. The newest member to the fellowship was Ryan. Ryan was... I loved playing this game. Well, judging by his bespoke designer frames, expensive watch, clean-cut appearance, quirky and irreverent ways, I would've said that he was a fashion designer. Wrong! It turned out that Ryan was a leading Danish architect.

As the chit-chat bounced around the table, I couldn't help but notice that the moon had come out to play. It was huge and appeared to be to be closing in on our table. As if it was trying to eavesdrop on our plans. Not that we cared, we were all too busy bouncing with excitement about the days ahead.

Then out of nowhere, someone mentioned the 'G' word. Bollocks! There I was, hoping to get through the whole first day unscathed. Sadly not. But as both Dan and Ryan raised it, I thought I may as well listen.

Dan, it would appear, had had God 'on hold' on a dodgy connection for the last few years. Which wasn't surprising from what he'd told me. But I could see he was still prepared to offer 'G' an olive branch. Ryan, on the other hand, had grown up feral. By feral, I mean without religion (the lucky bastard). He was now in a place in his life where he wanted to see, hear, learn and explore the possibility of it all – and if 'G' was for him.

I leapt on this instantly, as I knew it would deflect any 'G' chat away from me. I quickly pointed out that Ryan effectively, to use a golf analogy, was playing off scratch. His SIN SCORECARD was zero. If he didn't believe, in essence, he could argue that he'd never sinned. Well, that would need correcting – and pronto.

In fact, many of us, me included, were out there trying to reduce our SIN SCORECARD. Therefore, he needed to start and in earnest. Otherwise, it would totally defeat the point of walking to Santia…(I hadn't earned the right to mention its name), as he wouldn't have sinned enough to have his slate wiped clean.

My advice was simple – start sinning. That was enough to send both Dan and Ryan into fits of laughter. They then started to brainstorm what sins he should commit first. Jesus! What had I started? While this was going on I ordered another beer.

Our fellowship was now formed. It would be us three. Two sinners and one work in progress. Tomorrow at 7:43 am, we'd take on the 'Sleeping Giant'.

CHAPTER 4: SLEEPING GIANT

30th August, Saint-Jean-Pied-de-Port to Roncesvalles, 25km

I woke at 6 am exhausted in a pitch-black room. A combination of the previous night's beer, dehydration and discombobulation had put the kibosh on sleep. As I lay staring into the void, cool mountain air nipping at my exposed toes, I couldn't help but feel intimidated by the eerie silence that was hanging like a blanket over me.

Outside there were no ambulance sirens. No nee-nah-nee-nah sounds of police cars chasing drug dealers up the block. No yellow warning lights from the council's mechanical T-Rex as they picked up and tore bin bags limb from limb. Even the pigeons outside my window flew by in Airwolf 'Whisper' mode.

As mornings went it was very un-Brixton-like. As I lay there, my mind stirring, I tried to recall the last time my body woke naturally. I couldn't. Ten years of living in Brixton had me hard-wired to sleep with one eye open, forever walking the tightrope of REM sleep, but never quite getting there.

By 6:30 am I was up, showered, dressed and ready. But before I headed off, I wanted to experience a pilgrim breakfast. As it had been seventeen hours since my last feed, all my stomachs were hungry.

On the floor above, I could hear the shuffling and stumbling of sleep-deprived pilgrims. Hunger, no doubt, had woken them too. I knew it wouldn't be long before they started prowling the halls and descending the stairs.

When they did, I needed to be ready for the stampede that followed. If I got my timing right, I might have been able to muscle my way in amongst them all. But if, on the other hand, I got my timing wrong, I ran the risk of being trampled under the heavy hooves of twenty famished pilgrims.

Luckily for me I had size on my side, so muscling and jostling for position came easy, as we trounced down the corridor to the breakfast area.

What caused the stampede to come skidding to an impromptu halt was the sight of a sad, sullen-faced Korean lad. He couldn't have been more than eighteen years old. He was sitting, looking broken-hearted, at the breakfast table.

Even before I had a chance to ask what was wrong, the likely culprit appeared in the shape of a plump and joyless-looking French host. He obviously wasn't a fan of the morning, and he was keen to let everyone know it by bashing tables, scraping chairs and thumping the day's food offering down onto cheap, white side plates.

The term 'food offering' is used in the broadest possible context. In reality, I was greeted with the sight of:

→ One semi-stale French baton, last used during the 1789 Revolution
→ One slice of moist, freshly sweating cheese
→ One glass of eye-tinglingly sharp orange juice.

"Dear Father, for what we're about to receive (and it isn't much) may the Lord make us truly thankful," I said sarcastically.

When the "Amen" came, it was accompanied by sniggers of disbelief. Sadly, the fun soon faded further when I bit into the rock hard, jaw-shattering French baton.

"What the fuck!" I said in disgust.

I thumped the inedible French baton back down on my plate. What the hell was going on? It was meant to be a day of joyous celebration. Yet all around me were the sad, dejected and glum-looking faces of hungry pilgrims. All of which was made worse by the presence of our host, who I had loathingly named Mr. Bumble, after the miser in Oliver Twist.

With no food for comfort, I could see people's minds start to turn inwards. The battle for the day had begun. On one side of our minds' battlefield was hope, adventure, newly-formed friendship and optimism – while our inner demons lurked in the shadows. Always ready to shake my belief system and plant seeds of fear, doubt and uncertainty, my demons did that via my conscience's endless line of questioning:

→ *Do your boots fit? Like, really fit? They feel a little loose. If they're loose, they'll rub your feet red raw.*

→ *Seriously, what are you doing here, granddad? Can't you see that you've almost twenty years on the racing snakes and whippersnappers around the table? Wouldn't you be happier on a Saga holiday? Where you could spend your day sipping Sangria or walking on white sandy beaches?*

→ *How far realistically do you think you'll get today on zero sleep and an empty belly? The end of the road? Halfway to Huntto? I'll be generous, I'll give you one or two kilometres – max.*

What my conscience didn't know or understand, was the fact that I quite enjoyed its verbal jousting. Why? Because its antagonistic ways only added to my sense of clarity.

With regards to my boots, they were half a size larger than usual. This decision to go large was based on a discussion I'd had with Des, the store manager at Ellis Brigham in Covent Garden. He was quick to point out that in extreme heat, my feet could expand anywhere between a half to a whole shoe size.

I was well aware of my age. But my age was of no significance to the whippersnappers. They seemed more concerned with texting or obsessively checking their Garmin watches were synced, than asking me if I was lost. Or if I was looking for a local Mecca Bingo.

But my conscience was correct about my hunger levels. I was raging. Sod getting to the end of the road. If I didn't eat, and soon, I'd struggle to make it off the chair I was sitting on.

"Excusez-moi, monsieur," I said nervously to Mr. Bumble. "Please, could I have some more?" I said, with desperation in my eyes.

"Zis is ze traditional pilgrim breakfast. If you are still 'ungry afterwards, may I suggest you try ze local boulangeries. Zey open at 7:30 am," he replied bluntly.

"So, that's a no then?" came my equally blunt response.

"Well lads, you can't say I didn't try," I mumbled in disbelief.

With food not forthcoming, there seemed little point sitting about listening to the dawn chorus of grumbling tummies. With that in mind, I got up, scraping my chair petulantly, before I retreated back to my room.

By then it was 7 am, which left me only thirty minutes until I met Dan and Ryan outside Auberge du Pelerin on Rue de la Citadelle.

There was only one thing for it. It was time to break into my emergency rations. The very thought of food, in any form, was enough to make me salivate and cause my eyes to bulge in demented delight, much like Gollum in *The Lord of the Rings*.

"Gives it to me precccciiiioous. I wants it."

My hands dived into my pack, until I felt the silky, smooth and squidgy packaging of my Wayfayrer All Day Breakfast pouches. Little sausages bathed in bean juice – lovely. My hands traced over the words on the packaging as I read them aloud. 'Real food, Ready to Eat, Enjoy Hot or Cold.'

With no time for pleasantries, I tore open the pack, cranked my neck back and poured the contents down my gullet. Within minutes, the first pouch had been consumed. Followed minutes later by the second pouch.

All of which had left my shirt caked in dinner medals and my mouth dripped in bean juice. Not that I cared. I'd just inhaled nine hundred-odd calories, which would be more than enough to power me to Huntto.

With food taken care of, I shouldered my pack and headed out the door to meet the lads. They were beside themselves with glee, having spent the last hour feasting like kings on cereal, bread, cheese, yoghurt, fresh fruit and lashings of fresh coffee.

Righto, which way? A quick butchers at my SILVA compass said we needed to head down Rue de la Citadelle towards the 14th century church – Our Lady at the End of the Bridge. Seemed simple, or so I thought.

Neither Dan nor Ryan seemed convinced. While waiting for me, they'd been passed by several groups of pilgrims headed the other way up Rue de la Citadelle. That to me made no sense. But it was still early, and I wasn't up for a debate. Plus, in my head the worst-case scenario if they were wrong, would mean spending an extra ten or fifteen minutes in Saint-Jean-Pied-de-Port – which seemed fine to me.

As we wandered up Rue de la Citadelle I was struck by the tranquil nature and sense of timelessness to this place. From the magnificent white, stone-washed houses with thick, grey granite stone window frames with red beams and slatted shutters, to the pristine cobbles that fanned out before our feet. Nothing much would have changed here in a millennia, and I hoped it never did.

Just past the sandstone brick Bishop's Prison (now a museum), the street split. Now where? Did we head right, following the sign for La Citadelle Zitadela up the ramparts (which was said to have unparalleled views over the surrounding area)? Or did we head out, under the Porte Saint-Jacques? We chose the latter.

Of all the sights and sounds I had expected to see, nothing could've quite prepared me for what came next.

As we wandered out and through Porte Saint-Jacques, we were met by the sight of clapped-out Fiats, prehistoric Citroens and the shuffling masses of tourist crusties. If I didn't know better, I could have sworn that we had just gatecrashed an illegal pensioners' rave.

Up above, in God's Bar, I could hear Mitch cackling wildly. I wasn't sure even he could believe that we'd gone the wrong way within two hundred metres of setting off. This seriously didn't inspire confidence for the seven-hundred-and-ninety-nine-kilometres that lay ahead.

"Le chemin, le chemin," came the sound of a beautiful French voice.

As I looked up, a young, petite lady started to rush down the road towards us. In effect, saving us from being being accosted by ass-pinching pensioners.

"Le chemin, le chemin," she said, pointing back the way we came.

While I still had no idea what she meant, I did know it was time to get gone. As three men, hanging round a car park dressed in fleeces and shorts looked, well, suss. The last thing I needed was to get lifted by the local gendarmes and charged with being a dogging enthusiast. Nor did I fancy being mauled, cupped or fondled by the wandering hands of some raving pensioners.

Once through Porte Saint-Jacques everything became clear. Jesus, how blind were we? Everywhere I looked I saw Camino signs. They appeared on gates, doors, signs and even sprayed on the corner of a house. I was mortified. No wonder the locals, who were sitting on the wrought-iron benches lining the street, shook their heads in disbelief.

Basque bunting in red, white and green criss-crossed from house to house above our heads. The bunting connected the houses in an unwritten show of unity and pride, as it led us down towards Our Lady at the End of the Bridge and the clock tower.

Our eyes drew skywards, above the terracotta rooftops, where we caught our first real glimpse of the mountain ridges. They rose angrily from the earth like giants. The day's path would dance perilously close to all of these. My hope was that when it did, these giants would still be sleeping.

At the bottom of Rue de la Citadelle, we were greeted by the sight of two colossal-sized, eight-foot high, four inch thick, metal-studded wooden doors. The doors were flung open as if daring (or inviting) us to step through them. We all knew these were more than mere doors. They were portals. Our gateway out of this world and into another – the world of the pilgrim.

"Shall we?"

This was it. This was the moment I'd waited for since that first "Buen

Camino". I could feel the adrenaline surging through my highway of veins and arteries. I could see the same wide-eyed excitement in both Dan and Ryan, who suddenly transformed before my eyes into their twelve-year-old selves. I noted the time in the clock tower overhead – 7:42 am.

"We shall," replied Ryan sarcastically. Much to the delight of us all.

We stopped on the bridge for a few selfies, and also to fiddle nervously (and needlessly) with our packs. Once over the River Nive, we crept along the cobbled street on our way up and out of town.

We wandered passed shop keepers, proudly mopping their front step in preparation for the day ahead. We also passed delivery drivers, darting from one shop to another. All of whom were laden down under a mountain of fresh bread (I knew a place that could benefit from that). While overhead, on balconies, people were busy watering their plant pots in preparation for the fierce heat that lay ahead.

Lost in the excitement and newness of it all, I barely registered that we had begun to climb. Then within minutes, we were all confronted by two enormous stone pillars. These marked the old stone walls from times gone by.

Here the fan-shaped cobbles gave way to newly laid tarmac. On our way up the road, we passed what appeared to be a nursery and some large family homes. The road suddenly split. Now, which way was it going to be? In this instance we allowed fate to decide – via a coin toss.

Heads: if the coin landed on heads, we would turn right on Chemin de Mayorga, before taking the gentler, more mind-numbing road to Valcarlos. Though a safe route nowadays, it was anything but that back in mediaeval times. As back then, light-fingered upstarts would use the camouflage of trees to hide out before leaping out and rinsing pilgrims of all their worldly goods.

Tails: if the coin landed on tails, we'd continue onwards to Refuge Orisson along Route Napoleon. This route included a fierce, leg-wobbling ascent up to the Col de Lepoeder, the gateway to Spain, before it dropped down steeply through a pine forest into the mythical-looking Roncesvalles monastery.

The coin when flicked, seemed to hang in the air as if in suspended animation. All eyes looked to the heavens expectantly. Come on you beauty – do me proud.

"Tails."

"Well lads, tails it is. But just one thing before we head off. Not that I'm trying to sway the decision in any way, shape or form, but do either of you know how many of 'Old Boney's' battle-hardened soldiers perished walking this route into Spain during the Peninsular War?" My question drew blank looks, just as I had hoped.

"Well let me tell you, shall I? Lots. Yes, lots died. According to historical documents, most deaths were attributed to dehydration, exhaustion, blinding fog, frostbite or disorientation – sound familiar? Those who were lucky enough to make it to higher ground unscathed. Then they had to run the gauntlet against being picked off by wolves, vultures or famished buzzards. So, bearing that in mind, who's really up for Route Napoleon?" I said.

"I wasn't before. But I am now" came Ryan's enthusiastic response.

"Me too. I can't wait." said Dan.

"*Fantastic*," came my muted response.

Though I hated to admit it, there was something romantic about the idea of following in the footsteps of Napoleon. But by Napoleon, I meant Napoleon's horse. As 'Old Boney' wouldn't have been caught dead traipsing through the mud. No chance. Nor would he have risked getting his knee-high boots or his thick, grey, calf-length greatcoat dirty. Then again, why should he have?

After all, he had an army of scuffers to do all his donkey work for him, moving the munitions, food and supplies. In fact, I'd dare say the heaviest thing he would have wielded would have been a letter opener used to prize open the latest musings from his beloved Empress Joséphine.

Within seconds of choosing Route Napoleon, the road cranked up savagely. The morning pleasantries soon evaporated, to be replaced by the sound of wheezing, heaving and Orca-style blowing. Such was the steepness that I wasn't entirely sure that the road hadn't been transformed into some airport-style travelator as pilgrims who'd set off long before us started to slither and slide down the road towards us.

"Jesus, lads. If this is... the warm-up... I... can't... wait... for... the... main... event," I said between wheezes. I looked for comfort and reassurance in the eyes of Dan and Ryan – but saw none. This was game day, and already the Pyrenees were kicking our arses.

In an attempt to offset the rising anxiety and my quickly fatiguing muscles, I knew I needed to switch focus. It was then that I was reminded of a trick from the old days. The trick was to focus on the ten feet in front of me. Though this idea was hardly revolutionary, when combined with counting each step, it did a lot to calm my mind.

Within ten minutes of counting one... two... three... four, I could feel my mind calm, and I was given my first glimpse out over the Pyrenees.

Below to our left, the hillside fell away to reveal fields, thick with lush bracken. Some of the larger stems had been caught by the sun's stinging rays, bleaching them gold. Beyond the bracken, the landscape was a rich, quilted patchwork of fields. Each field with its own distinctive hue, framed artistically by a small cluster of trees. Dotted amongst the undulating landscape, white flecks like a painter's brushstrokes marked out farmhouses, out-houses and distant hamlets.

"Imagine waking up to this every day, lads?" I said, feeling my smile widen.

Not only was the scenery spellbindingly beautiful, but the mountain air just made you feel so much more alive and invigorated. It was a world away from the intoxicating, chemical-filled London air, that stuck to your throat and had everyone coughing.

With my mind overloaded with the intensity of the scene, a new question came to mind. Where was everyone? So far, we'd hardly seen a local, a cow or a barking dog. Where were the kids playing in driveways or building dens in nearby fields? Even the wisp of the wind as it fluttered by seem confused by it all.

So surreal was this feeling, as I looked out across the hills that shimmered in the heat haze, that I had to ask myself – was this real? Or was it just another of my lucid dreams? It was only as I turned, seeing the same shell-shocked looks on the lads' faces, that I realised. They were asking themselves the same question.

With all our minds agreeing on our new reality, we all started to relax. Slowly, three walking paces became one and the brotherly banter and friendly piss-taking from the previous night resumed.

Ryan had the sharpest mind and the quickest wit. Therefore, he was the first to fire off a few rounds – in my direction.

"So, Paul, I'm just wondering. How far along are you?" he said pointing at my stomach.

"And what about names? Have you given any thought to baby names yet?" quipped Dan.

For a second, I was in shock. I knew I was in for being baited today. My hope had been that it would occur at the end of the day – not the start.

"Obviously lads, it's time I came clean. Not that I need to, as you've already twigged. Yes, it's true. I'm six months gone."

With that, I placed my right hand protectively against my stomach.

"And if you really want to know how I'm feeling. Let me tell you, shall I? Currently, I'm experiencing mild cramps, hot flushes, shortness of breath and my nipples are raw. Any more daft questions?" I said coyly. By then Ryan had already started to chuckle, as had Dan.

And while everyone was attacking me, a poor defenceless pregnant man, I had a few questions of my own.

"Righto, Dan. Where did you hide those Orc bodies yesterday? Are they strung up in the woods somewhere, slowly maturing for twenty-eight days? Or did you sell a job lot of them to the goblins, as they'll eat anything? And what's the craic with your pack? Are you really only carrying pilgrim supplies? Or are you involved in the murkier world of smuggling Oompa Loompas across county lines?" I could feel myself winding up nicely.

"As for you, Uncle Travelling Matt. Where the feck is your pack? You can't seriously expect me to believe you've crammed everything you need into a pack that weighs only three and a bit kilograms? I have lunches bigger than that! What have you really got in there? A crusty T-shirt, a pair of shorts, some cheesy socks and a leather codpiece with more streaks than a subway map?"

Far from making any attempt to defend himself, which was wise, Ryan simply opted to chuckle. To me, that was the chuckle of a guilty man, with sin on his mind.

While the road we were on seemed keen to play games with us, darting one way then the next, the sun was not. It had already begun to collect scalps. Even at this early hour, people were beginning to shudder and falter. Though the temperature couldn't be more than 20C, it was the combination of gradient, packs, plus physical exertion that made it feel a damn sight hotter.

The higher we climbed, the closer to the sun we got, which had begun pouring down rays upon us. Our only hope of surviving the day was to delay our exposure to its evil clutches for as long as possible. With this in mind, we crept along the road like nervous vampires, using whatever foliage cover we could find.

I was ready for Huntto, a little hamlet on the hillside. It surely had to be around here somewhere. Suddenly the road began to slope away from us towards a bend. Was that a fleck of white paint I could see?

Urged on by excitement, and the growl of my belly, I set off. In my mind, that fleck of white paint must have been Huntto. It had to be. I could feel my mind start to race as I imagined all the food options I'd get to pick from.

So, what would I order first? Fruit cake, carrot cake or tortilla cake? Was tortilla a cake? Who cared – I was hungry. All I cared about was that cake equalled calories. Which was what my body was screaming out for. And what would I have to drink? I was gagging for a glass of freshly squeezed orange juice, in a tall glass with ice. How heavenly did that sound? I wanted it. I wanted it so badly I could almost have tasted it.

"Bollooooccccckkkssss!"

Having taken the bend at breakneck speed, I finally came face-to-face with my imaginary cafe. Which turned out to be a small barn piled high with hay with a growling tractor sitting out front.

To make matters worse, we were now out on exposed ground with our next tree line five hundred metres up the road. Was it just me, or did the moisture rising from the road make it look as if the road was steaming? There was nothing for it, we were going to have to make a run for it. Driven primarily, at least in my part, by the fact that spontaneous combustion wasn't covered in my InsureandGo travel policy.

But in order to make it to the tree line we first had to tip-toe around the carnage of pilgrim debris lying in it. The masses were sprawled all over it with their packs off, socks off and knives out. The knives were being wielded to cut a single slit along the instep of people's boots. This was undoubtedly done to create space for people's ever-expanding feet to breathe. Those who weren't wielding knives were sitting and watching or changing socks; or staring in disbelief at the early onset of blisters.

Under normal conditions, I'd have made an effort to stop – but not today. My body was steaming hot, there were already enough spectators, and we were having enough troubles of our own. No sooner had we hit the tree line than a bombshell was dropped.

"Boys, I'm done. Seriously boys, I'm cooked."

I turned to see a dejected-looking Dan. His face and shoulders were hanging low in acceptance. He was right – he was done. But I knew it wasn't the climb that had cooked him. It was the combination of a six-thousand-mile schlep across multiple time zones, little sleep and small meals.

We offered to divvy up his gear between us. I'd take the clothes and snacks while Ryan offered to escort the soon-to-be-smuggled Oompa Loompas. Sadly, Dan was having none of it. For safety, we stopped and topped up his bottle and I gave him a half pack of sweets. Hopefully, that would at least power him to Huntto.

"See you at the bar in Roncesvalles later?" I said, unable to hide my disappointment.

"And I'm buying. So don't be too late," Ryan said with a cheeky wink.

With that, we reluctantly shouldered our packs and headed up the road. Saddened by the loss of Dan, we trudged along in mourning for the next twenty minutes. But we were soon brought back to life by the sight of a building up ahead, just clipping the top of the hedges – this had to be Huntto.

But what was that up ahead? Sitting on a patch on grass beside a farmer's gate were a small group of pilgrims. At first glance it looked like a teddy bear picnic. It was only as we drew nearer that I realised this wasn't a picnic, but a pilgrim fly-tipping party.

"Seriously Ryan, would you look at these wankers! Who the feck do they think they are, dumping their shit on the side of the road? What, are they expecting the locals to run out and pick up after them? I get it. It's hot and everyone's packs are heavy. But it's their feckin' kit, they brought it. Therefore, they should carry it – end of..."

"...and another thing. You don't see Dan dumping his shit, do you? Why is that? I'm bloody sure given the option he'd love to. But no, he'll lug his kit to Roncesvalles. Where he'll either decide to post it on or gift it to others. Unlike these selfish gobshites. They're right bang out of order."

Ryan, sensing my growing frustration slowly started to manoeuvre himself between me and the didicoy pilgrim rabble. As I wandered by, I stared on in disbelief as hairdryers, novels, shoes, jumpers, even writing journals were ditched and left at the roadside.

"Wankers, absolute wankers, every last one of you," I muttered loudly.

In an attempt to distract me, Ryan clapped his arms around my shoulders, while placing another on my tummy.

"What have I told you? Stress is bad for your baby," he said smiling.

Ryan's wit did wonders to defuse the situation. A situation that was reignited two hundred metres further up the road, just before Albergue Ferme Ithurburia. Why? I spotted a bin. Not that I was advocating binning shit. But at least that was better than littering the pristine countryside.

I knew there and then that we wouldn't be stopping there. I was too wound up. To make matters worse, the alberuge had a large, shaded decking area complete with table and chairs. That would have been a perfect spot to rest my weary bones (while keeping a beady eye out for Dan).

But my rage didn't go to waste. Soon after we passed Huntto, the road rose savagely to the point that Ryan and I felt like Adam West in seventies Batman. All we were missing was a utility belt and a cable to help us scale it.

While I'd read this section was short and sharp, I knew the path would soon settle, before traversing the mountain and dropping down for the run into Refuge Orisson.

The sense of relief from having survived those first eight kilometres to Refuge Orisson was hard to put into words. Orisson looked like a classic French ski lodge. The bottom two-thirds of the building was made up of sandy and copper-coloured stone, designed to keep the savage Pyrenean winter at bay. Breaking up the stonework were four double windows complete with stained oak shutters.

The top third of the building was covered in wooden slats. Slats which were broken up in places with large panes of glass to allow light to flood in. My guess was the upper floor was where the rooms and dormitory were.

There was a viewing platform across from the refuge, complete with tables, chairs and a retractable canopy. I couldn't think of a better spot for elevenses. AKA, second breakfast. With that, my stomach let out a huge growl of approval.

After the fierce heat of outside, the inside of the refuge was baltic. The effect of which caused an army of goosebumps to ping up all over my body. All of this was quicky forgotten the moment I looked across the wooden bar counter and spotted a juicing machine, spinning fresh oranges.

"It's official. I'm in heaven," I said grinning at Ryan.

I proceeded to order a glass of freshly squeezed orange juice, a nuclear-strength coffee, two chocolate bars and a slice of tortilla.

"Quieres un sello?" said the smiling guy behind the bar.

Did I want a stamp? I gawped back at him blankly. Did I want a stamp? What would I need one of those... my thought was interrupted by the bar man who pointed to my right-hand pocket with my Pilgrim Credencial.

"Si, señor," I replied, feeling my face redden with embarrassment.

While the Camino was essentially rule free, there was one thing you MUST do, if you planned to obtain your Compostela (a certificate of proof of pilgrimage). You MUST collect:

→ One stamp for every day spent on Camino between Saint-Jean-Pied-de-Port to Sarria.

→ Two stamps for every day spent on Camino between Sarria and Santia... (I still couldn't say it, for fear I may jinx it).

These stamps provided the tourist office (where we could get our Compostela) with a record of our journey. Our Credencial also enabled us to gain access to pilgrim only accommodation along the way. It also had the additional benefits of reduced admission at exhibitions, cathedrals and points of interest. Plus, it offered the chance for us to get the pilgrim meal, which was often a set meal for roughly €10-12.

I watched in awe as the bar man fetched his ink blotter and slowly rocked the rubber stamp backwards and forwards over the ink. Everything seemed to go in slow motion as he slowly peeled open my Credencial, pointed at the empty squares, all desperately waiting, and thumped down the stamp. When he lifted it away from the page, I saw:

Refuge ORISSON 06 81 49 79 56

Below this, he wrote the day's date. As he handed me back my Credencial, I could feel myself bursting with pride. I was now a fully-fledged pilgrim. With my Credencial tucked back into my pocket I took my food and drink and headed out onto the terrace.

The next few minutes were utter bliss. Ryan and I were so comfortable in each other's presence, that we both ate happily in peace. When the silence did break, and it did often, it was broken by the sound of Ryan's laughter. What had set him off was anyone's guess. I didn't ask, nor did I need to know. All I knew was his laugh set me off laughing.

A few minutes later, we attempted to stand. My first attempt involved me standing, trembling, then collapsing back into my seat. My second attempt was much stronger. But even then, I felt shaky as my calves had begun cramping. I knew this would pass. Before we set off again, we both threw a glance back down the road. All in the hope of seeing Dan, but to no avail.

Typically, I wasn't one for stopping when I'd go walking. But today's pitstop was very much needed. So far, we'd fought our way up through the steepest sections and survived. Now with those climbs in our back pocket we were ready for our next challenge. A challenge which would involve us taking on the unrelenting sun on open ground.

With the gradient having eased, and me not talking like a forty-a-day chain-smoking donkey, I got to hear a little more about Ryan's tale. I liked Ryan, I liked him a lot. He was quirky, smart, laid-back and had the wildest imagination.

He was the Chief Architect of his own firm. He talked calmly and thoughtfully about his love affair with shapes, form, buildings. nature and his job. He also talked about the challenge of having global clients and the effect that had had on his life, with him often being away from his wife and only home for a hundred days a year.

Ironically, just that morning he had decided that that life wasn't for him anymore. He said it wasn't fair on him, his wife or the relationship he wanted to build with her. He had decided the time had come to scale things back and focus on projects closer to home. When I asked him what it would mean to leave his architectural mark on the Danish landscape – his face came alive.

The excitement that poured out of him as he spoke about his vision for the future was a joy to hear. His love for his craft reminded me so much of my own love for creativity. Like Ryan, creativity was my first love. We both agreed that there was no better feeling than picking up a pen, grabbing a sheet of paper and putting an idea down on it. It didn't matter what it was. Whether it was architectural plans, poetry, song lyrics or an advert, creating was our happy place.

So lost were we in our conversation, that the next ninety minutes floated by, like passing clouds. When we did finally look up, we noticed that the whole landscape had transformed.

Gone were the farmhouses, outhouses, telegraph poles, driveways, drystone walls and tree lines that once offered us protection. In its place was a single, thinly etched piece of tarmac. Tarmac that looked like a fresh scar, cut into the skin of the mountain. Yet at that altitude, with thinning air and only an aquamarine sky above us, it felt as though I could have reached up and touched heaven.

The sun seized on this opportunity to bear down with full vengeance. The effect of this, when combined with the energy-sapping, bone-crunching tarmac reduced our pace to little more than a shuffle. But shuffle we did.

Such was our focus on covering ground and finding shade that it wasn't until we'd hit the grass at Croix Thibault that we realised we'd missed the statue of the Virgin Mary – The Virgin of Orisson.

While the frazzled part of my mind was desperate to see it, the unfrazzled part of my mind asked – *do you want to do a three kilometre round trip to see a statue? Can't you just Google it later?*

"Save the statue for your next Camino, Paul," said Ryan, chuckling.

"Next Camino. I'll let you know. This is a one-way trip, Ryan."

We stopped briefly by the Croix Thibault to admire the cross, prayers, offerings and coloured ribbons tied to the protective guard rail. I could see that many of the prayers had been left by pilgrims who'd lost loved ones. Ones who'd been taken way too early. I sure as shit knew how that felt.

"Oi, fat lad! What are you mincing about here for? Get a shift on, will you? And stop crying about the heat. It's hot for everyone Saddlebags – not just you." Mitch's voice came through with his ever-familiar chuckle. He did, as always, make a good point. It was hot, and we still had ten kilometres to do.

Once onto the grass, we followed a dried dirt track as it headed between two mounds. What I needed now, more than anything, was not to see any cliffs or sheer drops (as me and heights were by no means friends).

What I didn't expect or plan for, as our path cut between the mounds, was to be accosted by a rogue band of wild, sandy-coloured horses. Sheep perhaps. But where the hell did the horses come from?

In all, there were seven of them, and only two of us. We were out-gunned, out-hooved and surrounded, with the horses taking up position on the higher ground. In short, we were fecked. We had wandered onto their turf with no warning or permission. For that, I had a feeling that safe passage would come at a hefty price.

The horses' swagger told me they were well-versed in the art of the stick-up. They coolly and confidently went about their business, relieving us of our water, snacks and energy bars. As muggings went it was textbook stuff. All of which was made worse by the fact that they insisted on being patted and stroked while robbing us.

After a further ten minutes or so, I could feel the horses growing bored. They'd taken what they wanted. They had no need of us. Plus, from the braying and twitchy nature of the horses, I suspected more pilgrims were headed their way. Therefore, they wanted us gone, before turning them over too. They didn't have to ask twice.

Our path now took us along a shaded woodland path. But where was the border? Did we need to have our passports ready? Would there be guards? Or simply a monument to convey the transition from France into Spain, with possibly some plaque and inscription about the route being used by Napoleon?

Not quite. Instead, we were greeted by a single, rusty cattle grid and a water fountain. Could the authorities be any less arsed?

The stone water fountain was a thing of beauty. Around the top of it was a brass ring about three inches in depth. Inscribed into it, in an old-worldy script font were the words – *Fontaine de Roland*. Beside the fountain stood a long, carved stone bench.

I wasted no time getting acquainted with the water fountain. I dumped my pack, ran over to it and hung my head under it, before Ryan punched the brass tap head. To my surprise and delight, ice-cold water gushed out, numbing both my head and body within seconds. I kept my head under for a good minute before resurfacing. When I did, it finally hit me. We'd made it. We'd beaten off the sun, the gradient and Sleeping Giant. We were now about to enter Spain for real.

The sense of giddiness and pride as we crossed the cattle grid into Spain was off the chart. Once across, the world and everything in it became lighter. I could sense us both finally relax as we followed the gently rising path up to the top of the Col de Lepoeder, which was marked by a strangely designed bench.

Ryan wasted no time in bagging the bench, leaving me to scratch around on the floor. In our heads the day was done. So, what better way was there to celebrate, than to down tools and get a battle kip in.

We woke up twenty minutes later, aware that there was one final decision to make. Should we take the steep and treacherous woodland path down to Roncesvalles? Or should we take the safe, boring road? And with that, out came my lucky coin.

→ **Heads:** we would take the steep woodland path

→ **Tails:** we would follow the road.

Heads won. So, over the road we went, before we began the most treacherous and dangerous part of our day. What made it so dangerous? Two things. The first being, we'd both started thinking of a warm shower, a bed, a lie-down and an ice-cold beer. While I was aware most expedition injuries happened within sight of home, I couldn't stop myself from dreaming of that first sip of beer. Or my body sinking into a bed.

The second thing that made it dangerous was the density of the forest canopy, which was so thick that in parts the sun failed to penetrate it. That meant that a lot of moisture and dew still clung to the surface of the rocks, making them lethal.

For the next hour we edged our way tentatively down the descent. We both knew all it would take was one misplaced step and it would be game over. The rocks knew this too, which is why they were baring their teeth, keen to snag a passing ankle.

When the descent finally levelled off, I felt physically drained and mentally exhausted. But that feeling soon disappeared as we cleared the forest and came out by a small stream. There before us was Roncesvalles. Which, for all intents and purposes, looked like a pilgrim version of Hogwarts.

We followed the road to the side of the building towards the front. There we were met by signage reading 'Pilgrim accommodation'. I could feel my mind trying so hard to savour the moment and take it all in, but my brain was shutting down.

Inside the reception area, it was cool and dark. To our left we could already see a queue had formed for beds. Neither of us had the energy to stand, so we threw our packs down and sat on the cold stone floor. In fairness, I'd have been quite happy to kip there. The floor was cold, and the thick, impenetrable walls would keep out the wind. What more could I have asked for?

For the next thirty minutes we sat there, our minds in a near catatonic state. Every so often my ears would tune into some murmuring. But before I'd grasped it, the thought was gone. I'd become so detached, I barely moved or registered the woman who collapsed two or three spots before me. All I recalled was the thump as she fell backwards, hitting her head on the glass partition wall, before she slid down it. And what was with the Irish fella? He was chuntering at a thousand miles per hour saying sporadic words: hunger, thirsty and bugs.

After what seemed like an age, we were asked for our Credencial for stamping. We were then led by a staff member down into the basement, where we were shown our allocated bunk beds. Ours was set in amongst a group of eight other beds.

Once I found my pit, I collapsed onto it. Now it was just a question of waiting for the pain to subside and the world to stop spinning. I also knew deep down that the day wasn't done by any stretch of the imagination.

Yes, the walking was done. But I still needed to shit, shower, shave, prep my kit and find food. And after 41,355 steps and seven and a half hour of walking, I would need a serious feed.

While the shower in the grey Portakabin did little to revive me, it did just give us both enough energy to hobble over for our pilgrim meal at Casa Sabina, the local bar and restaurant.

With nothing better to do, and with minimal strength to move, we decided to pitch up early and while away the afternoon looking blissfully at the setting sun. We reminisced about the beauty and the beast of the day – blissfully unaware that we'd left our packs unguarded on our bunks. But feck it, if someone wanted to rob me, they would. At least that would be one less thing to carry tomorrow (not that anyone did).

"Feck me, Ryan. That was harder than the London Marathon," I said as a matter of fact.

Ryan was too tired to talk, so he simply nodded his approval. During the course of the afternoon, one beer turned to two and two turned to three. By the time the pilgrim meal arrived we were ravenous and wasted no time getting stuck into a starter of soup, a huge basket of fresh bread (Mr. Bumble take note), a belly-busting plate of pasta, yoghurt and a large glass of wine.

By 9 pm we were half-cut and broken. What we needed were our beds. To our delight, as we shuffled back to our bunks, we caught a glimpse of Dan. Had he just arrived? Jesus.

With our fellowship reunited and the 'Sleeping Giant' conquered, we only had one final thing to conquer – sleep. And something told me that sleep was prepared to let this one go without a fight.

~~CHAPTER 5: HONEYMOON~~

31st August, Roncesvalles – Larrasoaña, 26km

As sleeps went, the night before was a non-event. A deadly combination of exhaustion, dehydration and a slowly dipping temperature with only my coat for warmth had put an end to that.

While the mattress had provided blessed relief from the day, it could do little to prevent the torture that the bed-beaters would bring. Though I couldn't see these critters, I could feel their presence. At first, they seemed to stand around my bed, silently observing me as I slept. Then I could hear one of them start to write, noting down all the areas where my aches and pains were originating from. Once they'd compiled their hit-list, they devised a plan of attack.

Prior to any attack, they needed to tool up. They did this by loading socks with soap bars. Once filled, they wrapped the head of the sock tightly around their invisible knuckles – and took up position. Then they launched a devastating attack, pummelling and thrashing my calves, ankles, knees, hips and lower back.

When the night finally shuffled off its mortal coil, I was left beaten and bruised. Not ideal preparation for what came next, let alone the day ahead. Suddenly, the darkened brick arches above my head were illuminated by a piercing search light. Within seconds, it was joined by two more beams. WTF was going on? Had I travelled back in time to an underground London tube station during the Blitz? Or unknowingly invited to an impromptu, 5:30 am Jean-Michel Jarre concert?

One thing was for certain, revolution was filling the air. This occurred the moment the beams tracked down the wall and onto the faces of crusty-eyed, sleep-deprived pilgrims. Any eyes attempting to resist their glare were met with a cacophony of ear-splitting sounds. Courtesy of the search light trio, a group of Italian pilgrims.

While they appeared blissfully unaware of the danger they were in – I wasn't. In fact, I couldn't wait for the reaction from the undead. All of whom were now waking and in need of a feed. The undead didn't care where they got their calories. Whether it came from bread, croissant or olive-skinned Italians.

"Idiots."

Ryan mumbled from the bunk above. He, like me, was hungry, tired, grouchy and in no mood for their nonsense. So, we got up, grabbed our kit and headed out to the grey Portakabin to clean ourselves up. Once washed, we shuffled back over to Casa Sabina. Though the morning air was biting hard at my exposed skin, the relief of being out of earshot from Super Mario and friends more than made up for it.

"Ryan, mate. I've got to ask you, as this is killing me. How! Just how, the feck is your pack only three point seven kilograms? I don't understand how that is even possible."

I was shaking my head in utter disbelief. But Ryan steadied his gaze and replied thoughtfully.

"Be honest with yourself. How much stuff do you really need...?"

Here we go, this is what I had been waiting for. I was about to be schooled in the Danish Art of Packing.

"...you see, I can only wear one thing at a time. I walk all day in one set of kit. When I arrive at my new accommodation, I wash my wet, sweat-stained kit. Then change into my dry clean kit. That's it. Well, that plus..." I wasted no time and jumped between his pause.

"Your spare leather cod piece? Your dog-eared copies of Juggerknockers?" I said in a vain attempt to put him off.

"...and my sleeping bag liner. I bet you wish you had brought one of them last night. As the bunk shook all night from your shivering," he replied, smiling.

"Well, aren't you the smart-arse?" I replied, waspishly.

"You see, I believe that in many ways your packs represent the sum of your fears," said Ryan, shooting me a zen-like stare.

"Packs! You're barely carrying one mate? Don't start making out that you're carrying two – you cheeky upstart." I said laughing.

On that note, the front doors to Casa Sabina blew open while I was prepping to fire off another few punchline jabs. That thought got intercepted by my eyes, which were feasting on the sight of fresh bread, jams, pastries and freshly squeezed orange juice. Then it hit me, the heavenly scent of rich, thick and aromatic roasted coffee.

We wasted no time and loaded up on food. Once done, we legged it back to the tables outside to watch the world wake up. In the fields opposite (on the other side of the N-135 road), low-lying fog, hung around lazily – unsure what to do next. The fog, much like the cattle, was showing no real enthusiasm for the day.

Above our heads, the sky was a shepherd's delight, full of tangerine orange and fiery reds. For several minutes we sat open-mouthed as we watched the greatest show on Earth unfold – sunrise.

"What the fuck am I doing with my life?" I mumbled, thankfully incoherently.

How many of these moments had I missed over the years? And for what? Just to grab a thirty-second head start on my day. Or to beat the commuter masses before they gathered at Brixton tube station? Surely there was more to life than chasing my own arse.

As the minutes ticked by, the undead started to appear. I heard them long before we saw them. My ears had picked up the sound of tired, lead legs and boots scuffing along the stones on the pavement. They, like us, had been broken and remade. Forged again by the sleeping giant we had walked upon.

While their bodies and minds creaked, there was no hiding the jaded sense of pride in their half-smiles. Yesterday's strangers were today's firm friends, bound forever by the road we had all walked upon. Around us, they laughed, smiled and embraced like long-lost relatives.

"Righto Ryan, let's get down to business. Who do you think is going to kick things off today?" I said, while scanning the masses.

"Either the Germans or these two!" said Ryan, who pointed at two Austrian girls, limbering up with a mini yoga session on the roadside.

"Well, one thing's for certain – it won't be our feisty, retina-burning Italian friends. Talking of them, where are they? Do you think they made it out alive? Or do you think the undead have consumed them and hidden their bones under the bunk beds?" I said with a smile.

"No, they're probably still in bed and giving the light bulbs a migraine," came his reply.

"Well, welcome runners and riders to today's exciting edition of the Camino Wacky Races. I am your host, Paul Middleton, and this is my co-

commentator, Ryan. The front row of the grid is starting to fill up as people take their positions. All competitors have started their engines. Now all we are waiting for is the signal three... two... one – and we're off.

"First out of the blocks and making a lively start to today's uppy-downy-kinda-stage is No.2, the twenty-year-old Asana-loving, Austrian pair from Amstetten. Followed eagerly by an early chaser, No.5, the Gebildbrot-loving Germans from Glaubitz. Hot on their heels and making the most of the slipstream is No.3, the High-Five-Howdy-Doody-Americans from Houston. While still on the grid and making no attempt to move whatsoever is No.7, the Chunky-Monkey-Jamboree combo from the UK and Denmark.'

"Fancy another brew, Ryan?"

There was no way the Chunky-Monkey-Jamboree was going anywhere fast today. Not least until we'd refuelled properly.

"Count me in!" he replied.

Suddenly, off to our left, we heard a series of coughs. Drawn to the sound, we both turned. There was Dan. I looked at Ryan and he looked at me in disbelief. Were we seeing a ghost? Or a resurrection? Unsure of ourselves, we started to pinch Dan excitedly. Just how was he up? How had he managed to rise this early after yesterday's thirteen-hour schlep?

With three brews ordered, Dan took a seat in the commentary box to watch the race unfold. We sat for another few minutes as the undead fired off down the road. It was Ryan who called time on our loafing. The crew of No.7, the Chunky-Monkey-Jamboree, assembled. We grabbed our packs and headed off in the direction of a road sign, where every pilgrim had stopped to take selfies and gawp.

SANTIAGO DE COMPOSTELA 790

Seven-hundred-and-ninety-kilometres. Fuck.

The numbers on the sign seemed so ridiculous, all we could do was chuckle. Was it right though? More importantly, what kind of sick bastard would shove up a sign metres from the start saying you've only got seven-hundred-and-ninety-kilometres left to go?

I, like everyone before me, draped myself around the sign like a conquering hero. The irony was I'd barely survived the Pyrenees, so it was a little premature to be declaring victory.

But today would be a kinder, sleepier day. We were trading the nerves, anxiety and excitement of the Pyrenees for a slower, undulating amble through fern-lined forests and tracks through Navarra's heartland. A region known as much for its unprecedented beauty as it was for being infamous as the home of gastronomy.

After taking photos, the gravel path gave way to a fern-lined forest floor. The sense of relief and lightness underfoot was magical and in complete contrast to the seismic shocks of the road that felt like shards of glass moving underneath my shins.

And talking of magic, the surrounding woodland was once home to just that. Hidden in and among the branches were mysterious Wicca dolls. These dolls were a nod to a witch's coven that existed here in the 1300s. I could only imagine the welcome greeting that the nearby Catholic congregation gave them. But I'd say their welcome was probably better received than when the 1478 Spanish Inquisition came rolling into town.

Once we'd cleared the wood, we picked up a small narrow track that ran adjacent to the N-135. Thankfully for us, the trees buffeted us from the road noise. As we wandered along, my mind was drawn to my question of the day: What did I learn yesterday? And how could that make the day's walk easier or better?

My two main takeaways were:
→ Forage wherever I could
→ Fill my water bottle at every opportunity.

The timing of these answers couldn't have come at a more apt time. Moments later, on the opposite side of the road, we came across a huge, white-washed building with green timber beams. Above the door, emblazoned in red letters were the words:

SUPERMERCADO - SUPERMERKATUA.

Even though I'd barely finished scoffing half an hour before, I was already planning my next meal. While I had no real reason to go inside, it surely couldn't hurt to have a look. After all, looking didn't cost anything.

Five minutes later, and several Euros lighter, I emerged. Laden down with two packs of TUC biscuits, a can of Coca-Cola and the day's star prize, a pack of Haribo Goldbears.

"What?.."

Ryan looked at me in disgust. He was standing and shaking his head with his arms folded and feet planted.

"...you said it yourself, Ryan. I'm eating for two – remember? Plus, I have to replace the emergency rations I lost yesterday. Courtesy of that tight-arse, Mr. Bumble."

Outside the supermercado some of the early frontrunners, No.3 and No.5 had already pitted. They'd downed their packs, undone their boots and were lying sprawled out along the grass and picnic benches.

I was keen to join them, but I was stopped in my tracks by a brood of rowdy chickens guarding the picnic area. Their look said the picnic area was full and they weren't taking any newcomers. And although their beaks didn't say it, their eyes said, "Jog on, fatty".

If we kept moving, we'd soon hit Burguete, which was yesterday's intended destination. I'd originally chosen it because I am a huge Ernest Hemingway fan. In my head, I had planned to explore the intricate streets that he called home in the twenties that inspired *The Sun Also Rises*. But my body had failed me.

So instead of spending the whole evening tootling around, admiring the colossal-sized homes, imagining what life would've been like back then, I got a few minutes.

I was struck by the colourful window boxes, along with the small gullies in front of the houses on either side of the road.

As we wandered along, curious locals came out en masse to greet us. While many were happy just to smile, wave or whisper "Buen Camino", a few brave souls called us over for a chit-chat.

While my grasp of Spanish could hardly be described as fluent, I knew enough to get by, and I found it easy to pick up. The key thing of interest here was the church of Saint Nicolás de Bari. Not far after that, we needed to keep our eyes peeled for a Santander bank. It was there we were told to turn right, before following a path down towards a small stream and over a bridge.

Sure enough, a little further down the street we spotted the ever-familiar red and white signage of the Santander bank. Beside it was a tiny, blue and yellow tile with an arrow and Camino sign on it. The slate cobbles around our feet also featured a set of arrows which pointed towards the sound of water, just as the locals had said.

The path led us down to a stone staircase with an old, rickety wooden bridge at the bottom that would carry us over the trickle of water that was the River Urrobi.

Once safely across, we were thrust back among the lush green hedgerows and low-lying fields. Fields which were full of a large herd of sandy-coloured cows and framed by the not-so-ominous mountain ridges, which looked almost laughable in size when compared to the previous day's beast.

While Dan, 'Joyous' Joy (an aptly named Canadian lady we'd met during the pilgrim meal) and I were happy to bimble along, it seemed that Ryan was on the charge. A mass pile-up of pilgrims had gathered around us. The effect of which had spooked Ryan and sent him scarpering up the road, seeking solace.

For a while Ryan remained attached to us by an invisible thread of elastic. He'd ping up the road, a hundred metres or so before stopping. He'd then wait, casually glance over his shoulder like a child seeking reassurance, before he came pinging back to us.

With each stretch of the elastic, the bonds between us started to loosen. And although no one mentioned it, it would only be a matter of time before the elastic P-I-N-G-E-D and snapped.

All that was left was one final wave from Ryan, then poof! He was gone in a plume of dust and smoke. And I for one, though gutted, couldn't have been happier as just that morning he had shared his anxiety about his lack of sleep, along with his longing to see his wife.

He knew that a certain amount of his apprehension had been brought on by the newness of his surroundings, the size of the task and the unfamiliarity of this new world. He, like all of us, was out of sorts and out on a limb. We were all a million miles outside of our comfort zone and a million steps from Santia... it still wasn't time to say it. All we had in our armoury to offset these fears was a smiley face and a lifetime of half-baked, shaky beliefs.

But melancholy had soon turned to delight last night when during beer number two, Ryan's phone had leapt from the table and into his hand. He knew instantly who it was from and his whole body softened as he read the message.

I'll see you in Santiago in thirty-five days xx

His wife had booked a surprise flight from Denmark to cheer her boy home. The message had utterly flawed him. So much so, that he kept reading and re-reading in shocked disbelief.

It had been this text, along with the thought that every step brought him nearer to his wife, that powered him now. My only hope, selfish as it was, was that somewhere along the road, either at Espinal or Viskarret, we'd meet again. Or failing that, we might possibly catch a glimpse of him in one of the albergues en route, either at Zubiri, Larrasoaña or Pamplona.

While Zubiri and Larrasoaña were the more likely choices, I couldn't rule out him pushing onto Pamplona as he'd spent months leading up to the trip running marathons, swimming in lakes and mud wrestling Danish Jersey cows at cattle markets (okay, I made that last one up).

As he slipped away, I hoped we'd meet again, but accepted we wouldn't. So, what was my Camino lesson for the day? Acceptance. While I was sad to see him go, I was grateful to have met a kindred spirit. Our chat and the secrets we had shared would forever remain safe. Blowing freely on the wind, high up in the Pyrenees, under the watchful gaze of the Sleeping Giant.

With Ryan gone, I dropped in beside Dan and Joy who were busy gassing about life state-side. I was happy to tag along, zoning in and out of their conversation. It was still too early in the day for me to be bothering with humans. No matter how nice they were.

I, like Ryan, just craved space, silence and freedom. In many respects, I craved everything my life lacked. I could feel myself slowly burning out. My mind was simply exhausted by the 24/7 fight for survival in London. Brought on by the fight to make the bus, avoid the rush, inhale food, answer emails, present work, then fight to get home. Being always on was slowly eating me alive.

By far the greatest drain on my energy was the creative agency I worked for. Every day was a constant battle, as senior bods stalked the halls posturing and pontificating their greatness to anyone who would listen. Instead of focusing on the job at hand, which was making great work.

As I wandered, I could feel my mind whir with these tired thoughts. But it wasn't the day to address them. My thoughts should be free to come and go on the breeze. All I wanted was to look, see and take everything in – while taking nothing in.

With that, I quickly switched my attention to what was before me. I marvelled at the path that stretched endlessly before us. I savoured the crunch of stones underfoot. A sound that reminded me of Rice Krispies popping in a bowl.

For the next twenty minutes I just drank in the scenery as it chopped and changed. One minute we'd be wandering along a wide gravel path. The next, we were fighting our way through dense undergrowth, being attacked by thorns or skipping over two-metre-long bridges and discarded wooden railway sleepers.

Espinal came with the sight of gardeners, busying themselves in their allotments. Some were working away under their polythene tunnels – watering, weeding and checking for pests.

A Camino sign just after the allotments directed us along Calle Iturrizahar, towards a T-Junction. From there, an arrow sprayed onto the road directed us right onto the Pamplona - Roncesvalles Road.

With a third of the day done, distance wise, all thoughts turned to what could be an early second breakfast at Toki Ona. It looked like a classic Swiss chalet; monstrous sized, yet stunningly elegant building. The bottom half was made up of polished stone while the top half had been plastered cleanly and painted yellow, topped with a rich red roof and matching shutters.

Outside Toki Ona, pilgrims were already making their pit stop (some of whom were crashed out). Most notable among them were the two Austrian girls, whose weary legs were sprawled across the aluminium chairs. While Dan contemplated which restorative coffee to have, I ventured off to check out the facilities, armed with my bog roll (and just as well).

Little did I realise or appreciate how valuable a commodity double-ply, baby-soft toilet roll was. It wasn't until I saw the look of disgust on a fellow pilgrim's face as he exited trap number two that I realised how lucky I was. It would appear that some light-fingered pilgrim had only gone and half-inched the remaining loo paper. A horror that was more than enough to keep me awake late at night. So, what I could spare, I did. In return for a seat around one of the tables afterwards.

For the next half hour, we lounged like lords, sipped coffee and pretended much like everyone else (who were also playing bluff), that yesterday hadn't been that hard. Which was bollocks, as all around me people were wincing, groaning and taping up bits of their body.

Beep-Beep! Beep-Beep! Beep-Beep!

NEWSFLASH! There was an electrical storm headed our way. The news when it came was delivered by none other than one of the feisty Italians from that morning's early raid. How had they got ahead of us? I didn't see or hear them pass us on the road. It all seemed a bit too dastardly and underhand for my liking.

With this news we tried to convince Joy to join us. After all, two's company, three's a party. But she was having none of it. It was her Camino 'honeymoon' and nobody, not even a biblical storm would convince her otherwise.

So, we headed up the road, our eyes eagerly scanning the buildings and street furniture for clues. About three hundred metres further along we saw a pedestrian crossing. It seemed to be directing us left, back into the woods.

Here the road soon became track. Our bodies urged us onwards as we attacked the two-hundred-and-seventy-foot ascent of Alto de Mezquíriz. While the gradient had nothing on yesterday, the lactic acid soon started to flood our muscles. The effect of which left my legs feeling like they were being dragged through wet sand.

As we headed deeper into the forest, the sense of claustrophobia started to grow. Trees reached out their spindly fingers in an attempt to snag or snare us. Meanwhile, the thickness of the foliage, when combined with a lack of air, sent our pulses and humidity levels through the roof.

By the time we'd made it to the top of Alto de Mezquíriz, I was bog-eyed and bollocksed. In my exhausted state I saw the road but didn't register it fully. Not until I was halfway across the N-135. Thankfully, God was on my side – at least today anyhow.

Having made it safely across the N-135, we now faced a steep three-kilometre woodland descent into Viskarret, in which we'd frustratingly concede every millimetre of height gained. But on the plus side, the track was dry-ish underfoot. Thus, making our descent a whole lot friendlier.

Thankfully, towards the bottom where it was at its steepest, the leaves, stones and wood shavings were replaced by perfectly laid, honeycomb-shaped, stone slabs. These provided the sure footing our ankles and feet craved. It also gave me a chance to break out my slalom skills, as I swished round bends before crossing over the River Erro and into Viskarret.

Behind us, I could feel the change coming on the breeze. The shepherd's delight skyline that had greeted us at the start of the day had been cast aside like an unwanted prop. The sky now was black and truly menacing. I could feel the air particles charging as we walked. Whatever was going to be unleashed would be of biblical proportions, that much was for certain.

From my perspective, the 'honeymoon' was over. There would be no more flower-sniffing, buttercup collecting or lollygagging between here and Zubiri. And as much as I despised the idea, we were now about to undertake the mother-of-all foot races. So, sod the Camino, sod the camaraderie and sod the high-fives. From now on, it was everyone for themselves.

I recall saying "hi" to Viskarret, then "bye" to Viskarret – that was it. The same could be said for Linzoain, a place that I had originally earmarked as the spot to enjoy second breakfast. That plan wasn't going to happen. As if to confirm, the sky let out its first belch of thunder.

Soon after Linzoain, we were sent back into the woods again. The animals, having gotten wind of God's plan were going apeshit. Overhead, panic-stricken chicks in nests called for their mums. While on the forest floor, squirrels and voles were busying themselves searching for their waterproofs and making umbrellas from oversized leaves.

Up through the forest we went, our pace getting more frantic by the second. Any thoughts of second breakfast had been binned. There would be no stopping today. Anything that could be consumed, would be consumed – while on the run.

It was as we crested the last ridge that broke the treeline, that I noticed two electricity pylons covered in satellite dishes. This was it; we had made it to the top of Alto de Erro. Our path from here crept along the treeline before dropping down the gravel path towards the bend in the main road. On the far side of the bend was a makeshift caravan serving snacks to a long line of food-ravaged pilgrims.

"Sello, sello?" shouted the cafe owner as we crossed the road towards him.

Yes, I'd need a stamp for my Credencial. But I wasn't prepared to hang about here in the open, not with...

Boooooooooooomm!

Suddenly, a seismic roar of thunder was unleashed. Its tremor so powerful that the ground and rocks around us shook. I turned and looked skywards, where I was greeted by the nastiest, gnarliest and most menacing skyline of my life.

Boooooooooooomm!

There came another crack of thunder and the temperature plummeted. My body, which had been sweating like an old dog, was now shivering like a homeless one. In seconds, goosebumps began to pop up all along my arms. While my teeth chattered violently, the wind started to whip up mini twisters from the dust, which left us momentarily blind as we rummaged in our packs for our wet weather gear.

Once found, the next job was to get the gear on, which was nigh-on impossible, as I couldn't see through the dust. Nor were my fingers working as a result of the sudden cold snap.

Boooooooooooomm!

But feck it, I just closed my eyes and tried to do it all by feel. Once dressed, I took a quick butchers at Dan's guidebook. According to his book, Zubiri was a good four kilometres away, which on a good day, would take roughly an hour to bash through. But on a not-so-good-day like this day I wanted to get it done much quicker.

We attacked the downhill with everything we had left in our limbs. The storm was closing in by the second. It wouldn't be long before it was upon us. We couldn't outrun it. It was more a question of how close we'd get to Zubiri before all hell let loose.

Come on... three kilometres to go. A slip followed by a slide. Two kilometres to go. At that point our legs had gone feral, and we had no control over them. They were just pushing and pushing. We were both way beyond being in control – but feck it. We, much like the storm, were committed now. This shit was about to pop off. One kilometre to go.

Boooooooooooomm!

The air around us was positively sparking. There seemed little point counting between claps. The storm was upon us and sitting ominously, inches above our heads.

Boooooooooooomm!

There was no way this could be held back any longer. Just as we hit the bottom of the climb and eyeballed the sign saying 'CONCEJO DE ZUBIRI,' the heavens opened. Within seconds of reaching the bridge, we were pelted with rain. Behind us, our path now resembled a stream. With the wind gaining pace and beginning to howl, we needed to find cover.

"Right," I muttered, unsure whether to head off to Plaza Mayor or up the street.

Are you off your tits? Just get your ass out of the rain you wally!

My conscience wasn't messing about. We opted to leg it straight down Calle Puente de la Rabia to Plaza Iglesia. Here, I noticed a arch set in front of a row of shops. This would do nicely. From there we could regroup, layer up and get warm.

"Dan, is that what I think it is?"

By luck, I eye-balled a shop with a whopping great illustration of a cup on it. Cup to me spelled coffee. Hallelujah, we had been saved.

The initial waft of heat as we opened the door hit us in waves. Waves that instantly made me feel nauseous. But within minutes, the nausea dissipated and my skin changed from Poppa-Smurf blue to rosy-red cheeks.

Although the locals greeted us warmly, wishing us all 'Buen Camino,' I could see in their eyes the question they really wanted to know – were we loco?

We quickly ordered two coffees – each. The first got dispatched within seconds, its job: damage limitation. While the second coffee was to be savoured and enjoyed. We sat back and watched nature lose its shit.

Above our heads the clouds grew blacker still, causing the shop's lighting to flicker and the streetlights to ping on. But their illumination was short-lived, as their tungsten lights were snubbed out by Evil's dark hand.

Boooooooooooomm!

Then the rumbles started again. It came low at first, as if toying with us. Then slowly its growl started to build, made more menacing by the gutter-like howl of the wind. A wind full of murderous intent.

Boooooooooooomm!

With that came the first crack of lightning. Its blue, thread-like veins tore across the sky as if searching for a victim. The lightning provided fuel for the next barrage of rain. Rain shells peppered the rooftops and cars hard pow... pow... pow. The noise was deafening, and its intensity set off nearby car alarms.

Boooooooooooomm!

Another crack. This one much closer to home. The forked lightning fizzed down from the heavens and struck a nearby tree. Whoever Evil was targeting, one thing was for sure – his aim was starting to get a lot sharper.

Through the streaks of rain on the window I saw an orange, yellow and blue shape out on the road.

"Are you shittin' me?"

Only a few metres from where the lightning had struck stood three pilgrims. What the feck were these clowns doing? Surely to feck they weren't contemplating walking in this. That was feckin' madness. All it would take was for Evil to adjust his aim slightly, and we'd have three deep-fried pilgrims. Then again, that would also free up some beds.

But what could I do? These weren't my monkeys, and this wasn't my circus. Plus, I had to think about our Plan B. Plan A had been to walk (though canoeing was a distinct possibility) to Larrasoaña. But there was no way we were going out in this. Therefore, our choices were to sit it out or stay in Zubiri. That would mean sacking off my accommodation in Larrasoaña.

We chose to wait it out. After all, there wouldn't be many times in my life when I'd get to witness a storm of this magnitude. I may as well enjoy it while it lasted.

Luckily, about ninety minutes later, there came an undeclared ceasefire. It started at five minutes. Then slowly eked its way out to fifteen minutes. At that point, we decided we would make a run for it.

We headed back over the bridge, before turning right up the path. With more rain imminent, No.7, the Chunky-Monkey-Jamboree set off at pace. I'd seen enough woodland paths, cattle and voles for the day. So, there was no need for us to stop. Now was the time for stomping. The Magna industrial plant was churning away as we passed it. A plant that looked pre-historic and totally out of whack with everything in the surrounding area.

Our road gave way to path and path gave way to woodland in a never-ending game of Pass the Pilgrim. The one thing of note along our way was a huge barn. One that proudly exclaimed in capitals – WELCOME TO THE BASQUE COUNTRY.

As we neared Larrasoaña, the path started to get narrower, giving thorns one last chance to snag our shorts or tear at exposed flesh.

Then suddenly, after what seemed an age, the path turned right. There before my eyes, as if in a dream, stood the Larrasoaña bridge. In days gone, this was a popular place for bandits to hang out. Shit! Where was a bandit when you really needed one? Had we arrived just as they were swapping shifts? If so, I was more than happy to wait, if it meant losing three or four kilograms from my pack.

Once over the bridge, we wandered into the village and up Calle San Nicolás, where we noticed the restaurant, Perutxena Taberna. Perfect. It was shut. But I bet with everything I had that it would open later. With the cold biting at my brain and my body aching, I headed off to Pensión Tau while Dan went off in search of his albergue.

"7:30 pm, Perutxena Taberna. See you there, Dan?"

"Ok, bud."

The relief of arrival at Pensión Tau was hard to describe. I was met by the owner whose warm smile couldn't hide her concern for the danger we'd all put ourselves in.

"*Tienes frío?*"

She offered me a cuppa. Frio. What did that mean again? I fought my mind's tiredness as I tried to figure it out. Frio… fridge = cold. She'd asked me if I was cold. Hence the tea.

With tea in hand, she invited me in and kindly showed me through her house. I stopped at the doormat, in a vain attempt to get my boots off. But my hands were frozen, and she told me not to worry. Once into the warmth of her beautiful home, she showed me up the wooden staircase to my room. A room which was both warm and cosy.

Once she'd gone, I quickly stripped and put my wet kit on the radiator. Screw washing my kit today. I just needed it to dry. Tomorrow I'd be honking – but so what!

By the time I'd washed, dried and squared my kit away. It was time to hit Perutxena Taberna. Over a few beers and a meal of chips and burgers we agreed that as honeymoons went – it had been spectacular. The good times and the sense of self-rediscovery were just about to begin. With that, we chinked our glasses in honour of our mate, Ryan (aka Uncle Travelling Matt).

Cheers, Ryan – wherever you are.

CHAPTER 6: POOHSTICKS

1st September, Larrasoaña – Pamplona, 15.5km
Boooooooooooomm!
I was shaken awake at 3 am as a thunderous crack of lightning tore open the Prussian-blue sky. Everything in my room shivered white momentarily, before scattering like fairy dust back into the darkness from which it once came.
Boooooooooooomm!
Evil had returned. He was back and full of murderous intent. I could sense the pot of hatred simmering within him. It had been made worse by the fact that his previous day's work had been cut cruelly short in Zubiri. For that, the world and everything in it, was about to burn.
Boooooooooooomm!
Another crack of lightning came. Evil's cobalt-blue fingers fizzed and flickered as shafts of light tore across the night sky. Just like before, Evil hadn't come alone. With him was his willing accomplice – the wind. Its low, gutter-like growl and rumbling were starting to get louder. It was as if Evil himself was standing behind a huge curtain prodding, poking and whipping it up into a frenzy.
Boooooooooooomm!
When the wind was finally unleashed, Evil moved to a vantage point high on the rooftops. From there he sat back, with a Death cigarette in one hand and a cheap bottle of whiskey in the other. He admired his handiwork.
Boooooooooooomm!
For the next two hours the wind howled, and the windows shook. Then suddenly, out of nowhere the world fell silent. During this pause in hostilities, I took the opportunity to get up from bed, as I was keen to inspect the casualties outside.
Within seconds of my feet hitting the carpet my legs and calves locked up,

as if shackled in irons. Their unwillingness to carry me meant that I was forced to drag my legs across the floor like an apprentice leper, hoping that one day I'd graduate and receive my bell.

I was suspicious. Why the ceasefire? What was going on? I peeled back the thinly veiled white mesh curtains. What was Evil up to? Was he pissed? Had he grown bored and tired? Or was he, as I suspected, merely toying with his audience before reaching the climactic crescendo?

Then, from behind the curtain of cloud, came the wind. It divebombed swooping along the hedgerows, gathering pace with each passing metre. It was only as it came within striking distance that it pounced, striking the windowpane.

That was the signal the rain had been waiting for. Within seconds, my window came under attack from a barrage of rain shells. They thumped hard against the glass, making it difficult to see out without squinting.

Outside in the garden, the dark silhouettes of trees had gathered. They had come together in a semi-circle for protection. Their limbs were long, their branches heavy and their heads bowed low in defeat. There was no way they could sustain this onslaught. Nor could they fight back. Their only hope of survival lay in their ability to plead for their lives.

But those pleas would go unheard. Evil wasn't there to listen to pleas or take confession. That was a priest's job. Evil had come to wreak havoc.

While the comfort of my room protected me from the worst of Evil's deeds. It offered no protection from the bed beaters who it seemed had travelled down with me from Roncesvalles (hidden in my pack). They waited again for my body to come to complete rest, before launching another devastating attack on my lower back, right hip joint and calves.

"Why me? What have I done wrong?" I said pleadingly into the darkness.

I think it's more a case of what haven't you done... came the bullish response from my conscience.

You haven't trained. Admit it, you've turned up here with your big-boy-Brixton attitude, a few North Wales expeditions and two sleep-inducing tales of London Marathon success. And you arrogantly think – you've got this.

Yet here you are crying and whimpering while hanging out of your own arse. These beatings are mere reminders of the price you will pay for your arrogance.

Somewhere in and amongst my scolding, I dozed off, only to be crudely woken moments later by the sound of my alarm – 6:30 am. As I lay on my back, relieved that the beatings had stopped, I took time to gather my thoughts as I prepared for the day ahead.

My first challenge would be the shower. The troubling question lingering in my mind was – did I have the hip strength to lift my legs up and into the bath? Or would I have to opt for a battle wash? Which would do little to remove the ground-in, salt-soaked pilgrim pong I was emitting.

But that morning, I felt more optimistic about achieving a shower. As I stood before the bath, I could feel my legs start to sway backwards and forwards like a seasoned high jumper. Ready or not. I was going to launch myself, Fosbury-flop-style, at the bath.

My first attempt ended in disaster. My poor timing, when combined with my leper legs, sees my big toe crunch hard against the beige, enamel bath side. The crunch of bone turned my face white with fright as I hopped manically, whistling like a tea kettle.

My second attempt fared only marginally better. My run up was good. But my leaping leg was still weak and crumbled beneath me, sending me crashing to the floor.

"Everything all right up there?" came the concerned voice of the owner.

"*Sí, señorita*. Just a fat man running at a bath, nothing to worry about," came my reply.

By my third attempt, I decided to ditch the fancy foot work and opted instead for brute force. In my mind: speed + girth + momentum = into the bath I go.

Once in the bath, I slowly hauled my broken carcass upright. It was then that I noticed everything in my world had turned beige. Beige tiles, beige bath, beige floor – even my skin was beige. I'd always found beige very calming, so I stewed for a few minutes, letting the warm jets of water soothe my creaking body and restore me back to life.

Having washed, faffed, and faffed some more, I hobbled down the stairs – clean, whistling and feeling fine. To my delight, the breakfast table was empty. Suddenly, my mind reminded me of a scene I'd previously deleted. It happened within moments of entering the house the day before (sodden, defeated and piss-wet through), where I was greeted by the sight of three smug pilgrims, all dry and lounging in chairs. They'd looked up nonchalantly and had asked, "What took you so long?"

Now, if Mitch had dropped that line on me, I'd have undoubtedly laughed it off. But the only words on the launch pad I had ready for them were, "Oh, do feck off". Thankfully for me, and due to the warmth of my greeting by the owner, I never used them.

While the pilgrim weebles had clearly wobbled off, I was at least grateful to them for not having hoovered up all the breakfast. In fact, judging from the overwhelming generosity of my host, they'd barely put a dent in it. On the table before me was enough food to feed the five thousand. But with the five thousand stuck in traffic, I felt compelled to eat as much as I could on their behalf – naturally.

By the time I finished masticating I could barely see, let alone walk. But with no nap forthcoming, I shouldered my gear and headed for the door. On the way out, I thanked the owner for a real home-from-home stay. In return, she shoved a small handful of mini muffins in my paw. More food – Jesus. Was she trying to make me pop? Or maybe she'd meant these to go to Dan? Well, that's how it felt anyhow. But we'd have to see about that.

"Morning bud..." came the sound of Dan's friendly Californian drawl, as he thundered up Calle San Nicolás towards me.

"...did you see that crazy-ass storm last night? Holy shit, the whole albergue shook."

His eyes were wide with excitement as he recounted his sleepless tale. A night filled with rain pellets, fork lightning, gatling gun snoring and the dawn chorus of farting.

While one ear was tuned into Dan, my eyes were busy scanning the ground around me. WTF. Where the hell was the carnage? I had expected to see downed branches, ripped off roof tiles and upturned cattle. But there was nothing. How was that possible? Had someone come along in the dead of night (maybe one of Dan's smuggled Oompa Loompas) and swept all the debris under the night's skirt? The more I looked at the newness of the scene, the more disturbed I became. This place was giving me the heebie-jeebies.

But on the plus side, the sky was clear, the temperature mild and any sign of rain had long since legged it. This came as much as a relief to me as the trees that lined the path. Gone were their sad, forlorn looks and brow-beaten branches of yesterday. They were standing proud; trunks erect and ready to embrace the day.

On paper, the day looked a doddle. A gentle fifteen-kilometre bimble along forest tracks following the gentle sound of the River Arga as it passed through the sleepy hamlets of Akerreta, Zuriain, Irotz and Zabaldika, before finally arriving at the hallowed castle gates of Pamplona.

In fact, the most challenging part would be the ferocious battles fought across the five, or was it six, bridges over the River Arga – where we would decide who would be crowned the Camino Poohsticks King. I knew having been trained in the dark arts of Poohsticks from an early age that I was the nailed-on cert to win. Dan, God love him, was an American. What more was there to say?

With that happy thought in mind, we set off, passing the San Nicolás de Bari Church and towards the bridge we arrived across the day before. Once near the bridge, we both quickly foraged for any available twigs. With the stream flowing slowly, I opted for a slight, dried twig. It looked both nimble and nippy. While Dan on the other hand opted for something way sturdier – typical amateur.

Five... four... three... two... one... go!

As soon as our sticks started their descent, we darted to the opposite side of the bridge and began cheering. Come on... come on... come on. But nothing. What was the hold up? It was only when I looked down that I saw a few worrying obstacles – a metre or so before the finish, there was a thicket of weeds and heavy stones.

"If your stick gets caught there, Dan, you... are... so... fecked."

Not that Dan heard me. He was too busy leaning over the bridge, his nose six inches from the water. Why was he bothering? He obviously wasn't going to win. A fact that was confirmed moments later as my stick swerved a stone, danced around the reeds and moon-walked over the finish line.

"Get in there, you beauty..."

"...Dan. Dan any sign of yours yet? Is there? Is there? Is there? I'm only asking as we've only thirteen hours of daylight left?"

Dan mumbled a response, which didn't seem to include the magic word – congratulations. God, was there anything worse than a sore L-O-S-E-R? With first blood to me, I danced up the gravel path, shimmying and shaking while blurting out Tina Turner's classic, 'Simply the Best.'

To the right of the path were two signs. The first sign hung from a red T-shaped steel frame. On it were four yellow rectangular mini signs showing four destinations. Three of them were for accommodation in Larrasoaña.

Been there, done that. The other showed Akerreta, straight on. About six feet beyond that there was a traditional Camino stone marker. I could only assume that it had been placed there to help clueless, dumbasses from getting lost (like we did on day one).

The morning air that greeted us was fresh. So fresh in fact, that its purity stung deep inside my nostrils. It was the kind of fresh and calm that only came after a torrential storm. The sense of calm in the day was already having its effect on me.

That was a far cry from my typical day, where traditionally, my inner calm was stolen within moments by the sounds of sirens, screaming and tube line brakes screeching. But those thoughts were mere second-class citizens inside my head.

Instead, my morning was filled with the sight of low-lying forests bursting with colour, trees shaking the rain off their leaves and the sweet, soft sound of birdsong.

Within minutes of following our path, the hedges started to descend upon us. By the time we hit the final bend (leaving Larrasoaña behind), the hedges had us surrounded. Our only way now was forward, up towards the Parish of the Transfiguration that loomed large on the horizon.

As we drew near, the path decided to snake to the right and rise savagely. If we were going to enter Akerreta, we first needed to earn that right. Our arrival into the hamlet was somewhat short-lived. Upon entering, we were greeted by the sight of an eye-watering allotment (that Samwise Gamgee would have been proud of) and a beautiful, rustic, renovated white-washed building – Hotel Akerreta.

A hundred yards beyond the hotel, the road split. Which way now? A question that always hurt first thing in the morning. Luckily for us, we spotted a Camino stone marker loitering with intent outside one of the houses. That marker led us down a gravel path and passed a barn where, suddenly, we were plunged into semi-darkness.

For the next few minutes, we battled with encroaching branches, ever-aggressive thorns and unevenness underfoot. Then finally in the distance, we could see the first shafts of sunlight illuminate and warm the tips of the tree branches.

Once free of the undergrowth, the path and the scenery opened up again. To our right was an endless treeline of forest, that stretched out for miles, creating the illusion that heaven, along with Mitch's commentary, seemed closer.

With serenity and calmness all around, I could feel my mind start to relax and be at one with the forest. From the birds taking breakfast orders, voles picking up the fruits from the wind's labour, to the sight of a magnificently coloured beetle, sitting nonchalantly on a wooden tree stump.

It was decked out in its Sunday best and seemed to be enjoying the hospitality of free hors d'oeuvres, as midges unwittingly flew just a smidge too close to its mandibles. Whatever the beetle had planned for the day – whether it was joining a high-powered executive of the Woodland Gathering, or a few games of whist – one thing was for certain: it wasn't going to be rushed.

After an hour of ambling through the forest, things started to level up and thin out. We were now wandering along single file tracks, with cattle looking perplexed to our left. To our right, was the steady trickle of the River Arga. I knew roughly from our pace that Zuriain, and more importantly, our second game of Poohsticks couldn't be far away.

With that in mind, my eyes began to eagerly scan the forest floor. I was 1–0 up and keen to pile the pressure on Dan. He knew if he didn't find a game-winning stick, and soon, he'd face another barrage of one-liners and punchlines.

Just as we approached Zuriain, I saw it, the game-winning stick. It was an absolute beauty. It was long and slim, with the perfect streamlined nose. It would cut through water effortlessly and surely deliver me the victory that was so rightfully mine. Except there was one problem. Dan's hulking, man-mountain of a frame was blocking my path.

Surely, he'd see it first, but what could I do? My mind quickly ran through the series of scenarios available:

➜ Rugby tackle him to the ground

(The guy was five inches taller, sixty pounds heavier and built like a brick shithouse. No. Bad idea.)

➜ Poke him in the eye with a sharp stick

(You don't need to poke him with anything. You just need the stick.)

➜ Kick his back legs.

(A little harsh, also immature and shows really poor sportsmanship. So, a contender.)

Unbelievably my conscience had got the better of me. While I disagreed wholeheartedly with the idea of playing by the rules, I did know any attempt to pass him would be foolish. All it would take was one swipe from his pendulum-swinging-pack and it would be game over.

Sensing I was up to no good, Dan stopped and began scanning the ground. The next thing I saw was him on his hands and knees, sweeping his hands along the floor. What was he looking for? A woodland IED? All it would take now was...

"Gotcha," he claimed.

To my horror and Dan's delight, he found my stick. Now we were only minutes away from the bridge. Dan had the winning stick, which left me scratching around for what would be, a shit stick.

Dan could sense that I was flustered. As we approached the bridge, he started to strut and showboat, (like he'd found the Holy Grail).

He won't be laughing if his shit stick performs like his last one, will he?

My conscience was right. All it would take was a stone, a few weeds or a renegade duck and his luck could change on a six-pence.

Five... four... three... two... one.

He let go of his stick and it landed perfectly in the water. Of course, it bloody well did. Mine hit the water hard and sank quicker than the Titanic.

Dan didn't waste any time in starting his celebrations, making whooping sounds, clapping and giving out high-fives to invisible passers-by. All that before his stick had even crossed the finish line. When it did, he finished his celebration with a Baloo-style dance routine, thus, ruining *The Jungle Book,* one of my favourite films, forever. Watching the whole spectacle from grey plastic chairs outside La Parada de Zuriain were the pilgrim masses, who made matters worse by joining in with Dan's clapping.

1–1.

Now I was depressed. While the La Parada de Zuriain albergue-cum-diner looked cool, what fascinated me was the iron sculpture of what I could only presume was a pilgrim that greeted us. Somehow it looked vaguely familiar. But how was that possible?

Then it hit me. The sculpture reminded me of Death, from the animated sequence of The Three Brothers in *Harry Potter and the Deathly Hallows: Part 1.* While the idea that Death was following us was undoubtedly true, the idea that Death may well have been clinging to my pack, even as I walked, gave me the heebie-jeebies.

1–1. WTF.

The day hadn't officially warmed up. But there was a hive of activity on the porch. The pilgrims began to furiously unclip their packs and rummage for their fleeces. When I closed my eyes, I felt like I'd entered the studio during a Run-DMC scratch session. Once the warm gear was found, the usual flurry of greeting hugs, high-fives, air kisses and back slapping resumed amongst the group.

"Dan, is that Ryan?" I said curiously.

Somehow my eyes were drawn to a silver-haired fox moving through the crowd. Whoever it was, he certainly looked and moved like Ryan. But at that distance, I couldn't tell if he smelled like Ryan – who after three days with only two bits of kit, may have been smelling a little, how should I say, ripe.

With the exciting prospect of seeing him again, I set off through the crowd in hot pursuit to the main door. No sooner had I inched the door open, I got hit with a tsunami of noise, the shock of which made me release the door instantly. With the noise trapped inside, the world felt peaceful once more.

Your mate's in there and there's food to be had. What are you waiting for?

Egged on by my conscience, I opened the door again. The noise seemed to blow me backwards. But somehow, I managed to close my ear flaps and enter. Not even that could have helped to prepare me for what I would see next.

All around me, pilgrims stood open-mouthed, motionless and transfixed. They'd foolishly fallen victim to the television's tractor beam. Upon seeing the damage, the television had done, I redirected my gaze downwards, while trying to scan the bar. No Ryan. Which only left the possibility that Ryan, or Ryan wannabe, had shuffled off to the khazi. While I waited for the outcome, I wasted no time in ordering two coffees and two tortillas.

When possibly - Ryan finally emerged, I was gutted. He wasn't the same make and model Ryan we'd met in Saint-Jean-Pied-de-Port. He wasn't even close. Now all that was left was for me to break the sad news to Dan.

I'd probably only been in the bar for about three or four minutes, but when I emerged, it felt like I'd entered a whole new world. All the hugs, high-fives and happiness were gone. Replaced by the nervous looks and anxious faces of those staring longingly into the depths of their mobile phone screens.

Dan's face was a picture. He, like me, couldn't quite believe it. With each passing second, more and more pilgrims began to get pulled down the technology rabbit hole. Pulled into a faceless world of likes, shares and tweets.

"I've seen enough of this shit, Dan. Let's go."

We quickly necked our coffees and demolished our tortillas before heading up to towards the main road – the N-135.

Hoooooooonnnnk! Hoooooooonnnnk!

Thundering towards us as we turned left onto the road was a white, thirty-foot, honking juggernaut. Its exhaust was spewing its guts into the air and right into our nostrils. Nice. Ahead was an arrow-straight road. Our safety was now in the hands of a white, continuous line not much thicker than a tightrope wire. This represented all there was of a hard shoulder.

In the distance we could see a small pocket of pilgrims fighting for yards. All the while they walked, they were being bashed and blown about like skittles in a cheap bowling alley. If the trees and the forest represented my version of heaven, then these aggressive truck drivers, choking fumes and their unbending refusal to give us an inch represented hell.

Thankfully, after a few minutes of bracing and buffeting, the road forked off to the left, where a large blue Camino sign directed us away from the N-135 and on to the NA-2339.

With each passing step, the roar of the juggernauts lessened. Our road was little more than a single car width, cutting between two fallow fields. Framing the scene and the skyline was a humongous, densely covered ridge, thick with trees. The angle of the ridge tore a ninety-degree tear in the sky's curtain – which had caught Dan's attention.

Mine had been caught on the sign up ahead that said RIVER ARGA.

With Dan distracted and only metres to the bridge, I had the pick of the sticks. By the time he realised what lay ahead, we were already at the bridge, which left him scrambling for any stick lest he lose the game by forfeit.

"You ready?" I said confidently.

Five... four... three... two... one.

Again, his stick hit the water first, diving then rising like a salmon, before steadying itself. My stick seemed more than happy just to be bobbing up and down like some fat biffa in an aqua aerobics class.

"Don't just feckin' bob up and down, you clown. Get after Dan's stick."

Not that that did anything to motivate my stick. It was in full-blown mañana mode – typical.

"Dan, what is it with my sticks? What is it they don't like? Are they afraid of a little hard work? Or do the buggers just not like water?"

Dan obviously heard none of this. He was too busy chanting as he ran up the road.

"2-1 to the Mighty Dan. 2-1 to the Mighty..."

I couldn't cope with much more of this. What was going on? Not only was I losing at Poohsticks, but I was also being out-thought and out-sung by an American. This thought was still raging in my head as we passed the hamlet of Irotz. Luckily, I was still in shock and Dan was too busy celebrating to remember we'd crossed another bridge.

With Irotz gone, my next big opportunity would come at The Battle at Zabaldika. Here the River Arga widened significantly, and its water course ran faster. As we were both standing poised on the bridge, I tried to look for patterns of current and flow. I needed this next win. I needed it badly. Otherwise, I'd never hear the bloody end of it.

All I needed was one good stick. Just one. One that wasn't afraid to give it go and had no inhibitions. And if need be, one that was willing to cheat.

"Come on, you beauty. Show this Oompa Loompa-smuggling, Orc-slaying directionally challenged fool what we, the half Irish, can do."

With that, I kissed then blessed my stick. With both God and the Irish nation on my side, how could I fail?

Five... four... three... two... one.

Our sticks got tangled up the moment we both let them go.

"Nooooooooooooo!" I screamed.

Who's would break the surface first? Come on now... you lazy, work-shy, good-for-nothing gobshite. With that, Dan's stick surfaced. No problem, nothing to panic about – yet! His stick started to drift towards the slower-moving current. While mine had somehow managed to steer its way into the current's fast lane. That was more like it. I knew deep down, when push came to shove, God would always side with the Irish – well, half Irish. All my stick had to do was hang on... two metres... one metre.

Suddenly, my stick got caught in the undertow. I could see it wriggling, trying to wrestle itself free.

All the while, Dan's stick was just cruising, like it was out on a Sunday drive down the Pacific Coast Highway.

Come on, come on, just right yourself you beauty you still have...

"Yeah, boy! U-S-A! U-S-A!"

To my horror, Dan's stick floated effortlessly across the line.

"Why? Why do I always get a friggin' warped stick? Seriously, what's wrong with these things? Why is it, no matter how hard I look, or how hard I try, I always end up with a friggin' warped one?" It was then that I realised I'd morphed into Governor Lepetomane, Mel Brooks' character from *Blazing Saddles*.

"U-S-A! U-S-A!" continued Dan.

Honestly, the whole day had been rigged from the word 'go'. There was no way I was going to accept that Dan was the Camino Poohsticks King.

Above, in God's Bar, I could hear Mitch chuckling while spitting his pint everywhere. For the first time in my life, I was utterly speechless. I had no comeback, no witty retort – nothing. I just had to face the fact that I was a L-O-S-E-R.

As if to pile on the misery further, the road now led us down to the path which ran adjacent to the River Arga.

"Hey, Paul buddy... buddy... is that your stick...? No, seriously, I think I can see it. No, wait a minute, maybe it's that stick over there. You see it? No, not there, THERE! It's the shitty little one, that looks half drowned. Maybe you should go rescue it? But if you do, don't take all night. It gets dark here around 10 pm."

While Dan was laughing wildly, I had to do the walk of shame beside the river. The underpass, our entry into Zabaldika Park, couldn't come quick enough.

Upon leaving the underpass, we were confronted by legions of pilgrims. They were stretched out among the stone benches and picnic area – sorting out their food, redressing wounds and hobbling to the bathroom.

From Zabaldika Park, there were two paths that led skywards. The official one started to the right of the red information boards. The crudely made pilgrim path (and at half the distance), started just after the toilet.

The climb up and out of the park was gentle enough. Someone had thoughtfully put down cement sleepers to help our footing until the golden path levelled off. When it did, we were treated to great views of the lush green valley below. The only thing to contrast it was the scar gouged into the earth by the blue-grey N-135 road.

Our path started to weave along the mountainside as we crunched along the path to Arleta, which was little more than a mansion house and an adjacent barn and had now been commandeered by anxious pilgrims, keen to escape from the furnace-like temperatures of the day.

On and on the path went, until finally we came to a narrow, clammy tunnel carved into the hillside. Once through, we could see that the hillside had been split in two, in an effort to make way for the ever-present N-135. Beyond this, set amongst a patchwork quilt of green and brown surrounding fields, was Pamplona.

Pamplona. The thought left me with mixed feelings. On the positive side, life was good. We would arrive battered but injury free. I was also ready to enjoy my first rest day. I knew that I had it in me to continue, but I couldn't shake the old saying: eat before you're hungry, drink before you're thirsty and rest before *you drop dead*.

Plus, it would also be good to wander through the streets made famous by the San Fermín Festival, the running of the bulls. It would be lovely to take the time to gaze in wonder at the beauty of the cathedral and the old citadel. Or to just hang out by the bandstands in Plaza del Castillo and watch the world go by.

But there was another part of me that selfishly wanted to remain in nature, in silence – in my bubble. I could feel myself just starting to come down from the manic nature of London life. Did I really need to be thrust back in, amongst the hustle, bustle and mayhem of two hundred thousand people?

By the time I'd walked down the hill towards Trinidad de Arre, a low-lying, six arched medieval bridge, I'd accepted my fate. After all, it was all well and good finding peace in nature or meditating in the wilderness (that, to me, was a piece of piss), what I needed to learn was how to carry that same sense of peace with me, regardless of the environment I was in.

Once over Trinidad de Arre, nature slowly started to disappear, to be replaced by narrow streets, pastel-coloured apartment blocks with brown shutters and balconies full of washing.

Having grown used to the simplicity of one track and one arrow, my eyes now had to compete with the world of street signage. In this urban jungle, with a tired mind and weary feet it was easy to take a wrong turn. The problem with any wrong turn (especially in big places) was that it could easily add an extra twenty minutes of walking onto my day. A thought that was excruciating and one that would most likely prove true.

Somehow, we managed to pick our way through the streets, crowds, parks and abandoned lanes until we finally found the enormous Magdalena Bridge.

Once that was spotted, I could feel my weary body start to shut down and relax.

While my eyes were keen to take in the beauty of the old city walls, the Portal de Francia and the drawbridge, my body was starting to scream, "Can we please just – stop".

The drawbridge that formed the gateway into Pamplona looked like the entrance into Helm's Deep. And judging by the height and girth of the city walls and gate, I'd say it could have easily held off an army of Orc, Uruk-hai or whoever else fancied their chances.

Once through the gate, we entered the belly of Pamplona. There we were hit instantly by the sound of a workman's angle grinder screaming for water. That was soon followed by the waspish sounds of scooters as they bounced over the defective cobblestones.

The first Camino tile I saw was high on the corner of the building on Calle Carmen. Feeling reassured, we wandered down the ever-narrowing street, lined with apartments painted lovingly in pastel shades of blue, orange, red and ochre.

The only people we'd seen for three days were pilgrims. We all looked the same, dressed the same, smelled the same. And by and large, we all walked in the same direction. Here everything was different, with people leaping out at us from all angles. On the whole, it felt as if I was swimming upstream, against the current and directly into the path of shoals of tourists and locals.

Slowly, we picked our way down Calle Carmen, Calle Mercaderes, Calle Chapitela before we finally came to the incredible Plaza del Castillo. Wow! The Plaza del Castillo was an enormous square, complete with bandstand. Surrounding it on all sides were bars, restaurants, patches of grass and trees. Here I could imagine that families, colleagues and friends would gather after work to enjoy a coffee, a cigarette break or just to sit out on yet another balmy Spanish evening.

As we headed through the Plaza, I spotted Café Iruña. Of all the things I'd researched, that was one of my must places to go. The café was one of the iconic spots in Pamplona. It was famed for its Belle Époque decor, its beautiful wooden panelling, dainty columns and decadent lighting. It was also a place where back in the day, Ernest Hemingway would while away an hour or two.

Invigorated by the sight of Café Iruña, we ploughed on up Avenue San

Ignacio until we came to the night's haven of peace and sanctuary, Hotel Avenida. Once checked in, we both headed to our rooms to collapse and grab a battle kip before we headed back out.

The day hadn't been long, but it had taught me a thing or two. The first being to never play Poohsticks in Spain. The sticks were warped, anti-Irish and I was never going to win. It also taught me a valuable lesson about inner peace.

While any old numpty could find peace and tranquillity sitting alone, cross-legged halfway up a mountainside banging a tambourine, I needed to learn how to carry my peace with me. As it was in this space, in this calm, where my life's riches lay.

~~CHAPTER 7: DREAM TO ME~~

2nd September, Pamplona, 0km

Where are you now, Jo Hills?

I woke into the abyss at 5:32 am tired, confused and pinned down by my three-hundred-pound opponent. I tried to move but couldn't. The sleeper hold on me was too strong. So strong in fact, that it'd left me wheezing, coughing and gasping for air. This was a fight, I knew I simply wouldn't win. My opponent was too soft and too strong. I was left with no other option than to tap out.

Thud! Thud! Thud!

That was the sound of my palm slapping the mattress in submission. Upon hearing it my opponent, the white linen duvet, slowly released its grip. With victory assured, it collapsed exhausted into my weary arms like a star-crossed lover. There we lay in mutual bliss, before I slowly drifted off into what I'd hoped was a deep, impenetrable sleep.

Thump! Thump! Thump!

I was woken sometime later by that sound. Even before I'd had chance to scrape my eye bogies away, my mind was conjuring up possibilities. What would I see when I finally opened them? Would it be:

→ Evil peppering rain shells at the hotel window?

→ Dan's midget marching band striking up?

OR

→ Alice's white rabbit thumping its back leg hard in frustration before disappearing back down the rabbit hole?

"Breakfast, bud?" came the shout from Dan through the door.

"Yeah... uh," was all I could muster before my mouth gave up.

Slowly, exhaustedly, I rolled over and sat up. What the hell was wrong with me? My body felt like it'd been hit by a train. As for my mind, that was lost in a sea of thick fog.

Oh! Deary dear. Would you look at the sorry state of you?

While I was relieved, we'd made it to our day off. I only realised how exhausted I was when I was stopped halfway down the corridor by two anxious-looking English oldies.

"Are you alright, dear?"

I tried to reply to the Jawa-sized, smartly dressed pair. But words failed me.

Well, this isn't awkward – much!

In an attempt to break the Mexican style stand-off, the same lady tilted her head to one side, before whispering to Dan, "Are you taking him out for the day, dear?"

"Yes, ma'am. I am." Dan proclaimed.

"And between you and me, I'm taking him on a little adventure... first to Plaza del Castillo. He just loves open spaces and people watching. And then, if he's a good boy, I might just buy him an ice cream. You love ice cream, don't you?"

Dan's face, much like the ladies', was beaming in wild delight.

WTF! When did I turn into Ruprecht? The trident carrying, one-eyed gimp made famous by Steve Martin in the classic *'Dirty Rotten Scoundrels'*.

"Then afterwards and depending on how tired he is (because he gets grouchy if he doesn't get a nap), I might take him down to Calle de la Chapitela before heading towards Plaza de Toros de Pamplona to see the bull ring."

"That sounds lovely. You two boys have fun!" said the ladies before waddling off.

I was relieved when we finally made it outside. While Dan was in fits of giggles, my attention was drawn elsewhere – to the sight of churros trotting up the street, attached to the hand of a fellow human. Criminally, he seemed more interested in his phone than his churros.

I'd soon sort that – no bother. All it would take was for one of those bad boys to come within striking distance. When it did, I'd paw swipe it and steal it. But as I raised my hand to strike, my hand hit something hard – Dan's forearm.

Seriously! Someone was taking his carer role a little *too* seriously.

Righto! Enough of this nonsense, I was hungry. I tried to conjure up where I'd seen a cafe the day before. In my mind's eye I could see it. It was situated nearby, on a street corner...

Could you BE any less specific?
...opposite a pedestrian crossing...
That's narrowed it down.
...and I remember it had a maroon-coloured awning with white-out letters. And out front were three oak barrels huddled together, like old men in a boozer.

As we creaked our way along Avenue de Zaragoza, my eyes were drawn to the gently spitting fountain on the roundabout. Surrounding it was a beautifully manicured lawn and flowerbeds bursting with colour. That was more than could be said for the surrounding buildings, which all seemed to have endured death by a thousand licks of beige.

"There it is, Dan. Cafeteria Jamaica."

Situated on the corner between Avenue de la Baja Navarra and Calle Emilio Arrieta, the cafe – exactly where I said it would be.

That wasn't how you described it at all.

We only managed to get halfway over the crossing, before I was struck by the heavenly scent of coffee. The intensity was enough to draw us inside, where we were directed to two empty bar stools.

"What would you like to order?" said the barman.

"*Toda,*" I replied in Spanish while waving my hands. I wanted it all.

For the next hour we chomped, chuntered and chatted while Dan tried to reformulate the plan for the day. Why? He'd promised me ice cream. I wanted ice cream. He'd also said he'd take me to sit in the open at Plaza del Castillo – he'd promised.

Granted, Pamplona had so much more to offer beyond the Plaza, such as:

→ University Museum of Navarra
→ Pamplona Cathedral
→ Taconera Gardens
→ Citadel of Pamplona.

But I (Ruprecht) was tired. The last thing I wanted to do was get be dragged around on my knuckles on a must-see tourist excursion. Bollocks to that. If I was going anywhere today, I wanted to be carried through the street like a Roman deity.

With our bellies full and minds defogged, we settled the bill then headed off down Avenue San Ignacio towards Plaza del Castillo.

Even though it was still early, about 10:45 am, the place had started filling up with casual joggers, coffin dodgers and people watchers. And as we'd had no bags to carry, no arrows to follow or pilgrims to kick, knobble, or sneer at, we decided that if we couldn't beat them, why not join them?

One thing I'd begun to notice and love about the Spanish is they always seemed to be smiling. But that in some way unnerved me. What was wrong with them? I got it, a smile goes a long way, but all the time. Imagine if I tried smiling in Brixton? Within seconds I'd be glared at, sworn at or labelled a f-u-c-k-i-n' f-r-e-a-k.

But here, everyone was at it. So much so, that I'd began to think the city was embroiled in some secret game of pass the parcel, with the parcel being a friendly smile. I sat transfixed, watching a smile passing from one face to another. Had I somehow stumbled across one of Pamplona's best kept secret?

With my smile restored and my bones warmed by the sun, we set off down Calle de la Chapitela, a street lined with beautiful, pastel-coloured apartment blocks. At the bottom of the road, we turned right, along the cobbled and shaded Calle de Mercaderes.

I tried to imagine the riotous spectacle that would take place every July during the eight-day Running of the Bull Festival. When six or seven one-thousand-pound rampaging bulls would tear along these claustrophobic and cobbled streets at 15 mph. Their target, the bull runners (known as mozos), who'd be dressed head-to-toe in white with red accessories.

The very thought of the festival was terrifying. Not only from the mozos' perspective, but the bulls'. I tried to imagine the life of the bull. One minute it would be enjoying life in the Spanish countryside, chewing grass, chilling out or getting its end away. The next, it would be plunged into the alien and oppressive heat of the city, subjected to the blood-curdling screams of a million testosterone-fuelled fans.

Their route would take them along Santo Domingo, passed the City Hall, Plaza Consistorial and along Calle de Mercaderes. Treacherous as fuck under hoof in the wet. All of this would occur before the sharp right-hander onto Calle Estafeta. From there it would be a seven-hundred-metre dash down an arrow-straight street, devoid of sky, to the bull ring.

The sight of the bull ring made my blood run cold. The cold, concrete, lifeless exterior reeked of death. It felt like a gladiatorial arena from days gone by, where death was delivered over three crowd-cheering acts, or tercios.

What was it about bullfighting that was so admired? I wasn't judging. I was just curious. I knew that culturally, bullfighting had existed here for well over twelve hundred years, dating back to 700 AD. But who had brought it here? And why? I was also keen to learn why bullfighting was still popular in some regions yet loathed in others.

With no one to ask and my in-tray of questions starting to pile up, I decided to park any further thoughts for the day. Instead of ploughing on needlessly or seeking the knower of truth, we sought out the peace and tranquillity of the side streets. Trying, where possible, to avoid the noise and trappings of modern life – and tourist crusties.

Over a few days, I had noticed that two topics in particular, religion and first loves, seemed to bubble up in our conversation. While I was keen to hear Dan's thoughts on the first, I was particularly keen to hear how he navigated the waters of first/true love.

I was also painfully aware that my interest in his interest meant that sooner or later the focus would shift back to me. Something I was nervous about. Why? I tended not to talk about feelings. But something was going on out there in that sacred place, that was hard to explain. It felt as though the Camino was drawing these stories out of us – like a sting.

"So, my brother. You've danced, distracted or distanced yourself around this subject for long enough now. Now's the time to talk. I wanna hear about your first, real love," Dan said, before pointing to a bar he'd spotted.

"How much time have you got?" I said reluctantly. Hoping it would've thrown him off course.

"Several beers worth," said Dan, batting it back.

"Reckon you're gonna need every one of them," I said nonchalantly.

With our table commandeered, we undid our boots, aired our feet and rested our weary bodies. I ordered dos cervezas por favor and waited for the words to come.

"Her name is… Jo. Jo Hills."

Just saying her name was enough to light my whole face up.

"We'd met in the summer of '95, during orientation week at Camp Saginaw, which was situated in an incredible, three-hundred-acre woodland site in Oxford, Pennsylvania. I had gone over during the university summer holidays as part of a European contingent of Camp Counsellors UK. My primary role would be to teach archery and look after the sixth and seventh graders.

"Are you sure you want me to continue? It's our day off after all." I said hoping to convince Dan to change his mind.

"Stop stalling. Keep talking," replied Dan, as he drew his chair near.

"We met on day two of orientation, just after lunch. I remember it just like it was yesterday. I was standing by the water cooler near the open-fronted canteen. At the time I was attempting, but failing spectacularly, to waterboard myself.

"As I looked up, I spluttered wildly as three girls went by. They were making their way towards the wooden, maroon-coloured steps that led down to the pool. I recognised the two ginger-haired girls instantly – which is hardly surprisingly, as seeing one ginge is quite rare. But seeing two together, in the wild, that's pretty much unheard of.

"The taller of the two was Elaine Spooner. I remember her as she had the most incredible, porcelain-coloured skin and piercing eyes. All of which was offset by a head of beautiful, free-flowing, fiery red curls. She looked like she had stepped out of the canvas of a Pre-Raphaelite painting. The other ginge, Michelle, was similarly blessed. Her gift was a laugh that could light any darkness. Yet sandwiched between the two was another girl. That girl was Joanne... Jo.

"Have you ever done a summer camp, Dan? Well, let me tell you, the first week is utterly incredible. It's a frantic week of learning everything about camp. From what activities the campers could do – which in itself was exhaustive. They could do everything like arts and crafts, archery, softball, soccer, canoeing, basketball, tennis and waterskiing – to where these activities took place: Lower Field, The Hill, and Saniford Hall to name a few.

"Added to this was a hundred new names and faces, attending inductions, cleaning bunks before the campers arrived. All of which, when accompanied with jet lag and the heat of summer, left little time for anything else.

"The early skirmishes between me and Jo resembled little more than sly glances, a half-smile or a "hi". We were like two ships in the night, destined never to meet.

"Not that I minded. In fact, I welcomed the distraction. A distraction was exactly what I needed, as my head was spinning. This was brought on, no doubt, by the seismic attraction between us. A fact that hadn't gone unnoticed by any of the lads in the Inters and Juniors Division.

"Jo was exactly my type: five foot six, sporty, with brown shoulder-length hair. She possessed the heartiest of laughs. But what felled me were her eyes. I could almost swim in them. They were a piercing shade of blue with tiny flecks of green, like jewels. Those eyes, when combined with her warm smile, cute dimples, quick wit and calm thoughtful nature meant only one thing – I was well and truly fucked.

"Towards the end of orientation week, I could feel myself flagging. I continued to take notes and listen during the inductions, but my mind was slowly beginning to drift. I was forever wondering when and where I'd next catch a glimpse of her.

"You bored yet – I can stop anytime you want?" I enquired. Dan simply smiled back at me. I could tell the innocence of the story had got to him.

"But things were about to change for the better. The Camp Elders, aware that we'd had a great week, and prior to the campers arriving, announced a free night bus to Christiana Mall. It would then take us on to Newark, Delaware.

"I knew Christiana Mall well. What many of my fellow counsellors didn't know was that it was my second summer in Camp Saginaw.

"I also knew where the best bar was at the time in Newark – The Deer Park Tavern on 19 W Main St.

"The Deer Park Tavern was a huge, three-storey red and white, brick and timber building that dated back to the mid-nineteenth century. Out front it had a large porch and seating area. What I loved about this spot was that it sat fifty yards from a train track. So, every once in a while, an old freight train would roll steadily by, blowing its horn.

"The inside of the tavern was made up of several lively, stained wooden bar areas. The first bar, on the left as you entered looked straight out of *Cheers*. It was small with single seats lining the bar edge. This bar was very laid back, warm and welcoming. The place you'd head to chill after a hard day's graft when you wanted to relax. So definitely not where a bunch of mouthy, milk-bottle-tanned European gobshites should be. We preferred their open bar where the music was lively.

"When the evening finally came around, I was like a cat on a hot tin roof. I couldn't focus at all. I could also feel my mouth was permanently dry. Such was my state, that upon hitting the Deer Park, I broke from the group to go out onto the porch. There I was greeted by a gentle waft of breeze and the sight of the sun losing its fight with the day (oh, the irony).

"Within minutes of the sun slipping below the horizon, my old friends the fireflies came out. Now they knew a thing or two about romance. They didn't mess about. If they were after a mate, they'd simply give it a few short, sharp flashes of their arse and bosh – all available fireflies would come running. Well flying, but let's not split hairs.

"Meanwhile back in the human world, I had to face the reality that I didn't possess a light-emitting arse. Nor could I find a way to get closer to Jo. She was surrounded by what could only be described as her Close Quarters Protection Team, who seemed to follow her wherever she went.

"I decided to make my move and asked the CQPT if they wanted a drink. Success. I got three yeses for small soda and limes. I mean, it was eighty-five degrees outside and humid as fuck, so they were as likely to accept a drink off me as they were a one-eyed, toothless soothsayer dressed in rags – but it was still a success.

"It also taught me that to get to her, I had to get to know her team. So, I knew by offering to buy drinks, I'd bought myself half a yard inside the circle. Moments later, that unbelievably seemed to turn into one yard inside as two of her loyal team decided to do one. Two down. One to go.

"Now all I had to do was crack Elaine Spooner. This would be a damn sight trickier. It turned out that Elaine happened to be Jo's best mate at home and at university, in Bournemouth. But I knew if I held my nerve, stood my ground and didn't get too waspish or sarcastic, I stood a chance.

"One minute went by... two minutes went by... and I was still standing. Not that this meant anything. These were two switched on, sassy women who were sharp as feck. Each time I opened my gob, I could feel myself wobbling on a highwire. All it would take was one wobble, a gust of wind or one inappropriate comment (which I am famed for) and that would be me gone.

"In an attempt to calm things, I decided to switch tack by asking Elaine a whole load of questions. She saw through my strategy in seconds. But instead of calling me out for it, she responded in kind, by upping the ante and clapping back at me with some even more quick-witted questions.

"I have to admit I admired Elaine. All she was doing was pre-screening me to see if she could trust me with Jo. Minutes later, after what seemed like an age, she conceded. Finally, after five long days, endless skirmishes, and a million sly glances, I'd finally get a chance to speak to Jo.

"Now what? There was silence. Typical. All week long I'd been preparing for this moment. And now that it was there, I was utterly speechless.

"I couldn't believe I'd blagged it this far. I also couldn't quite get my head around why a posh girl would seem interested in a cheeky scrote, like me. But now here she was. I couldn't take my eyes off her. She looked stunning in a white sleeveless top that exposed her lean, sun-tanned arms. Her cream linen trousers seemed to cling to her bum every time she swayed her hips.

"The next few hours were surreal. With each passing line of conversation, I could feel this protective bubble starting to inflate around us. To the point that everything outside of it appeared distorted and muffled.

"After the pub, our chat continued first on the bus, then long into the night. We discussed everything from music, her family, goals, dreams, wanting kids, one day owning a black labrador and her apprehensiveness at finishing university. By the time I finally crept into bed, I was exhausted, but utterly exhilarated.

"Beer, Dan?" I said wearily.

"Three pints' worth," came his witty response. "And hurry up, I want to know what happens next."

"Our time together in camp was magical. The days were long and sometimes the evening activities conspired against us. But we always found a way. Either by word-of-mouth, through letters or notes passed between our campers.

"By week four I was properly loved up. But my happiness came with its demons. My conscience was always at me, clawing away. For the vast majority of the time, I could keep it under control and on a leash. But it was sneaky, it knew my weak points. It knew where to hit or what lines to feed me to stir my insecurities. It knew, like I did, that sooner or later it would get its chance.

"It's chance came, the day a gang of ten of us headed off to Atlantic City for two days. These would be our first days off, away from camp and without any campers in four weeks. I was exhausted. All I wanted to do was get away, enjoy some beers and have a lie in with Jo. To add to that, I had also planned a surprise picnic for us. But before all that, we headed out en masse for a few quiet drinks and that's when my conscience's whispering started.

"Having fun, are we? Enjoying playing happy families? It must be nice to know that while you're here, living it up in la-la-land, Magic is home – all alone. Do you ever think about her? I don't think you do. Because if you did, you'd be home with her right now, like any good son would be. But no, not you! You're too fucking selfish. You'd rather spend your time making daisy fucking chains and looking gormless at some girl. Who by the way is a million leagues above you.

"This was my conscience tightening the screw. Each barb cut a little deeper – a little harder. It hurt because it was true. I should have been at home with Magic. Our world had been blown to bits that year when my dad left. We were both still trying to find our feet in this new world.

"I tried to disguise it, but I was broken both mentally and physically. To the point that I wondered, if I tripped and fell would I shatter into a thousand pieces? The only person I wanted to talk to about this was George, my best mate. But he was on active service in Bosnia. Thankfully for me, he wrote often. George was, is, and always will be – my rock.

"Yet no matter how many times I tried to tell my conscience I needed a break; it just came at me harder. I could hear George's voice telling me to shift my focus. To focus on the here and now. But my conscience simply wouldn't stop. The best way I could think was to drown it with drink. This flawed tactic I'd used successfully at university, where I'd drink 'til I blacked out.

"At least in the numbness, I wouldn't be able to hear or understand what my conscience was spitting at me. I still remember a flicker of a look on Jo's face when I stumbled back into our motel drunk after the night out. If I didn't feel shit enough already, one look at Jo's face just broke me. We'd waited four weeks for this night to spend some quality time together, and me and my demons had fucked it all up.

"Though I owed her an explanation, I simply couldn't tell her the whys. Not because I didn't want to, but because the whys didn't excuse my selfish behaviour. She deserved so much better than that – and me."

I stopped to breathe, blowing heavily as I inhaled and exhaled. This story had been in my vault for twenty years, untouched.

"It's all good, my brother. Let it all out," said Dan, patting my shoulder.

"When I got back to university I couldn't focus. I struggled with my course, my eight flat mates and the absence of Jo. Though we'd often talk and try to arrange a visit and vice-versa, work always got in the way. Day-by-day I could feel her slipping away. Until foolishly and regrettably one night, we let go. I was utterly floored."

"Wow," replied Dan.

"Well, hang on in there, Dan. There's a bit more if you can stand it?"

"We'll need another beer. Back in five, bud."

He returned with some fresh beers, and I continued my tale. "Where was I... three years passed. Then out of the blue I get a call. It was Jo. At the time I was seeing someone, who just wasn't Jo. Within minutes of talking, we were back in our bubble. She spoke about her pride in bagging her ideal job, head of the hospitality division for REED Recruitment. No sooner had the call ended than radio silence again.

"Nine months later, I get asked by my brother if I fancied a weekend in Bournemouth. He was heading down to do a Tony Buzan mind map course. A weekend away. Yes – I was in.

"Within seconds of agreeing to go, I got on the phone to REED Recruitment. It was a long shot, but was Jo there? The lady who answered the call, quite rightly couldn't confirm or deny if this was the case. Which inadvertently told me that Jo was still there.

"My very next call was to Interflora. I ordered a stunning bouquet of flowers and added a simple note: *Fancy a pint? I'm arriving in Bournemouth via high-speed donkey on Saturday. Paul xx.* Underneath that, I scrawled my phone number.

One day passed. Two days passed – nothing. Then on the day I travelled down I received a two-word text as a reply: *Yes. Jo xx.*

"I arrived in Bournemouth like a returning king. That night I headed to the pub early. I was nervous and twitchy. I could hear my conscience willing me to have a drink to calm me down.

"There was no chance that was happening. My dark days of drinking myself into oblivion were gone. I now stood in The Last Chance Saloon, and I was determined as fuck – not to fuck this reunion up.

"Then through the doorway she came. Suited, booted and looking every bit as beautiful as the day I'd met her. I could feel my stomach starting to tie itself in knots. I ordered her a large white wine, while checking out her ring situation. There wasn't one. Phew. Once the opening few gags were fired off, we both settled down. It was like old times, except without her Close Quarters Protection Team. Or so I thought.

"No sooner had I said that Jo pulled out her phone to take a selfie. 'Now Paul, who do you think I'm sending this to?' she said, giggling hysterically.

"I didn't need to guess; I knew straight away – Elaine. After the pub shut, we headed back to her top floor flat on Frances Road. There we sat up until the wee small hours, laughing, talking and listening to Evanescence. Jo teased me about how her young campers at Saginaw would tease her by asking where and when we were going to get married. A reply that came back with the response, 'Well what's a girl to say to that,' as she winked at me.

"Come the morning she left for netball, and I headed to my hotel. We kissed. We hugged and off she went – again.

"I felt sick as soon as I returned to my room. Something felt wrong. What the fuck was I doing? Was this it – again? I got out a piece of A4 paper and scratched down a note, then slid it through her letterbox (one she shared with three other flats). Having just re-established contact I couldn't let her go again.

"Did she get the note? Did she read it? Did someone else bin it? I guess I'll never know. Where are you now, Jo Hills?" I said.

"Wherever she is and whoever she's with, I just hope she's happy. If I was allowed one dream, it would be to see her once more.

"I feel lucky to have swum in her universe for what was the best summer of my life. I will always cherish her wild cackle and the bootleg copy of 'Everybody Else Is Doing It, So Why Can't We?' by The Cranberries she made for me. Even though I knew she disliked the fact that I found Dolores' singing voice heavenly.

"And as the famous line in 'Dreams' goes, "You're a dream to me.""

With that I paused and looked over at Dan. We both had tears running down our cheeks.

I do miss you, Jo Hills.

CHAPTER 8: SPIRIT

3rd September, Pamplona - Puente La Reina, 24km
Kikikiki...ki...wahhhh...wahhh...ki...

There was no mistaking that distinctive, yet familiar, high-pitched shriek on the wind. Goosebumps popped like champagne corks all over my resting body.

It couldn't be... could it? Could Spirit really have returned to my dreams? Though I was aware that my subconscious had been working overtime, it could do little to prevent my heart from bucking wildly in my chest at the thought of seeing her again.

Then I spotted her: a simple, black, silhouette with outstretched wings, three hundred feet above me – alone in a cotton candy sky. I watched mesmerised, my head swaying hypnotically in unison with her as she twirled first one way, then the other.

Wow! How she'd grown. As I watched transfixed, I could feel my mind bubbling with questions. Where had she been? What had she seen? But more importantly, why had she chosen now to return to my dreams?

Suddenly, my mind transported back to our first meeting in August 2002. She came one balmy night, a scruffy-looking, adolescent buzzard with twig-like wings, reddish brown plumage and piercing black eyes. Her presence in my dreams intrigued me. Why? Because as a nipper, I'd grown up on the teachings of Sitting Bull, Geronimo and Crazy Horse. I'd learned about Native American culture and had become fascinated by spirit guides, the forms they took and the roles they played.

What I didn't know though, was why Spirit had come. And who had summoned her? Traditionally, spirit guides didn't show up unannounced.

During 2002, my life was at a crossroads. I was about to place myself on one of two paths. My next decision would be pivotal, and one that could easily define my next decade.

The question was which path would I choose? The familiar path was of certainty, service and familiarity – Magic was a nurse, George was ex-RAF Regiment then police, while my older brother, Pete, was an ex-RAF Supplier.

→ **Path of certainty:** I'd been offered a place with the Dorset Police, starting that September.

Or would I walk the untrodden path of uncertainty?

→ **Path of uncertainty:** I'd also been offered a place on the PG Dip Creative Advertising Course at the University of Falmouth starting that October.

My head told me that a job in the plod would provide the security and certainty that I, as a twenty-nine-year-old, craved.

My heart on the other hand, told me to follow my dream. Ever since I was a child, advertising had fascinated me. I'd grown up in the era of sing-along ads: Mash-Get-Smash, Hello Tosh Gotta Toshiba, Shake-And-Vac.

The very thought that someday, someone would walk down the street humming, whistling or singing a tune I had written filled me with excitement. Why? Because creativity was my first love. It was my go-to happy place. A place I'd retreat to as a child, escaping the demons of a school system that had labelled me 'slow'.

But by choosing this path, I'd be offering up the thing most sacred to me. Was I ready to bury the labels of childhood? Was I ready to stand up with a few flimsy thoughts on paper to have them scrawled on, laughed at or crucified by the 'smart kids'?

For three weeks a battle raged hard inside my domed head. Every night around 2 am the Kangaroo court would sit for yet another session. The prosecution would set out its case against me: attacking my character, my inconsistencies and my previous failings. All in an attempt to manipulate me into choosing the easier path.

Yet all the while Spirit would come and sit quietly beside me. She was my ever-watchful guardian. Why had she come? What message did she have? What was she waiting for?

With the increase in pressure came the increase in the vividness of Spirit's dream. When she first appeared, she sat alone on a moss-covered rock. Then, with each subsequent night, a little more of the picture started to develop around her. Much like an image coming to life inside a photographer's dark room.

Behind Spirit, I was shown a lush, green mountainside through the morning mist. Then, as I looked down from on high, I saw the mist rising slowly up the mountain kissing the forest canopy awake as it ascended.

Then the image shifted, and I was shown lots and lots of symmetrically cut stones, before the final reveal – a huge slab of horizontal granite. This gigantic monolith of rock had somehow been carved by hand – how? Set into it was what looked like a primitive altar. On top of it was a single thirty-centimetre-high block of stone. It seemed to mirror the mountain in the background. There was something eerie about this monolith... like I'd seen it before somewhere. But where?

Then one night the answer finally came. I had seen the monolith. It was the Intihuatana stone, used by Inca High Priests during the 1400s to track the passage of time. Suddenly, I thought I understood what Spirit had wanted me to do. As if to confirm my thought, she let out a huge squawk of approval – before finally taking flight.

Three weeks later, Magic and I woke up at 5:30 am into the stifling heat of an Aguas Calientes morning. All around us, disgruntled mosquitoes of the Urubamba Valley were buzzing and generally trying their best to infuriate the fuck out of us.

Once dressed, we headed out, picking our way through the dusty, ramshackle streets, passed half-built, corrugated houses, dozing dogs and hombres heading home to sleep off their incoming hangover.

Somehow everything felt familiar, as if I'd lived this day a thousand times before. I knew where to twist, when to turn and where to find the bus. Just like I knew that when I found the bus it would be empty – it was.

We climbed eagerly aboard the bus and took up our positions on either side of the aisle. This gave us a three-hundred-and-sixty-degree view of the Urubamba Valley and the monstrous peaks that loomed like lords above us.

The bus set off slowly, bucking and billowing with smoke as it bounced along the gravel track. Our route followed the natural course of the river before coming across an old rickety wooden bridge which wouldn't have looked out of place in *Indiana Jones and the Temple of Doom*.

Once over the bridge, a sign directed the driver left, up a steep, tyre-spinning, mud-covered track. We held our breath. One minute the bus would zig and expose us to jaw-dropping views of the forest canopy and the slowly rising mist. The next, the bus would zag, leaving the tyres spinning and teetering millimetres from a drop, with the doors to Valhalla open and ready to receive us.

By the time we arrived at the gates of Machu Picchu my nerves were shot. But I still managed to leap from the bus and bound up the claggy, mud-covered stone path – resisting the mud's attempt to pull us back. As I walked, I could hear a deep rasp within my chest, like I'd swallowed a whistle. That was my body's way of telling me it was struggling to cope with the paper-thin air of the altitude.

With each step the excitement grew, to the point that I was almost shaking with anticipation. Suddenly, my whole world fell silent. Before me was one of the most mesmerising sights of my life – Machu Picchu.

Just... just... how?

How had the Incas built this? How had they moved these stones thousands of feet up a mountain? How had they carved these rocks without tools? How had they learned the secrets of advanced mathematics? And how had they learned to track the passage of time?

Everywhere I looked provoked another question. The more the questions came, the more my body started to vibrate. WTF was happening to me? It felt like every cell, every pore of my being was plugged into an invisible, yet intoxicating, power grid. Colours were brighter, my eyes were sharper, and my thoughts were clearer.

For an hour I wandered with Magic in a semi-comatose daze, through what was once the estate of Pachacuti. Why had this place really been built? Surely it was more than a weekend retreat.

Then I recalled a conversation I'd had the day previous with a tour guide at Ollantaytambo. He'd floated the idea that Machu Picchu was in fact a finishing school for all major religious leaders. And that Jesus, Muhammad and Buddha had all studied here before taking their teachings out into the world. Could that be true? Could this place really have been a place reserved for the greatest of minds?

What with the combination of endless questions and thinning air, it wasn't long before my head was spinning. I could feel it tighten as if placed inside a carpenter's vice. It was only a matter of time before I chose to sit or fall down. So, I found the nearest flat rock, put my head between my knees and closed my eyes.

Within seconds my mind was disturbed by a rustling off to my left. It was probably nothing. Just the remanence of my over-active imagination playing tricks on me. But as the seconds passed, the nothing soon became something.

Was it me, or was I being... watched?

Then came the gentle, undeniable flap of a bird's wing. In that instant, my whole body turned cold, as if someone had walked over my grave. Suddenly, I was reminded of my dream. In that moment I felt sick. WTF was going on.

Kikikiki...ki...wahhhh...wahhh...ki...

Slowly, reluctantly, I raised my head. I was too freaked to look towards the source of the noise, so I turned my head to the right in the hope of finding some solace. It was then that it hit me. I had unwittingly stumbled upon the Intihuatana stone from my dream. That meant the squawk could only have come from one source – Spirit.

As I turned, her eyes met mine. In that moment, I could feel my whole body wanting to take flight, but my legs weren't budging. I was rooted to my rock: confused, speechless and in utter awe at this majestic creature.

We both swam in each other's gaze. I was mesmerised. Why had she summoned me here? Was it to remind me of my true love, creativity? Or was it to warn me against the perils of choosing the easier path?

In that moment, I felt like I knew what she wanted me to do. But my mind was lost in this surreal reality. Was this actually happening? It was only as I turned and saw Magic, who was now sitting beside me, that I realised. This was madness – but it was real.

From behind I heard mutterings. To my dismay, I turned and was greeted by a posse of happy-snappy, Japanese tourists decked out in fuchsia baseball caps with their cameras trained on us. Their attempt to quieten the situation by shushing gave off the sound of a thousand kettles all coming to boil at once.

Then from behind me, I heard a gentle, undeniable flap of a wing. My heart sank. When I turned back to the moss-covered rock, it stood alone. Spirit was gone – possibly forever. Until she returned to my dreams on Camino.

The mood in the camp at breakfast was jovial. Dan and I had woken refreshed, rested and ready to step back on the Camino travelator.

Strangely, as we headed out, I couldn't help but feel relieved to have the weight of my pack on my back. It felt more like a protective shell than a burden. One that would keep me grounded when I got above myself. One that would protect me from the lashing rain, when it finally came. And one that would buffer me from life's crosswinds.

Outside, the morning air on Avenue de Zaragoza was chilly and tinged with the acrid scent of eau-de-car-fumes. While overhead, the clouds had gathered en masse to extinguish any hope of the sun making a breakthrough.

All this provided near-perfect conditions for our lumpy-bumpy, thirteen-kilometre schlep up to the day's high point Alto del Perdón – the Mount of Forgiveness. Where, if the weather held, it would reward us with mind-boggling views across the patchwork quilted valley.

Then from the heavens of Alto del Perdón (which sat at over two thousand four hundred feet), we'd descend through hell, with a ninety minute, gnarly, ankle-snapping, Camino-ending descent down to Uterga, passing through Muruzábal and Obanos, before arriving at our final destination – Puente La Reina.

On paper our escape seemed simple enough. All we needed to do was retrace our steps back to Calle Mercaderes. From there we could pick up Calle Mayor, shimmy passed the Taconera Park Gardens and out via the old citadel. Simple.

Within minutes we were lost...

Different day. Same clowns.

...and hemmed in on all sides by high-rises. Every move we made; they'd counter it in what was fast becoming a surreal game of Pilgrim Chess.

Luckily for us, in our bumbling we'd stumbled across three head-scratching, work-shy workmen. They were busy staring into the abyss, into a giant hole in the road. Theirs was a look of utter bewilderment, as if the hole had been created by an asteroid or the arrival of a new breed of Terminator. It was a hole, lads. See it, fill it, have a nap.

"¿Dónde está la ciudadela?"

Oi soppy bollocks, have you really just asked these fellas where the citadel is? You see that enormous, 16th century, high-walled structure right in front of your eyes? Yeah, that's the one. The one that's seven hundred metres in width, five hundred metres in length and looks very citadel-like. Well guess what that is, Numbnuts?

Luckily for me, I could see from the look on their faces that they hadn't quite figured out if I was being ironic or special.

I know which one I'd choose. It might also explain why that big hulking lummox beside you is following you everywhere. Go on, admit it, the old crusties were right. Dan is your care assistant, isn't he?

"For the last feckin' time..." I mumbled in frustration at my conscience's badgering.

With our route found and my humiliation complete, we shuffled off in the direction of Calle Fuente Del Hierro. The road was thankfully arrow-straight and lined with an abundance of trees, so it was hard to get lost.

When we passed under the trees, the leaves gently flapped in the breeze. Were they wishing us a fond farewell? The road stretched out ominously, down towards a large motorway bridge and beyond.

Within seconds of exiting from under the bridge, the hubbub of modern life, high-rises, and honking delivery trucks was forgotten and replaced by the sight of perfectly manicured lawns, clipped trees and the return of glorious technicolour. Our path was free to wander along Calle Universidad, passing the university grounds as we went.

I smiled as my mind served up a showreel of those who'd helped shape me and my career. The roll call of inductees into my Hall of Fame included:

➜ Tony Purcer and Andy Butler who, at Shrewsbury College, took me (a shy, timid, fledging creative with limited talent) and lit a fire under me.

➜ Ian Lovell (my best friend in junior school), who leant me his life drawings that secured me a place at the University of Derby.

➜ Gordon, Lynne and Dave de Leux at the University of Derby, who helped produce a book of illustrations based on Stephen King's 'The Dark Half'.

➜ Giles Winser who opened what was an almost impenetrable door into the world of marketing and advertising.

➜ Chris Lonie who filled my mind and fuelled my belief with his love of experiential and ambient ideas.

➜ George, Bear, Higgs, Terry Bush, Rosie Mills, Neil French and Simon Lane who had been the guiding lights in my life. Their wit, warmth and wisdom were constant reminders that work should be fun.

On our way through the campus grounds, I couldn't help but notice the empty, aubergine-coloured student accommodation blocks. They stood nervously, like expectant parents awaiting the arrival of their new brood of energetic, enquiring and untamed minds.

Once we'd passed them, we crossed over a small bridge over the River

Sadar, before picking up a dusty, gravel path lined with what looked like cypress trees, alongside the now bustling NA-7027.

Our first port of call was the hilltop village of Cizur Menor. I'd mistakenly mispronounced it as 'Caesars Manure'. A simple mix-up between brain and mouth, but not one Dan would let go of easily.

There was something timeless about these villages that I loved. To many pilgrims, these villages represented little more than distractions en route to their larger goal of the day. But to me, these forgotten places, with all their quirky nuances, were the jewels in the Camino's crown.

Within seconds of entering Cizur Menor we were greeted by smiles, waves and the inevitable shouts from across the street of 'Buen Camino'. The joy and pride the locals felt for their small part in our tale was reflected in everything we saw. The place was immaculate with freshly white-washed houses, pristine lawns and flowerbeds bursting with life and colour.

With our first stop reached, all thoughts turned to second breakfast. Which, at 10:15 am, felt a little premature. But the choices were to fuel up before the strenuous six kilometre climb to Zariquiegui or go without and run the risk of breaking down in no man's land, surrounded by mud with fellow pilgrims kicking up dust in our faces.

While Dan trotted off to the Church of San Emeterio and San Celedonio to check-in on God, I flipped a coin to decide what I should do next: **Heads** = second breakfast. **Tails** = second breakfast.

Heads it was. That was simple enough. And it was made all the more special moments later, when I spotted an empty bench on a patch of grass that provided a good vantage of Alto del Perdón. It was also the perfect spot to have some fun.

My aim here was simple. Get the locals hooked on Haribo. All I'd need was a hook to lure in passers-by. I decided to play the role of the ever confused, bumbling Brit...

That shouldn't be hard.

Within minutes I'd snared my first crusty, an old lady out for her morning constitutional who'd foolishly wandered too close for comfort. Once I'd reeled her in, all that was left was to introduce her to the magic of Haribo, before setting her free to wander the street happily once more.

Ahead of me was Alto del Perdón. I noticed the lower fields surrounding it were made up of some of the most unusual hues of green, gold and brown

I'd ever seen. They looked like they'd been mixed in haste by a manic painter.

Above the fields, the higher slopes became a densely packed forest, brimming with life. Perched (no, plonked) precariously above it all sat a fat band of water-bearing cloud. A cloud that looked as though it was ready to unleash itself at any given moment.

Dan's return from church came just as I was dealing out the last of the Haribo. With the village now tuned into the magic of those sugary bombs of goodness, I did what any responsible food sampler would do without a licence – I legged it.

Quickly, I bagged up my empty stash packets and scuttled off down the terracotta-coloured pavement, passed monstrously sized family homes, car parks and jade tiled walls of the European Forum Navarra Business School.

Not far after the business school, we came to a pedestrian crossing. Hardly unusual. But to the left of it were three stone steps which led down to a small, stone, pyramid-fronted building with a gabled roof. This building, according to Dan, who somehow assumed the role of unofficial tour guide (*carer, you mean*), once housed a much-needed water fountain.

Once over the crossing, our path cut its way through a grassy park before quickly turning right, then left, through eerily quiet streets. It deposited us at the bottom of Calle Camino de Santiago, where white arrows spray painted onto the curb and lamppost directed us forward – straight at the ridge.

With nothing to obscure our view, our eyes were drawn skywards. The sun, furious at being locked out of the sky, launched a fearsome fight back, firing shaft upon shaft of light into the clouds. Its ferocity soon began to punch holes in the cloud's armour, illuminating the fields below with white spotlights.

While our eyes were consumed by the heavens, our noses were ill prepared for the sudden, overwhelming and unmistakable stench of death.

It was only when I dragged my eyes downwards, that I realised we'd inadvertently wandered into a field-cum-graveyard of spent sunflowers. Their bodies, having been scorched by the sun, were standing limp and leathery, their heads bowed in defeat.

Contrary to my first thoughts, the path we were on wasn't going to be making a beeline up to the steepest part of the ridge. Instead, it would snake off to the right, cutting its way through fallow fields and up towards a small ridge consumed by trees – which undoubtedly hid Zariquiegui.

Beyond I could see the top ridge framing the landscape. Waiting on top were about twenty white wind turbines, which seemed to be gently whooping in delight at the sight of a new influx of pilgrim ants edging their way.

With our route found and my brain's work done for the day, I could relax. With each step and every breath, I could feel myself slowly starting to be at one with my surroundings.

Kikikiki...ki...wahhhh...wahhh...ki...

Then out of nowhere came a ghostly – yet familiar squawk. It stopped me dead in my tracks.

Kikikiki...ki...wahhhh...wahhh...ki...

Dan, alerted by the shriek, started to eyeball the heavens. But the combination of piercing light and dark clouds rendered him blind.

I didn't need to look up though, I knew who was responsible for that squawk. The thought of possibly seeing her again made my heart leap. But how... how had Spirit found me? After all, Machu Picchu was nine thousand five hundred miles and a world away from Cizur Menor.

Everything about the squawk, the tone, depth and cadence was as I'd remembered. Plus, her timing was extraordinary. She had only just returned to my dreams after a thirteen-year hiatus. Yet there she was, high above, keeping a look out for me.

The route up to Zariquiegui was a long, slow slog. The sliver of gravel we were on weaved first one way then the other. Ahead, peppering our path, were small pockets of pilgrims, busy feeding off each other like out-of-work vampires. All in an attempt to power themselves up the hillside.

I was in no mood to chase or keep pace. I was more interested in what was happening above. I couldn't stop thinking of Spirit, with her wings and tail feathers outstretched and flickering wildly, as she fought the invisible forces of the wind.

Where had she been? Why had she come? What message did she have for me this time? What hadn't I been paying attention to?

Thankfully, arriving at Zariquiegui provided both the sanctuary and sanity respite I needed. As soon as we entered the dusty village we noticed the beige-coloured, stone-fronted exterior of La Tiendica de Mertxe. Two chairs were going begging out front – but they didn't have to wait long before I threw my pack onto one and headed off into the cafe in search of... iiiccceee... cccrrreeeaaammm.

Suddenly, I was eight years old again. I could feel my eyes starting to bulge, my palms starting to sweat and my body starting to shake with excitement.

"Don't drop it, don't drop it, don't drop it," I mumbled wildly as I headed back to my seat. Even before I'd sat down, I'd already undressed it with my eyes. Slowly, seductively, I started to peel off its outer layer of clothes – the wrapper. Behind it, lay a dark, silky smooth, chocolatey body just waiting to be devoured. God, I loved the taste of a Magnum...

"Paaaaauuuullll!!!"

... Classic.

I was interrupted by the excited screech of Joyous Joy and Hwan, who I hadn't seen since Roncesvalles. Joy was, well, joyous. Hwan, on the other hand, was in agony. His body had taken a real good kicking. His knees were strapped, elbows grazed, and his socks were caked in dried-in blood.

"Jesus Hwan, have you been scrapping' with the Camino again?" I said only half-joking.

Hwan looked a beaten man on a paper-thin timeline that was disappearing with each passing minute. There was no way he was going to make it to the end in thirty-two days before his flight home. No chance. But the last thing he'd need was tea and sympathy, which was why everyone around him started to dish up large portions of sarcasm.

For half an hour we all sat about exchanging stories about biblical rainstorms, phantom snorers, sly farters, stingy breakfasts and glorious pilgrim meals. With each passing minute I could feel our energy lifting Hwan. Once the ice cream was dispatched and we'd refuelled on misadventures and powered up on hugs, we set off again. But not before Joy got in her parting shot, remembering how pitiful our sense of direction was.

"Hey, boys! See that big hill? The one with all the windmills on? Head towards that, just don't fall off the edge."

Joy's cackle could be heard on the wind for the next fifteen minutes. She made a fair point, our ability to get lost was fast becoming Camino folklore.

The slog up to Alto del Perdón along a metre wide, shale-covered path, lined with low-lying, ankle-biting bushes. The intensity of the climb came as a blessing as it offered us the chance to look back upon Zariquiegui, Pamplona and across the sprawling valley – painted in a thousand shades of autumn.

With each step the wind turbines grew larger, the path smaller and our legs heavier. Until finally, we could see the faint outline of the sculpture by Vincent Galbete, which made Alto del Perdón famous.

This consisted of twelve silhouetted pilgrims, spaced intermittently along one long line. The inscription on the piece read, 'Where the path of the wind crosses that of the stars'. I'd seen many pictures of the sculpture before yet resisted reading up about it. I preferred to look and interpret things based on what I saw and felt. Not what I was told to see.

What was interesting to me was the fact that the sculpture consisted of twelve figures. Was there any significance in that number? Twelve pilgrims? Twelve disciples?

The first two silhouetted figures represented modern day pilgrims. Both were decked out in sun hats and rucksacks. Had this been done to make the piece instantly relatable?

The next two characters looked positively medieval in appearance. The male was wearing a 'Continental' cocked hat, a long, heavy, knee-length overcoat and breeches. While the woman wore a handkerchief wrapped round her head along with a loose-fitting dress and pantaloons.

The next four characters appeared as a group. The lead boy (possibly a servant) was sitting on a donkey laden down with goods. Behind him, his affluent masters were sitting proudly on horseback. To their left was their ever-loyal dog, who appeared to be looking up at them for reassurance. Making up the rear was a girl (possibly a servant too) pulling a reluctant donkey laden down with additional goods. It was refreshing that there were people out here carrying more gear than me.

The last four characters, furthest from us, wore stylised outfits from days gone by.

What did they represent? What did it all mean? What message was the sculptor trying to communicate? Was he trying to imply the Camino was timeless? Or that now, in the age of mass distraction, the Camino was needed now more than ever?

Of all the characters on the sculpture, the one that resonated the most with me was the figure out alone. He/she was out in front. Happy and at peace with the world, lost in thought. Yet though alone, they understood that they were still connected by the invisible thread that tied us all together.

Kikikiki...ki...wahhhh...wahhh...ki...

Suddenly, a higher-pitched shriek went out on the wind. This, I knew, was a warning. Something, or someone, was fast approaching. To my dismay, I looked left along the road to see an army of tourist crusties waddling our way.

With no time to waste we rushed over to La Kontxa, a mobile caravan-cum-shop to get our Credencial stamped. Once stamped, we headed toward the eight-foot, wooden post bearing a blue plaque that pointed downwards. On it read the words – Puente La Reina ten kilometres.

From our spot in heaven, we now started to make our descent down through hell. The opening metres were deceptively pleasant. But that soon changed. In the space of one turn, the golden carpet we had walked upon was rolled up and put away. In its place came a gnarly track covered with fist-sized, arrow-sharp, boot-piercing stones.

Every step now was a calculated risk. Dan had walking poles, so he had the benefit of testing the ground before stepping. I, on the other hand, hadn't. Therefore, my eyes were darting from rock to rock, while my brain was racing with questions. Should I step here, or there? Did the ground look like it would hold? If not, what then?

Mentally, the effort required to hold my nerve was exhausting. I knew all it would take was one slip. One slip and I could easily break my ankle, dislocate my kneecap or tear a muscle. If that happened, my Camino, much like Hwan's, would be over.

With the increase in tension and tiredness came the fear. Worse still was the fact we could see the bottom. I knew from previous experience, that it was here when the mind started to switch off and where most injuries occurred. So, I fought every step to stay focused. I could hear and feel the pings of muscles as they tightened in the bodies of those around me.

By the time the path finally levelled off we were both battered, bruised and our minds were shot. But miraculously we'd made it through unscathed.

As way of giving thanks, we stopped off by the memorial garden on the outskirts of Uterga to offer a prayer. The garden took the form of a U-shaped cluster of trees, with some stone seating in the centre, facing a marble statue of the Virgin Mary on a cream-coloured plinth.

Having reached Uterga, we knew we'd broken the back of the day, with only six kilometres left to do. We wasted no time going to work on it. We tore along Calle Mayor, passed Camino Del Perdón and Casa Baztan before being directed onto Calle Mediodía and out the back of town onto yet another gravel path.

Muruzábal came and went. Somehow, my mind only stirred from slumber when we came to the Neo-Gothic Church of San Juan Bautista in Obanos. My eyes were drawn to the minimalist sculpture of Jesus on the cross, resting on a plinth in the middle of a brick roundabout.

From the church, we went under a stone arch, passed a modern statue of the pilgrim on Calle San Salvador and out onto Camino Santiago. At that point all other thoughts turned to Spirit and beer. But mostly beer. All I wanted was to sip an ice-cold beer, in an ice-cold glass, under a sprawling tree.

Only around half an hour later, we crossed over the NA-6064 and down the path, towards the newly-varnished gate of Albergue Jakue – we'd made it. The relief as we handed over our Pilgrim Credencial was felt through every pore we had.

The day had been both magical and brutal. How I'd managed to dodge an injury I'd never know. The descent down into Utegra was as merciless if not more so, than the descent into Roncesvalles.

With our Pilgrim Credencials stamped and beers bought, we settled back into the plastic chairs laid out for us. As we gave into rest, the tsunami of aches and pains started to stir. But in that moment, they didn't matter. We'd survived another Camino day. The route had been hard, the weather kind and the scenery sublime.

But the unforgettable sight of the day was that of Spirit. She had returned to my life, and I'd never felt happier. Why did she come? I didn't know. But her mere presence brought a deep-rooted sense of calm within my spirit.

I knew that as long as she was near, everything would work out just fine.

Cheers, Spirit

~~CHAPTER 9: SLOW DOWN PILGRIM~~

4th September, Puente La Reina - Estella, 23km
Zzzzz... sssssh
Zzzzz.. sssssh
Zzzzz... sssssh
I was cruelly woken at 3:21 am by the sound of 7.62 mm snore shells thumping hard against the darkened walls around me. The sound left my...
Zzzzz... sssssh
...senses disorientated...
...mind frazzled...
Zzzzz... sssssh
... and my ears ringing with a low-pitch whistle.
But where the hell were those shots coming from?
Cautiously, using the duvet for cover I crawled tentatively towards the head of the bed. Once there, I eased the pillow up several inches, before I slid my head underneath and looked out.
Typically, within seconds the world fell silent. Undeterred I lay there motionless and unfazed while I fought the uncontrollable leg spasms and twitching nerve fibres in my back. Five minutes passed, ten minutes passed – and nothing. Yet somewhere in my advanced state of readiness I drifted off.
Zzzzz... sssssh
Suddenly, I was shaken awake by a single crack of snore fire at 4 am. The sound warmed the air around me. Wherever the shooter was, they were close. Yet within minutes, I was fighting the sleep haze again, which had gathered like Dracula's cloak around my tired, beaten and sleep-deprived body. There I lay for the next ninety minutes, slipping in and out of consciousness, woken occasionally by the sporadic crack of snore fire.
By 5:42 am I finally conceded. I'd been out-gunned, out-thought and out-manoeuvred by my sharp-shooting snore nemesis. With that, I raised the white

pillow of surrender. Having freed myself from conflict, I fell into what I could only hope was a deep, impenetrable sleep.

Beep....beep...beep...

"For the love of God, what now?"

I threw off the covers and stared loathingly into the face of my beeping watch, which returned my glare with an equal measure of aggression – its face all red and lit up.

"Seriously! What the hell have you got to be angry about? It's not like you've been stalked through the night by a Vasily Zaytev-style sharp-shooter – is it? No! You were too busy getting your kip in. So, pipe down with your beeping otherwise we are going to fall out. And while we're at it, where's that slippery bastard anyway?"

With that, I got up and slowly started to search the room looking for where his possible hideout could be. Was it under the bed, behind the curtains and inside the dresser draw...

Dresser draw! Your sniper wasn't a rogue Oompa Loompa.

After ten minutes of searching, I admitted defeat – again. As I slumped dejected onto the bed, I noticed my rucksack, which was sleeping on the bed opposite – tassels out. It was then it hit me. I was alone. Alone in my hotel room, which meant...

"WTF. I snore."

This shock realisation caused words to form like cartoon clouds in the air. Reminding me of Wile E. Coyote moments before his demise. Meep meep.

I glanced at my watch. 7:51 am. Bollocks! I was late, and not a little late, a lot late. I threw on my gear and rushed down the wooden staircase to the breakfast area. I spotted Dan pacing backwards and forwards like a trainee dementia patient.

"WTF Dan... I snore."

So, no "good morning". No "sorry I'm late, mate". Just straight into talking about you, hey?

"I think I heard you," came his cackling response.

It was an alarming thought. Especially as he'd slept three floors below me.

"You mean you knew?" I replied, genuinely shocked.

"You mean you didn't?" came his smirking response.

"WTF, Dan. It's 7:52 am and my days already turned to shit. I've half a mind to sack it off and head straight back to bed," I said in a disgruntled voice.

"On a separate note. Where is everyone?"

I scanned the room and only managed to pick out one or two of the walking wounded. Reprobates from the previous night's feast in the Hotel Jakue restaurant.

But even before Dan had a chance to answer, my mind was gone. Transported back to the feast, held in an area of the restaurant I'd labelled 'The Great Hall.' Merely due to the fact that it looked like it had been plucked straight from the pages of a fantasy novel.

High overhead in 'The Great Hall' were monstrously sized oak beams. The room was decked out with wood throughout and featured two long tables with ornate chairs. Thirty, thirsty, sun-ravaged and ravenous pilgrims had sat their sweaty hides on these chairs, troughing down on fresh salad, pasta, steak and chips, fresh fruit, yoghurt and a mill's worth of bread. As feasts went – it had been monumental.

"Everyone left," came Dan's reply.

"People are twitchy. And you know what it's like. Once one person starts, the fear spreads – fast. Rumour has it, it will hit 32C. That's hot. And hotter still, when you think we're going to be out in it for six hours surrounded by almond groves."

"Isn't there any-"

I got halfway through finishing my sentence when Dan dived in.

"Shade? There is. And they come in the form of dry, airless and dusty farming tunnels which criss-cross under the main roads en route between Cirauqui and Estella. But that's it."

"Ok, Dan. Let's drink up and get gone."

With water now the priority of the day (and readily available), we made the most of it. Once finished, we loaded up and headed towards the exit. Even before we'd reached the door, we were met with the first, early licks of the sun's fiery breath. For a second, we stood at the door preparing ourselves. Then with one big, brave push we headed outside into it.

Whoooooooooosh.

The intensity of the heat that we hit caught us off guard. Within seconds, we were both scurrying back towards the safety of the main door, looking panic-stricken.

It was smoulderingly hot. To the point that I didn't dare fully inhale, for fear I'd burn my windpipe or set fire to my chest hair. Feck! If it was like this at 8 am, how suffocating would it be once we hit the open ground and hilltop villages of Mañeru, Cirauqui or Lorca?

As it was, we fought our way outside and along the slip road, which was lined with wilting ferns, none of which seemed to be faring any better than us. Once the road faded, we were forced to join the ever-bustling NA-1110, where once again we had to walk the one and a half metre wide tightrope. One that separated us from hellish sounds of thundering articulated trucks and the Gates of Hades.

Then, suddenly, out of nowhere, the whizz of the world erupted with a piercing screech, followed by the ever-familiar scent of acrid, burnt rubber. Instantly, my senses sharpened as my eyes took in a million small pieces of information at once.

Everything in the world paused hauntingly as I waited for the inevitable crunch of steel-on-steel and the ear-splitting shriek as shards of glass tore through the air.

As I turned, my eyes caught sight of Kamikaze Kev (in a red Citroen) attempting a death-defying overtaking manoeuvre. The result forced Skid Skedaddle (the car in front) to pull off a spectacular high-speed, emergency stop – which had been the cause of the blood-curdling squeal of terror I'd just heard.

If Skid hadn't been so cat-like in his reactions, Kamikaze Kev would be starting his journey to the afterlife forty years earlier than anticipated. Carried off, impaled on the polished, chrome grill of an articulated truck.

"HAPPY FRIDAY!" I screamed.

Any thoughts I had that Skid Skedaddle might savour his escape were sadly short-lived. Instead, he set off in hot pursuit with his eyes bulging, fists pounding and his mouth screaming obscenities.

"Seriously, Dan, what is wrong with people nowadays? This here demonstrates everything that's wrong with modern society. On any other day, these two numpties would be brown bread, as in dead. Simple as. Yet today, having swerved the Grim Reaper's dark clutches, how do they want to celebrate their good fortune? By chasing each other to the ends of the Earth before kicking the seven bells of shit out of each other. Some days, modern life and the numpties in it, get right on my..."

"Tossers!" Dan's grasp on English slang had come on dramatically.

"Exactly," came my reply.

Suddenly, I could feel an explosion of rage go off inside my head. Its intensity started to create white specks of light in my vision.

"Feck! I'm no better than Skid Skedaddle. In fact, I'm way worse," I mumbled in shock.

At first, my mind refused to entertain this notion. It countered the argument by serving up loving images of my early childhood on the nearby roadside wall:

→ Magic reading me bedtime stories

→ Me in my wigwam, wearing full Native American face paint

→ Magic winning five-a-side manager of the year, and me dancing uncontrollably with excitement

→ Me sitting in the RAF AFCENT library, legs swinging, face grinning and my nose inches away from the paper drawing.

What had I done? Who had I become? And why hadn't I done more to protect the timid, dreamy, buck-toothed, happy kid I once was? But more importantly, who was the angry imposter whose face I saw staring back at me every morning in the mirror?

I knew that inner city life had changed me immeasurably. If it wasn't the 24/7 sound of sirens, it was the insane levels of aggression that I could find within minutes of leaving the house. Most notably at the bus stop where I'd be met by a rag-tag army of bleary-eyed, anxious and strung-out commuter junkies desperate for a fix. A caffeine fix that was. And even though I'd usually arrive at the bus stop barely conscious, I still had to be alive to the threat that any look, tut or a mere touching of toes could cause. In any other part of the country, that would be met with a titter, a smile or an apology. But there, it was considered enough provocation to start the nuclear launch sequence and kick off World War III.

If I was lucky to survive the ride down Brixton Hill without windmilling or breaking up a scuffle, I'd be given a few moments to compose myself before taking my seat on the haunting horror ride – the tube. A ride where strangers, now devoid of social graces (these didn't exist underground), would carry out some of most heinous acts of human degradation, all within plain sight.

Bored commuters would start picking, flicking, rolling or wiping bogies on seats. But somewhere deeper down the carriage was where life's filthy bastards were. They'd use any cover they could, from the screeching brakes to the flickering lights, to disguise the clipping of their fingernails.

Bogey mining and pinging fingernails on public transport before 8 am. That would leave me only fifteen minutes of peace for walking before undertaking the main battle of the day – work.

So, was it any wonder, after years of hand-to-hand combat, verbal jousting and sleepless nights, that I was mentally, physically and spiritually exhausted?

WTF was I even doing on Camino? I knew in reality that I shouldn't be there. In days gone by, if someone had arrived on my DofE expeditions in a similar state, I'd have binned them off instantly. No questions asked. Why? Because I'd consider them a danger to themselves and the group.

Yet there I was, hanging out of my own arse, barely able to speak, too tired to listen and often unable to perform the simplest of tasks – like tying my laces.

Not only was I mentally exhausted, but I was also increasingly aware that I was under attack from my darker half, who was attempting to take my throne.

Was this why Spirit had returned? Had she come to protect me from me? If so, I'd need every ounce of her strength and support, as I had almost nothing to give. All I wanted to do was slow down, lie down and shut down.

Well good luck with that! You're already one hour behind the pack and sitting in last place in today's race for a bed. Of which, Estella has about five hundred. And I guarantee you this – they will go fast.

By then I'd grown bored of my conscience's wittering. So instead, I switched myself back to reality mode. Up ahead I caught the first glimpse of the moss-covered bell tower of the Church of the Crucifix.

Having read a little about the church (pre-Camino), I couldn't wait to cast my eyes over this 12th century Romanesque gem.

I was especially keen to see the exquisite, semi-circular arches and barrel vaults, as well as the depiction of Christ on the cross. Plus, there were some conflicting rumours that the church had some link to the Knights Templar.

After turning off from the NA -1110, we passed by the pastel-coloured walls of Albergue de Pereginos. Outside, they'd hung a huge banner to welcome in weary, weather-beaten pilgrims.

To the right of the albergue, I saw the first building connected to the church. It had a hexagonal roof, square walls, minuscule windows and rough brickwork. The walls intrigued me as each had a slice cut out of the corner (which reminded me of Magic's Christmas cake).

Architecturally, the church was a feast of styles and craftsmanship. As our path turned right along the cobbled street, we passed the cream-coloured plastered walls on which hung the banner Colegio - Seminario.

From there, it was a short walk to the church entrance. I was desperate to see inside, mainly due to my fascination with the Knights Templar.

I stared in awe as I placed my right hand onto the old, cold, knotted surface of the oak door, encrusted in metal studs. All it would take was one big shove and I'd be...

CLOSED.

"It's closed. You... have... got... to be shitting me, Dan."

While I was lost for words, Dan was lost for air, having descended into a fit of giggles.

"What's the bloody point? We set off out here at the crack of sparrows, much like a couple of starving orphans in the hope of salvation. And what thanks do we get? De nada. Nothing. Feck all. If I wasn't so paranoid, I'd swear this is starting to feel like a bloody conspiracy. Why is nothing ever open? Do the locals sit above, watching for the sight of my fat sweaty carcass before frantically shutting up shop? How do they alert the villagers? Secret handshake? Release a dove? Or do they have a chain-smoking donkey braying out the warning?"

Though I was only half-joking, I had to admit that Spain mystified me. To the point that I wondered if businesses were operating an I'll-only-open-if-I-can-be-arsed retail model.

"Righto, Dan. Let's be serious for a minute. And I need you to be honest with me. So, having missed breakfast, your fellow pilgrims and entrance into this magnificent church, is there anything else you desperately don't want to see before we crack on? Because I, Captain Cock-Up, can probably arrange that for you."

"No, it's all good. But if there is a chance to miss something ... count me in," replied Dan, a little too sarcastically.

"Great. Fantastic. Good to hear, Dan." I quipped.

With the nonsense now sorted and all thoughts of hope quashed, we trudged off down Calle del Crucifijo, Calle Mayor and passed Plaza Julián Mena, until I saw a small, stone arch. Now that was one thing that we couldn't conceivably miss. Unless it suddenly collapsed. Once through the arch, we made our way onto the jewel in Puente la Reina's crown. The breath-taking 11th century, Romanesque Queen's Bridge.

It was considered a remarkable feat of civil engineering – and one of the monuments of the Camino. Design-wise, it was made up of six sandy-coloured stone arches which pitched up towards the centre and spanned the width of the River Arga.

Back in medieval times, it played both a pivotal and strategic role as it was essentially the only route over the river. A fact that I was sure hadn't gone unnoticed by the queen who'd had the bridge built for King Sancho the Great. He was quick to promote the Camino, no doubt to relieve weary pilgrims of coin for their safe passage over his waterway.

It was as I stood on the centre of the bridge, appreciating the two sets of beautifully inset cobbles and listening to the gentle flow of the river, that it hit me.

My life was shit. And not just a little bit shit. It was a steaming cow-pat of festering shit.

It is. And it will continue to be so until you get a grip and stop hiding behind all your bullshit excuses. Ask yourself this, fatso! (My conscience was now in full flight.)

When you were a timid, dreamy, buck-toothed happy kid, did you dream of the day you'd walk down the street and hear mums, school kids or plumbers singing, whistling or humming one of your ad jingles? (Better still, do you remember dreaming of working at Saatchi & Saatchi?)

Or did you dream that one day you'd end up bobbing up and down in the creative toilet bowl of life, arguing and scuffling with gladiator-sized turds? Turds who you knew would never accept you, your ideas or your thinking.

Think about that, and while you're at it, ask yourself this: How much time, effort and energy are you wasting fighting the inevitable? It's time you listen, accept and move on. Change is no longer an option, it's a feckin' necessity. As every day you delay is one day nearer your spiritual death. One day nearer that your cancerous twisted darker half gets to take control over the inside of your head. Is that what you want?

I knew my conscience was right. And as I stared into the murky waters of the River Arga, I could feel a decade worth of pent-up anger, frustration and resentment bubble to the surface. Reflecting back on my lack of focus, growth, drive and inconsistency, the inevitable release came, and a thousand tears of dead ideas poured down my face.

"I'm so, so sorry," I blubbed.

The pain in my heart was almost too excruciating to bear as I stood shaking with anger. I was angry because I was aware of the talent I possessed. I was just furious that I hadn't accomplished even ten per cent of what I'd intended. But I had created this mess by my daily thoughts, inaction and poor focus.

Just like how I'd allowed my dark half, my imposter, space to breathe. It had been me who had invited him into my head to live rent-free. And it had been me that had fed him a toxic diet of negativity, aggression and self-loathing.

It was time to cut his cancerous tissue from head. I was tired, more tired than I'd ever been. I was tired of feeding him. Tired of him thieving my oxygen. But mostly, I was tired of hiding behind him. I wanted back what was rightfully mine – me.

"You ok, bud? You're shaking," said Dan.

"Yeah, I'm fine. I'm just having a senior moment." Which was true.

Where the hell had this come from? I must admit, I had felt the beginnings of something at Alto del Perdón. But at the time, it wasn't something I could quite put my finger on. Had Spirit played a part in this? Definitely.

I could feel myself slowly surrendering to the rigours and ritual of life out there. Was it these thoughts that were telling me to slow down? Undoubtedly.

In theory, I was done. I was done playing games, playing catch up or even trying to keep up with people. Whether at home or out there. If that meant redirecting my energy at home and shutting certain people out – that was fine. Likewise, if it meant hiding under a tree, cowering under a bush or seeking solace in the cool comfort of a church on Camino, so be it.

If my new 'go slow' meant arriving at Estella honking of sweat but happy, regardless of whether I'd bagged a good or bad albergue, who cared? Whatever came my way from then on, I was back in the director's chair – no one else. And as far as accommodation went, whatever God denied I knew booking.com would provide.

With my head lost in thought, I wandered across the Queen's Bridge. A Camino sign directed us left, back towards the ever-busy NA-1110. Once safely across, we picked up a leafy lane that passed in close proximity to a huge wall that contained the four-storey powerhouse of the Convent of the Comendadoras del Sancti Spiritus.

Just beyond the convent, a Camino marker directed us left, off Calle Zubiurrutia and onto a concrete path. The path passed by boundary walls, barren fields and huge electrical towers, before leading us underneath the monstrous NA-601 bridge.

Under the safety of the bridge and away from the incessant roar of traffic, wildlife was free to flourish again. All around us flew a hungry flight of swallows diving, bombing and swooping down and picking off lackadaisical bugs who'd been caught napping in the early morning sun.

While the swallows were hard at work, worker bees were plundering the hedgerows. They spent their morning hopping from flower to flower, filling up their pollen baskets like early morning shoppers.

I wandered in this dream-like state for an hour, paying no real attention to where I was, who I was with or where I was headed. I was lost in the simplicity, beauty and wonder of Mother Nature's finest work.

That wonder was still whizzing round my head as the path, having kicked upwards once again, came to a roundabout just on the outskirts of Mañeru.

The first thing that struck me as we stood on the edge of the town, was the tussle that had obviously occurred for domination of the skyline. A newly-built apartment block had tried to take on the 18th century Church of San Pedro – and there was only ever going to be one winner.

Off to our right, I couldn't help but notice a Camino arrow, sprayed crudely onto the bark of a young tree. Beside it was a board with a laminated map full of potential things we could miss today.

Having given this the once over, we tootled down Calle Mikelaldea and Calle la Luna. Towards the bottom of the street, we were directed by a large, wooden Camino sign right onto the noisy Calle Fe.

Upon entering, we were met by the sight of a large, triangular open area. Nestled in the centre was a wooden pitched shelter, surrounded by sprawling trees. Under it were the broken bodies and gaunt faces of weary, salt-soaked and sun-baked pilgrims, gathered around the water fountain like thirsty pigeons.

To stop or not the stop – that was the question. But having only walked for an hour, the real question was – did we need to? We had food. We had water. We had enough snacks to see us to Cirauqui and beyond.

So, on we went, down Calle Esperanza, passing not one but two albergues, both of which were swarming with pilgrims. The overspill continued down further onto Plaza de los Fueros, where the local's wooden benches that lined the stone square had been commandeered by pilgrims. The scene had turned into an impromptu E.R hospital. Everywhere I looked, people were trying desperately to revive their lifeless, exhausted and dying feet.

From Plaza de los Fueros, it was a quick shimmy left, then right, before we were onto Calle Forzosa and out into the wild again, where the crumbling remnants of a Roman wall cutting between wheat fields lined our route.

To the left of our path was an eight-foot high, white-washed wall, surrounded at the back by trees. With its position and close proximity to town, that could only have been one thing – the Mañeru bone yard (cemetery).

Beyond the cemetery, the surface underfoot changed quickly. Gone was the punishing, soul-sapping and energy-draining concrete that hammered our joints. In its place came the heavy, clay-coloured, nutrient-rich soil of the Navarra – vineyard country.

Suddenly, after cresting one last ridge, the rich valley basin opened up before us. There, like a mirage, sat row upon regimented row of fields brimming with lush green, shimmering leaves. And hiding beneath them were rich, fat, full and juicy grapes.

Just as we had expected, the sun struck. Having spotted us on open ground, thirty gut-busting minutes from Cirauqui, it hit us. Within seconds, it began firing ray upon ray down onto us, peppering the ground with smouldering hotspots. We found ourselves zig-zagging up the path to avoid them.

While we'd chosen to embrace it, a small group of pilgrims further on had decided to take evasive action among the vines. That only seemed to enrage the sun and redirect its efforts to those pinned down cowering under leaves.

While that was tough for them, it at least allowed us to slip from under its watchful eye and scamper away unnoticed.

In an attempt to offset the burning sensation, I was beginning to feel in my feet and salt-soaked eyes, I directed my attention to the two ridges in the distance.

The first ridge, which appeared off to our left, resembled a lunar landscape. It was barren, pock-marked and the only semblance of life came from a single row of trees. They drew our eyes seductively, from left to right, towards the second ridge. The front was awash with lush green vines that looked like they'd soon overrun the medieval hilltop town of Cirauqui at any minute.

Cirauqui was mesmerising to behold and reminiscent of Casterly Rock (from George R. R. Martin's *Game of Thrones*). The white and terracotta coloured kingdom was designed in a semi-circular defensive pattern, isolated in the landscape. Its main beacon of hope was the church bells of San Román and Santa Catalina.

By the time we'd shuffled our way to the outskirts of Cirauqui, our bodies were steaming. Thankfully for us, the strong shadows cast by the labyrinth of close-knit streets did wonders to cool the surrounding air.

We weaved our way through alleyways and opposing apartment blocks peppered with Camino signs onto Calle Carros, which rang out with the distant sound of laughter and music. Finally, we were spat out in front of the ochre-fronted facade of Café El Portal – which was overrun with pilgrims.

Many were crashed out on aluminium chairs, hugging or simply strewn across the street, lying on shadowed, cooling cobbles.

A quick scan of the masses told me everything I needed to know. There was no sign of Ryan, Hwan or Joy. Nor was there any room at the inn for newcomers, as all the seats were taken.

So, we decided to plough on (but not before catching a few eyes and throwing out a handful of 'Buen Caminos'), heading up towards a low, stone arch that marked the entrance to the heart of the town.

As I admired the impressiveness of the stonework, I couldn't help but be drawn to the gentle sound of squawking overhead. It was then, as I looked up, that I noticed a series of tiny windows cut into the face of the rock with a little ledge sitting beneath.

These windows had obviously been created by the master builder to encourage birds to nest, rest and raise their young. Such a simple nod to nature, but it was one that very much made my day.

Under the arch we went, my eyes now transfixed on the timeless cobbles in the centre of our path and the flagstones that framed them. Little did I realise that I would be transported back through time.

Calle Portal was beset by houses from a bygone era. Each of them had been thoughtfully and lovingly restored, and even though they were unique in appearance and style, they seemed to sit comfortably beside each other.

Their differences ranged from contrasting facades, stonework, design and window frames, with some adorned with Juliet balconies.

There was also a contrast in doors. From the highly polished, semi-circular doors encrusted in metal studs, to the square-fronted, panel beaten metal doors. Doors decorated with Moorish door knockers alongside castings of ghoulish characters.

At the top of Calle Portal, a simple tiled Camino sign beneath a gas-powered streetlight directed us towards Plaza Ayuntamiento. There a small Camino tile led us through the main building and out the other side (but not before we refilled our bottles and got our Pilgrim Credencial stamped).

Our path continued and dropped us down through Calle Markora and Calle Mayor, where two cream-coloured farming sheds provided the perfect frame of blandness to contrast God's main stage, which contained a multitude of fields set against a flawless, pale-blue sky.

Just a bit out of town, down a steep gravel track, we came upon the remains of a grand old Roman bridge. Though what remained resembled little more than a collection of grey mottled stones, it still had a presence. Considering the Romans first arrived in Spain in 206 BC – it was highly impressive.

Less could be said for its more modern, soul-less equivalent, the NA-1110, which appeared moments later.

Our path then turned left down a track and back amongst the vine-filled valley floor. With absolutely nowhere to hide our pace plummeted, our sweat soared – and soon even our water ran dry.

Thankfully we were rescued by a hawker who'd set up a table alongside another section of Roman wall. The hawker, much like the modern-day King Sancho the Great, was only too keen to relieve us of cash. In return, he provided us with an ice-cold can of Aquarius lemon drink (which was worth four times the €1.50 we paid for it).

Once we'd downed our cans, we set off again through the rugged landscape. Soon the almond groves gave way to hedgerows, which offered us a modicum of shade for a few fleeting moments. Until we hit the first underpass beneath the NA-1110.

It was far from being a dry, airless and dusty farming tunnel, but was in fact a modern cement tunnel that cooled the air to a near chill. It also provided the perfect spot for first breakfast.

Once refuelled, and before the lactic acid had a chance to take hold, we set off again. We wandered beside the NA-1110, passing under bridges, aqueducts and over bridges where pilgrims were busy baring all and letting off steam.

Soon after the bridge we were back fighting with the hedgerows, before finally coming to the colossal farming tunnel that seemed to appear in every guidebook. It was a masterpiece of craftsmanship – as well as being bloody freezing.

At the far end of the tunnel, I could see a golden halo of light, from which we popped out moments later cold, shivering and reborn – ready for one last scramble up a gravel track and into Lorca.

When we got there, we were met by the monstrously-sized, sandy-coloured stone masterpiece of the 12th century – the Church of San Salvador. A church that I'd guessed had undergone one or two minor procedures. But hadn't everyone these days?

As we wandered along Calle Mayor, I couldn't help but feel the love for the Camino starting to come alive. It was everywhere. It was on the plaster-cast vignettes of Jesus, St. James or the white Camino shell pinned above the entrance to people's homes.

It was also written into the lines on the faces of the elders who had come out to smile, cheer and greet us. I could feel something had changed deep within me. I didn't know what. I didn't know how. But something had shifted.

At that stage of the day, with my mind sapped by the heat, thoughts came and went on the warm breeze. But the one image that remained constant was the smiles on the faces of the elders. They had found their lot in life. They had found their happy place. All I could hope was that someday I would find the same.

After a short-lived reacquaintance with the NA-1110, our path dropped down onto a dusty gravel path. There we were greeted by a Camino signpost that told us Estella was seven and a half kilometres away – less than two hours to go.

With nothing much to focus on my eyes took to the horizon, to the sight of a huge three-thousand-foot beast, what must have been Montejurra. It was surrounded by a legion of trees, not to be messed with. For our part, we wouldn't be. We were merely passing by.

Villatuerta felt like an abandoned film set. Nothing moved. No cars, cats or the usual territorial guard dogs that stalked the front yards. Were the people in on the gag of 'shut up shop, get ya shutters down, fatty lummox Paul is in town'? If so, I had to take my hat off to them. They had all done a remarkable job.

Once out of Villatuerta, the dusty gravel path resumed, passing parks, over the River Ega and onto the outskirts of Estella. Its boundary seemed to be marked by a stone cross balancing nicely on a plinth.

The first building I noted as we headed along Calle Curtidores was the renovated hotel, Hosteria de Curtidores. It sat lovingly beside the tranquil River Ega. While we wouldn't be staying there, it was definitely one for the future.

Further down Hosteria de Curtidores and alongside a large open park was the Church of the Holy Sepulcher. It was a colossal beast, built with a mishmash of Romanesque and Gothic style. I didn't even look to see if it was open. I was bored of that game.

Dan, having arrived outside Albergue Municipal de Peregrinos, one of the first as you entered Estella, declared himself home. But I was hungry, and my bed for the night was at Hostal El Volante, on Calle Merkatondoa at the opposite end of town. Wasn't it always?

Having learned the shocking revelation of the day – that I snored – I didn't fancy spending the night surrounded by twitchy, sleep-deprived pilgrims. They'd earned a decent night's kip and wouldn't have welcomed the sound of semi-automatic snore fire, which based on my level of tiredness, was incoming. With that in mind, I said bye to Dan, and shuffled my way up the road. Safe in the knowledge that I had reserved a room all to myself. So I could snore without fear of reprisal.

The Camino today had carved me open. It revealed something to me that was hidden in plain sight – I was angry. Angry at myself. Angry at all those wasted years, but mainly angry that I hadn't done more to protect the timid, dreamy, buck-toothed happy kid I once was.

But that needed to change – and fast.

~~CHAPTER 10: DETOX~~

5th September, Estella - Los Arcos, 21km
Beep! Beep! Beep! Beep! (6:45 am)
"Stop it..."
Beep! Beep! Beep! Beep! (6:48 am)
"...I'm warning you..."
Beep! Beep! Beep! Beep! (6:51 am)
"...this is your last chance."
Beep!...
"Right, that's it. I've had about all I can take from you, you infuriating, manipulative, soul-sucking bastard."

Unknowing to me, I was about to launch into a tirade of Basil Fawlty style proportions.

"And don't give me that look either. You know exactly the one I mean. That butter-wouldn't-melt-in-your-mouth look."

"What – me?" Suddenly my voice had transformed into that of a 19th century Torquay fishwife.

"Yes, you. You with your annoying curves, sleek lines and nauseating adolescent neediness. You, you, you. Is that all you think about? Well, is it? Well... I for one am sick to my arse-end with your tantrums, sulking and constant craving for validation and approval. Why don't you do us all a favour and trot on? Go on, off you feck! Find another host to infect, leech off and suck the life force from. Because me and you, mobile phone, we are over."

"We... are over."

I whispered it again as I sat in quiet disbelief. Where had this rant bubbled up from? There was something in it that excited me. I could almost hear the clunk and rattle of keys, as if a jailer had unlocked and opened the door to my cell. Ushering in a new era of freedom.

Was this it? Were we really done, after almost two decades? Had I really called time on our toxic, timebomb of a relationship? I'd encouraged and fostered it through the misuse of social media apps that had stolen my time, my focus and many a childhood dream. All through clever dopamine manipulation and AI functioning.

If this was true, then I was free.

At least in that moment. But I knew it was only the start of my battle. It was easy enough to stand there all cocksure saying we were done. It would be a whole different ball game when it came to handing out eviction notices and demanding they transfer their hold and their power back to me.

When I finally came around, as my head was struggling to get to grips with what I was asking, I found myself shivering, with my hand cradling my phone protectively. My thumb gently stroked the screen. Jesus! If this was my body's initial response to the severing of the umbilical cord between us, God help me when the full fury of my digital detox kicked in.

But feck it! The fightback was on. There would be no more:

→ Staring lifelessly into my phone's darkened abyss – praying for validation

→ Salivating every time its red light flashed

→ Sweaty palms or itchy-twitchy fingers.

My hands had been primed like a practised gunslinger in a Spaghetti Western to 'Reach for it, mister,' within milliseconds of my phone vibrating. Surely, they too deserved a rest.

The question was, how should I mark my day of independence?

Should I perform a jig? Chuck my phone down the khazi? Or stove its head in with the heel of my size 11.5 boots?

Or you could simply try turning it off.

My conscience was right. Why not just turn it off? It wasn't as if it could stop me – could it?

"Oh, for feck's sake! Get on with it," I muttered, annoyed at myself.

With that, I grasped the neck of my phone and pressed hard on the power button. It let out one last gasp before it slipped into the darkness. That was it. I'd done it.

For those first few seconds, I sat in shock while a numb, uncomfortable silence slowly filled the air. This was followed soon after by the thump of my heart. Next came the nervous, clammy hands, and that ever-familiar feeling of dread and fear.

What the fuck was I doing? Why was I being so selfish? What if I needed to know something, anything, urgently? Or if there was an accident – what then?

Well, if it hadn't escaped your attention, you're right slap-bang in the arse end of nowhere. Eighty miles from the nearest airport. With no high-speed donkeys or 'Dons' to save you. I hate to have to tell you like this, but if there was a real emergency, people would either have to wait, or they would be fecked.

Listen, no one's suggesting you go full Luddite. What I'm suggesting is putting in some boundaries. Try phone off 9 am to 6 pm, then off again at night by 9 pm. These may seem harsh. Then again, they will prevent you from wandering about like an anaesthetised chimp. It will also create space and settle your mind. Along with giving you something other than your wrist to look at – no pun intended.

Right again. My issue was disconnecting myself from my work brain. A brain that was typically bombarded by emails, chat and interruptions. Most of which were totally unnecessary, if people took time to engage their brains rather than simply adopting the CBA (can't be arsed) approach.

I could feel myself getting feisty. But I understood this was my mind rebelling at the idea of a new, disconnected reality. In so many ways, I was just like any other addict, (on average, British adults check their mobile phone every twelve minutes). One who was in denial and simply looking for any lie, excuse or leverage I could gain, to justify using again.

The truth of the matter was that I was half excited and half bricking it. The idea of spending a day undisturbed, where I was free to enjoy the beauty and splendour of Spain sounded sublime. The idea of doing it, while going 'cold turkey,' with no support – that sounded terrifying.

But wasn't this one of the many reasons I'd come here?

I tried to prep my mind for the day ahead. I knew the first thirty-six to forty-eight angst-ridden hours would be horrendous.

Not only would I have to manage the mental side of withdrawal (irritability, frustration, mood swings, difficulty concentrating, anxiety – the lot), but I'd also have to deal with the physical side when the lack of likes, shares, retweets and supporting messages reduced my dopamine hits. I'd have to learn to manage this, while still appearing my same, semi-jovial and sarcastic self.

In many ways, it felt like the Camino had snatched the Etch-a-Sketch drawing of my life, before shaking it up and erasing it, and handing me a blank one with the challenge of starting over.

Imagine that! Imagine being given a blank sheet of paper with the opportunity to start over. Free from all your previous failings, misdemeanours and shortcomings. All that would be left would be to decide what to do with the time I'd been given.

Beep! Beep!

7 am.

My watch alarm sounded. This left me thirty minutes to wash, stretch and get gone. I headed out to meet Dan at the cafe with green awnings on Calle Mercatondoa Kalea, which I had fully expected to find open.

CLOSED

"You have got to be shittin' me?"

This time the exasperated, but inevitable, response came from Dan.

Instinctively, I could feel my hands dive towards my pocket, where my fingers began to seductively rub along the curved edges of my phone. All it would take was a few seconds...

Are you shittin' me?

... a quick on-off.

That's NOT going to happen.

No one would ever need to know.

Except me, of course. Here's a novel idea for you, soft lad. Instead of relying on your mobile for every thought, hope and suggestion, why not try an old-school technique? Like using your brain. Or better still – your eyes. Remember rolling through town when you first got here; what was the steel-fronted, swanky-looking, petrol station type thing on the corner of the roundabout?

"An AVIA garage," I muttered.

Genius! Now, if you lift your eyes out of the gutter, instead of scanning the pavement like an old-one looking for 5ps and fag butts, you'll see the garage is sixty metres away. May I suggest, when you do go in, that you focus purely on the food and not the clothes section? Unless you've a partial fetish for dressing like...

"Dan, Dan, Dan... I think I know where Ryan bought all his Uncle Travelling Matt Camino gear," I said, chuckling.

But it was already too late. Dan had steamed through the doors at the garage, where he proceeded to wade through the aisles of clothes, holding aloft Exhibits A, B and C from Ryan's Exclusive Camino Collection. But more worrying still, was the fact he was also eyeing up a trilby hat, poncho and a pair of khaki shorts with an elasticated waist band.

"What'ya think?" Dan's face was one of pure excitement, having donned the dark blue, all-in-one poncho.

"Seriously..." I replied, unable to read his expression. "You look like feckin' Quasimodo. And I for one don't fancy getting lifted by the law for having aided and abetted your escape from the bell tower of the Church of San Miguel. Nor do I want to be anywhere near you when Esmerelda's Roma family catch up with you." The look on Dan's face was one of sheer disappointment.

"Now, can you stop arsing about and focus on the job at hand – getting food?" I said matter-of-factly while pointing with excitement at the food counter.

When we finally exited the garage, some ten minutes later, we were laden down like a pair of drug-trafficking mules with Snickers bars, TUC Biscuits, Mini Babybel, Haribo Goldbears (standard) and a two-foot-long ham and cheese bocadillo.

All of this would help propel us up the nine kilometres towards Villamayor de Monjardín (the high point of the day), which stood at over two thousand feet and was surrounded by a ring of impenetrable forest. Perched on top of Villamayor, and offering unprecedented views across the valley, was the castle of San Esteban de Deyo.

Once we arrived our plan would be simple. We'd stop, catch our breath, check our pockets and re-zip everything before launching ourselves, roly-poly style, twelve kilometres downhill.

En route, we hoped to catch a glimpse of fallow fields, vine groves, terrified pilgrims, curious shepherds, and the look of a bewildered sheepdog, before finally arriving at Los Arcos in the late afternoon – dizzy, dusted, dazed, and ready for dinner.

From the AVIA garage, we sauntered over the pedestrian crossing, turning left then a sharp right. We were guided by a large Camino sign attached to a nearby lamppost, which directed us up and behind a local florist shop.

From there, we wandered along a tree-lined concrete path that cut its way through a modern, sleepy, suburban housing estate. To our right was the terrifying sight of many a childhood nightmare – an empty playground. Riderless swings creaked menacingly.

As we edged our way up and out of Estella, along Camino de Santiago, the houses soon began to fade and were replaced by monstrous, monotone-coloured factories. While initially these looked impressive in size, they soon paled into insignificance against the might of Montejurra – a three-thousand-foot sleeping giant, resting off to our left and dominating the skyline.

Soon after the factories, Camino de Santiago became Calle de Estella as the path ramped up yet again. It was there, at the entrance to Ayegui, where we were met by ochre-yellow painted homes, complete with matching white balconies, shutters and garage doors.

Onwards and upwards along Calle de Estella we went, until we stopped in our tracks from the ever-familiar sight of disoriented pilgrims, frantically darting left, right and back again.

Such a scene was typical of the first hour (often considered the worst hour) of any Camino day. When tired minds, battered bodies and aching limbs fought back wave upon wave of tiredness. Tiredness that left us all frazzled, nauseous and unable to follow the simplest instruction.

We watched the scene play out by two lads as they came up to a fork in the road, where they had to decide between Camino Santiago or Calle Mayor.

Somehow, the lads had failed to spot the single blue tile, directing them down and along Calle Mayor. They'd also missed the two Camino tiles stacked one on top of the other, just before Plaza San Pelayo.

Well, they'd either missed them, or worse, didn't trust them. Which in itself wasn't that unusual a phenomena. In fact, it was something I was often guilty of myself. Neither boded well, especially as we were still six hundred kilometres shy of Santia...

Alas, it was a case for Google. Before I had a chance to shout out directions, the two pilgrim gunslingers had drawn their weapons and began firing messages, peow peow peow, into their search engines. When they finally came around and looked up, they saw, less than three feet from them, the signs that had eluded them. Slowly, shyly they turned towards us.

"Jesus lads, what were you on last night?" I said smiling, and quite clearly envious of them.

One look told me all I needed. Both lads were hanging. Undoubtedly as a result of their previous day's effort. But probably not helped I'd say by a fitful night's sleep, empty bellies and a night's worth of beer, the scent of which seeped out through their pores.

As there seemed little mileage to be had in taking the piss (these lads would suffer enough today), we opted instead to wish them a 'Buen Camino', before we scuttled off down Plaza San Pelayo towards a stretch of lawn littered with fellow pilgrims.

To the right of the benches was a small, whitewashed stone monument. Inside the alcove was a scene depicting the crucifixion, captured beautifully by three plain wooden crosses on top of a stone mound. Curiously, beneath Jesus's cross, and at the bottom of the stone there appeared a hole.

Or was it a cave entrance? If so, was this intended to represent the cave where Mary Magdalene had gone to anoint Christ's body? Christ only knew.

"Forgive them father, as they know not what they do."

Those were the words written above the alcove, that much I did know.

"Well ain't that the feckin' truth, Dan?"

From Plaza San Pelayo, our path weaved its way down the roughly laid concrete street of Calle Zuloandia. From our vantage point, we could look down upon the NA-1110 or across the vine fields in admiration at the beauty of Montejurra.

Nestled in against the bosom of Montejurra, and just visible above the rooftops, was the 8th century Santa María la Real de Irache monastery. This masterpiece of stonemasonry was once home to an order of Benedictine monks, where it had served as one of the primary pilgrim hospitals in the area. Its role back then was to support, nurture and care for the brow-beaten, broken-spirited and battle-weary pilgrims.

"THE BELLS, THE BELLS!" yelled Dan.

Even before I'd turned, I half knew what to expect. As I did, I saw Dan hunched over, in a stoop with one-eye closed. He'd somehow acquired a lisp and was busy flailing his arms around theatrically.

"ESMERALDA, ESMERALDA!"

"For your bloody sake mate, it better not bloody be." I said, alarmed.

I nervously checked behind for any sounds of her family scurrying about in the shadows. Thankfully, this wasn't the case.

From Calle Zuloandia, the road dropped down towards a junction. There, we were directed right, then across Calle Carretera. Ahead I could just make out one of the rarities of the day – a water fountain.

"Never waste an opportunity to fill up," I mumbled under my breath.

This had been one of the many lessons drilled into us when we were young on expedition. It was one lesson that I religiously stuck to.

Having filled up our bottles, we turned left up Camino de Santiago. There we traded hard concrete for a sleepy, shaded, gravel path between two opposing vine groves. Ahead and to our left, was the domed Santa María la Real de Irache bell tower. While to our right, was an enormous four storey futuristic building peppered with forty, small, porthole windows.

This building (which formed part of the winery) was protected by a low, thick, concrete wall and an eight-foot-high steel fence emblazoned with the words BODEGAS IRACHE in huge white letters.

As we made our way alongside the building, my eyes were drawn to a dark slate plaque up ahead that was mounted onto a cream-coloured, roughly cut, stone wall. On the slate, sprayed in white letters were the words FUENTE DE IRACHE.

While neither myself nor Quasimodo knew what fuente meant. I was more than willing to take a punt that the word below it, vino, meant wine.

"Free wine?" I said excitedly.

"Free what?" came Dan's somewhat bewildered response.

"You know: Jesus juice, plonk. Devil's urine, yee old tongue looser... WINE. How crazy is this? It's 8:50 am. The sun's barely shown itself. We've a fierce day ahead of us. Yet how has the winery chosen to greet us? By cunningly trying to knobble our efforts by getting us rat-arsed on FREE vino. How dark is that?' I said, jokingly.

"I love it," came Dan's response.

"Me too, Dan." It really was a thoughtful and welcoming gesture.

And with that, we both steamed through the steel gates. Once through our eyes were drawn to a metal shield, with a drinking font set into it. Protruding out were two brass taps each backed onto a large conch shell.

The first tap offered vino.

The second tap offered *agua*.

I must not get wankered, I must not get wankered.

This was the thought being played on an endless loop inside my head. Or at least, that's where I thought it was being played. It wasn't until I looked up and saw the chuckling faces that I realised my internal thought had gone external.

"Bud, you know I won't let that happen," came Dan's waspish response.

From the devilment in his eyes, it was clear that Dan was talking bollocks. Not only did he want it to happen, but he was also itching for it to happen.

Dan already knew I had an incredibly low tolerance for beer. What he didn't know was I had zero tolerance for wine – nada. Yet there I was, foolishly contemplating a game of Russian Roulette. A game that would only have one winner – the Camino.

But judging from all the jostling and wild excitement of those around us, it seemed as though I wasn't the only one up for a gamble.

Ahead in the queue, eager pilgrims were scrambling to unhook their Camino shells from their rucksacks. I quickly split them into three groups:

Group 1 - would use their Camino shell as a receptacle to draw wine

Group 2 - were frantically ditching their water to make room for wine

Group 3 - (the real filthy skanks among us) were empty handed, preferring instead to wrap their salt-sweated gums around the tap and drink directly.

"I must not get wankered," I said, repeating my new mantra.

I knew if I had even one sip, that would be me done for. And if I did, I'd invariably be found some time later, face-down in a ditch, dribbling, snoring and covered in flies. Or worse, attempting to coerce others to join me in my imaginary boat as I belted out the hymn 'Michael, Row the Boat Ashore'.

Are you saying NO to FREE WINE?

I was and nothing could be said to tempt me otherwise.

Plus, by saying *NO* to *FREE WINE*, I was saying *YES* to being an active spectator in the day's sporting extravaganza – The Pilgrim Pile-Up.

The joy of watching the spectacle, as wasted pilgrims swerved, swayed and bounced along the path, while desperately trying to avoid the ditches was too good to miss. And as all-day, free entertainment went, it was a great one to watch.

While everyone was busy filling their bottles and gullets, we headed out the gate, where a small white sign saying *Museo Del Vino* directed us along the path, passed the colossal-size monastery, a small picnic area and alongside a dry-stone wall, overrun with ferns and foliage.

We followed the wall for about a kilometre as it slowly wound its way into the open. Finally, we were spat out onto a dry and dusty dirt track, into what looked like a scene straight from 'Gunfight at the O.K. Corral'. Three opposing groups had formed in the dirt, all looking twitchy, nervous and uncertain. WTF was going on.

I could feel myself being lured into their drama. I could feel the tension slowly rising within the groups as their twitchy fingers thumbed their shorts' pockets. I knew once one pilgrim drew, it would set off a nervous chain reaction, causing everyone to instinctively reach for their phone.

You keep your hands where I can see them, mister...

Suddenly, I froze.

Good...

My conscience was in no mood for messing.

Now what I want you to do, is slowly and steadily...

...lower your right hand towards your side pocket.

OK.

Take it real easy now....

...when you get there. Take out your guidebook.

But before I did, I was curious to find the cause of the stand-off. Over to the right of the path was the likely culprit, an eight-foot wooden stake in the ground. On it, pointing in two opposing directions, were the words: *Straight ahead - Los Arcos 17.2km and turn right - Los Arcos 18.2km.*

"Well, that's clear as mud isn't it, Dan?"

While I then understood the confusion, it did little to change the outcome. Suddenly, all around us, pilgrims began drawing their pieces and started firing off queries, checking apps, reviewing maps and reading online blogs.

"What's the problem? Both routes lead to Los Arcos, no?" said Dan.

He was right. But it did nothing to ease the uncertainty. It was rare for the Camino to offer up options. And after six or seven days of following without question, people looked genuinely dumbstruck at the prospect of having to choose. Yes, both routes led to Los Arcos, but I could still see from the look on their faces that everyone was questioning which way was the right one.

I knew, having consulted my guidebook, that if we chose to continue straight, we'd walk in the shadows of Montejurra along a quiet forest path. The dense forest canopy and foliage would offer protection from the steadily warming sun and the noise of the nearby NA-1110.

But if we chose to turn right along Camino de Santiago, we'd get to walk along a narrow path lined with houses on the left and barren fields on our right, with the only point of interest being a small, shaded picnic area that came complete with a fountain.

Of the two, the first route sounded invigorating. Both in terms of what it could do for our spirit and our weary feet. So naturally, we didn't choose that way.

Our decision to go right was driven more by necessity than anything else. We'd gone through a lot of our water. And although we were both still pissing like fire hydrants, the sun was beginning to sizzle as the sweat began to pour off us. And I for one was keen to avoid becoming a boil-in-the-bag pilgrim.

While our decision was easy, The Pilgrim Pile-Up crew were uncertain. It wasn't long before we heard the sound of their boots behind us. If they found this decision hard, their next had them all sweating.

So, what was it going to be lads, were you going to ditch it or down it?

To ditch it meant ditching the 250ml of wine they'd just filled their bottle with. Surely these wine connoisseurs (and judging by the patter, some of these lot knew a thing or two about wine) wouldn't do that? Not without a serious loss of face.

Yet to down it broke every wine etiquette rule ever created. Surely, they wouldn't be so uncouth or uncivilised; so, what was it going to be?

To my utter shock (and delight) they decided to try downing it – fantastic. This reminded me of the scenes of carnage from my student days in Derby, where university scrotes would gather on Tuesday nights around a bin placed in the centre of Berlin's Bar, waiting for their turn to take part in the Yard-Of-Ale Drinking Challenge.

Within seconds, the connoisseurs were coughing, spluttering and belching wildly. Bloody amateurs. This was followed by the slow reddening of their faces and rolling of their eyes. While they were busy with that, Dan and I filled our water bottles and tried desperately not to snigger.

Once we'd filled up, we turned to admire our soon-to-be-wasted pilgrim compatriots, who were now hanging onto their stomachs and gasping for air. They looked like they were ready to embrace the idea of a siesta, tramp-style, among the picnic benches.

While they shuffled off, we crossed the NA-1110, where we traded dirt for the unforgiving tarmac of Avenue Prado de Irache. This instantly made me question whether we'd made a wrong turn. If so, how many needless kilometres were we adding onto what was already down as a long day?

I could hear my phone's soft whispering growing louder. It knew where to go. It knew the way. It really wanted to help. All I'd need to do was ask. With each passing step, I could feel my mind slowly giving in to fate.

Then out of nowhere, appeared the Asador Restaurant, Camping Iratxe and a small Camino sign that seemed to be aimed directly at a giant-sized mole hill in the distance. I knew that somewhere hidden amongst the impenetrable forest that made up the molehill lay Villamayor de Monjardín.

Once we'd passed Camping Iratxe, our path led us along the hedgerows and underneath farming tunnels, before spitting us back once again, amongst nature. We were hit with a cacophony of sounds as birds chased the forest news update, chicks cheeped their breakfast orders and rabbits scurried.

We wandered in the shadow of Monjardín, our eyes following the swerving path of pilgrims. For the next fifty minutes we played peek-a-boo with Monjardín, until finally, we found ourselves on a sweeping path on the outskirts of Azqueta.

As we sauntered up the path into town, three things immediately caught my eye: The Church of San Pedro, small allotment plots to our left and two wily old fellas up to mischief.

It was the latter in particular that intrigued me. They greeted us with hearty shouts of 'Buen Camino' and welcoming smiles. But behind their eyes, I could see signs of pure devilment. And having spent a lifetime amongst pranksters myself, it didn't take long to figure out who the chief protagonist was.

The two old fellas, Gardener A and Gardener B, were hard at it in their allotments, trying to rid their patches of pests. Or at least, so they both thought. What Gardener A hadn't realised was the greatest threat to his crop was Gardener B.

As soon as he saw Gardener A's back was turned, he picked up a handful of his snails and pegged them into Gardener A's patch. The brazenness tickled me, as it was exactly the kind of thing Mitch would have done.

This was even more comical once Gardener A finally turned around. He simply stared in disbelief at the fact that somehow, his patch was suddenly overrun with snails. While curiously enough, his neighbour's patch, Gardener B, was pest-free.

When we passed, Gardener B placed his forefinger to his lips. It was a childish attempt to buy our silence. It worked. The effect of our bought silence brought about another huge roar of laughter from him, and he threw his arms (and snails) in the air in celebration.

His laugh was only just beginning to fade as we passed a renovated stone house adorned with a huge white tile, announcing in capitals: AZQUETA.

Azqueta was a sleepy one-horse kind of town. No sooner had we swept right passed the town hall, Bar Azketako and another eerie playground, then we were out the other side and directed down a rough track. We passed a derelict-looking farm before the path took a breath-stealing incline up the molehill.

"WTF, Dan," I said in shocked disbelief.

Suddenly, on our right, alongside a wall of giant boulders there appeared what looked like an abandoned Tardis. If there was ever a time for a time machine, that was it.

Sadly, Dan was only too quick to point out that far from being a time machine (which it clearly was), it was in fact the recently restored 12th century, twin-arched gothic fountain, known locally as Fuente de los Moro – Fountain of the Moors.

"So, definitely not a time machine," he muttered.

From the wannabe Tardis, it was only a few minutes' walk along a dusty track until we came into Villamayor de Monjardín, which was now swarming with The Pilgrim Pile-Up crew. They'd commandeered the benches and bus stop so they could draw their phones and hook themselves up for a fix.

"Dan, do you mind if we crack on mate?" I said, anxiously.

I knew the further away from temptation, the happier I would be. Luckily for me, Dan understood. He too was keen to embrace a little detox. So, while I fought against the pull of my phone, he shepherded me down Calle Santa Maria, Camino Romaje and along Camino de Urtala.

From there our path headed down the roughly laid concrete, where eagle-eyed Dan spotted a Camino marker sign hiding in the undergrowth. With the bulk of our thinking done, all that was left was a six-kilometre roly-poly downhill to Eduardo's Cafe for tea, coffee and light refreshments.

Once clear of Villamayor de Monjardín, we headed back in and amongst the hedgerows, wandering in single file, like ghosts in the landscape.

When we finally came out of our catatonic state, we caught our first sight of a small caravan on the outer sweep of the bend, Eduardo's - Café Móvil.

"Daaan! Paauul!"

The shout that tore through the silence came from the one and only – Joyous Joy, our Canadian friend who we hadn't seen since Zariquiegui. Before we knew it, she was up and out of her chair and rushing towards us.

After the initial hugs and kisses were dispensed, we found a seat. Once seated, a mutual silence fell upon us. None of us had the words. But no words were needed. I could read the story of their Caminos written all over their faces. It was a story of total and utter contentment.

When the silence did finally break, it was Joy again. She'd decided that with only six kilometres left, her day was done. So, she suggested that we cool our jets and mosey on into town together as one.

From Eduardo's, the path meandered lazily passed hedgerows, a forest and a sizeable, shaded picnic area. But we were all too lost in conversation to take note of where we were. It wasn't until we came upon a sign for Los Arcos that we realised we'd arrived.

Once through the outskirts, we picked our way down the narrowing streets of Calle Mayor. Why was it, and this had always amused me, that the last kilometre always seemed so much longer than any other? Did the Camino just do this out of spite? Or did it just enjoy the sight of my waddling as I dragged my fat, sweaty carcass to the finish?

At the bottom of Calle Mayor, a small Camino tile above an archway directed us onto Plaza la Fruta. Even before we hit it, I could hear the first rumblings of laughter and chitter-chatter, before we were spat out onto Plaza de Santa María.

Sitting in and amongst the chairs, eating, drinking and chatting loudly were many of The Pilgrim Pile-Up crew. If I thought they were looking rough earlier, they looked well gone now. Lining Plaza de Santa María was the impressive Church of Santa Maria of Los Arcos.

More importantly, at least from my stomach's perspective, were small shops full of snacks, fruit and provisions. I'd have to wait a bit later to get to those. Dan headed off to his albergue and I trudged off to Pension Los Arcos to get my siesta on.

I was greeted by the owner's warm smile, who was quick to ask if I fancied an ice-cold beer. As greetings went this was epic. On noting my general weariness, he opted to swerve the paperwork, at least for the time being, preferring instead to take the time to show me to my room.

Upon entering the room, I threw myself on the cool, tiled floor. It was bone-chilling, but welcoming. I didn't move for the next twenty minutes, as I waited for my heartbeat to stabilise and the first waves of exhaustion to hit.

Dinner that night was back in Plaza de Santa María. It was a celebration dinner. One of friendship and gratitude.

We celebrated the fact that we'd survived another day. I was also keen to celebrate getting through the first thirteen hours of my digital detox. I knew I still had a long way to go. I was by no way out of the woods.

But I was done with constantly feeling anxious, reactive and drained by the dopamine overload of digital life. From then on, the only thing that would be powering me was Mother Nature and Haribo Goldbears. Both of which I was utterly fine with.

CHAPTER 11: IT'S TIME

6th September, Los Arcos - Logroño, 28km
It's time.
I woke, cold and shivering into the dark eerie silence of my hotel room. I lay fidgeting and scratching – uncomfortable in my own skin. I was painfully aware of what my conscience was asking me to do.
It's time.
It had begun a few days before in the form of a low, slow and distant drumbeat. Like that of an Orc army, wandering menacingly through the deep caverns of my mind. But with each passing day, the drumbeat, and its message grew steadily louder – and clearer. To the point that it could no longer be ignored.

"It's time... to go it alone."

The words seemed to stumble, almost apologetically, from my mouth where they were met by a wall of shock-filled, guilt-ridden silence. What was I thinking? But even as I said it, I knew it was too late. The thought had been set free – there would be no taking it back.

"But seriously! WTF are you thinking?" I mumbled to myself.

And why? Why had I chosen the hottest day with the furthest to walk as the day to bin off Dan? It made no sense. Especially as we were having such great fun, and I was still reliant on his support to shepherd me through the emotional minefield of digital withdrawal. Plus, was I even ready to go it alone?

"Absolutely," came a voice of unshakeable confidence.

I recognised the voice instantly. It was that of my younger, twenty-five-year-old self, with his 'fuck it, let's do it' attitude to life.

With the decision made, I was eager to get gone. But what time was it? 5:50 am. While my body may have been raring to go, my older, wiser self was having none of it. There was nothing to be gained at this hour, only injury.

But it seemed as though not everyone was in agreement. Outside my window, I could hear the low mumbling voices as pilgrims started to gather. Then came the fizzing sound of a match being struck, followed seconds later by the familiar scent of death that only cigarettes brought.

The voices hung around outside, as if uncertain of what to do next. What were they waiting for, permission? Then came a large booming voice, presumably from the alpha of the pack. With the order given, I lay back and listened to the gently fading, clickety-clack of walking poles.

With first light still hours away, I stared up at the ceiling. I waited like an expectant cinemagoer, to see what images my mind would serve up as part of the Saturday Morning Matinée. The first image was of me heading out into the cool, still, tranquil morning.

Then I was shown the image of my eight-foot-long, elongated, alien-like shadow stretching out before me on a golden, sun-baked path. The left side of the path was beset by low, ankle-biting bushes and gnarly thorns. To my right, I could see a football-sized field bursting with grape vines. In the middle stood a single, solitary, twenty-five-metre-high electrical pole. Attached to it were three cables swinging like a skipping rope in the wind.

Above, in a flawless, aquamarine sky was a large, dark figure with her wings stretched out majestically. I knew instantly who it was. Just like I knew how Spirit had something to do with the messaging that told me – it was time.

Right, enough of the hippy-trippy bollocks. What I really want to know is...

Even before my conscience had finished, I could feel my stomach start to tighten.

...what the feck are you going to tell Dan?

Shit! Dan.

Yes, Dan. The fella you seem to have conveniently forgotten. The very same fella who's been by your side every step of the way since Bayonne train station. The fella who you've shared many laughs, beers, dinners and even a few tears with. Remember him?

What was I going to tell Dan? The truth – I guess.

And which version of the truth would that be, Don Quixote? The one in which you reveal you're being guided by a buzzard. A buzzard that's somehow crossed the divide between the spiritual and the real world. Good luck telling that story. Do you have any idea how bat-shit crazy this story makes you sound?

On second thought maybe I'd swerve the truth, at least for the moment. In the meantime, I needed to get my brain sparking. If I was going it alone, there would be no room for Captain Cock-up.

From then on, it would be all on me. I'd be responsible for my feet, my fuel, my focus, my hydration and my pacing. I'd also have to stay on top of where I was headed, which towns I'd pass and where to score food and water.

Of these elements, the one that concerned me most was my pacing. My usual tactic was to attack the day with everything I had, before slowly dying a death by a thousand cuts, stumbling, stuttering and crawling my way to the finish. I'd managed to wing it thus far on this tactic, but it would be too hot and dangerous today. What was required was a more sensible and measured approach.

I don't fancy your chances.

From the conversations I'd overheard the night before, the day was rumoured to have three water fountains in the three main towns en route: Sansol at seven kilometres, Torres del Rio at eight kilometres and Viana at eighteen kilometres.

If true, that would leave an eleven kilometre stretch between Torres del Rio and Viana where there'd be nothing – nada. If I forgot to fill up, I'd be sucking on fumes.

With all the main points covered, all other thoughts turned to breakfast, which came courtesy of a cheese baguette that sat perspiring on the nearby dresser. It had had a rough night.

Its exterior had hardened overnight and was now tooth-chippingly tough. The cheese, the star of the show, looked on menacingly. I could feel the anxiety in my stomach as I peeled it off the dresser.

Once in my mouth, the tussle began. The cheese licked, lapped and lashed at the corners and roof of my mouth in a vain attempt to steal all the available moisture, which made chewing quite impossible. For fifteen minutes I fought both the cheese and my gag reflex as I force fed myself calories.

With the baguette dispatched, I could feel my mind starting to calm. Or at least that's what I thought it was doing. It wasn't until I hit the fresh air that the reality of the day really hit me. This would be my last day with Dan.

The morning air that greeted me was cool and the clouds overhead were terrifying. A fact that hadn't gone unnoticed by the pilgrim herd who were firing through Portal de Castilla, over the bridge over River Odrón and up Calle Ruta Jacobea.

I only made it as far as the bridge before I needed to stop. My head was pounding, and my guts had begun to spin at 1400rpm, causing the acrid sensation of stomach bile sliding up and down my windpipe.

As I looked up into the light, I saw a lone figure standing outside Albergue Isaac Santiago. A figure lost in their own morning ritual of checks and re-checks.

"Morning, bud," I said, when I finally caught up to Dan.

"Hey, bud. How are you?" came his ever-cheerful response.

On the surface, Dan appeared his same jovial self. Yet beneath it, something else stirred. He was fidgeting, something he never did. He was also constantly eyeballing the blood-red sky. He was spooked and not without good reason. Heat was his kryptonite, and today the sun planned to rain down fire on us.

What's going on here then, tubby lad? Not two hours ago, you were pontificating about cutting ties, burning bridges and striking out alone. Now look at the state of you. You've folded easier than a seaside deckchair. You do realise that going it alone means no Dan?

I was in no mood for my conscience's waspish humour. I was tired, crabby and stressed enough as it was. But what the feck did it expect me to do? Was I meant to rock up to Dan, a man who called me brother, and tell him to jog on?

That's exactly what you're meant to do, you cloth-eared twerp.

Well, fuck you! That wasn't happening. I would be starting the day with Dan – end of. To me, this made perfect sense. Why would I want to kill off our energy? It was going to be a hard day. Why make it harder? In my head it made sense that we headed out together then allowed the day's events to unfold naturally.

Sounds like you've bottled it.

"Right, bud. Shall we?" I said, half mustering a smile.

With that, we set off up Calle Ruta Jacobea, passed identikit houses, Albergue Casa Alberdi and up onto a thin concrete path. The path was lined with proud, young saplings ready for morning inspection.

"What have we got here then?" I muttered in a mock sergeant major's voice.

Who the hell had dished out these haircuts? They were far from the standard issue short, back and sides. Edward Scissorhands (or whoever the tree surgeon was) had gone rogue, dishing out mohawks and mullets to this rag-tag tree army.

Soon after the trees, and before the boneyard, we came across a wooden display board. On it were topographical and elevation drawings, marking out the day's route. I roughly translated it to mean that Los Arcos to Viana would take five hours. And Viana to Logroño would take an additional three.

Once we passed the boneyard, I stopped to admire the gnarly and contorted beauty of the almond groves. Each tree lovingly sculpted by the seasons and the hands of Mother Nature.

Upon clearing the almond groves, barns and outhouses we were thrust out once again into the wilderness. We were greeted by warm, tender and loving kisses from the sun's rays. Like a scanner, they started working their way up our bodies, gently warming and easing the tension in our calves, hamstrings, backs and shoulders.

Ahead on the golden sun-baked path, our shadows danced with delight, reminding me of the silhouetted figures in the opening sequence of the TV classic *Tales of the Unexpected*.

On either side of our path (and much larger than they appeared in the Saturday Matinée) was a metre-high thicket of bush. Its thorns had already snagged a few passing ankles, taking sock fluff as victory trophies.

As we wandered through this sparce wilderness, our only company came in the form of electrical poles. Their role it seemed was to guide us down towards the only redeeming feature in the landscape – a small electrical substation.

Overhead I could hear the faint and familiar crackle of static on the line. A sound that took me back to my childhood. Back to the time when I thought the crackle sound was of coded messages being fizzed down the line.

Having passed the substation, the full splendour of the Camino was revealed. We were greeted by the sight of mile-upon-mile of undulating, regimented vines. Vines that rose up like an ocean wave, crested, before tumbling down and rolling in towards us. The mesmerising beauty of my exterior world seemed to contrast sharply with what was going on in my inner world.

This was fuelled by two factors:

→ My apprehension about my chat with Dan
→ The sight of pilgrim bait scurrying up ahead.

Will you just get on with it? You sound like an angst-ridden teenager contemplating a break-up. Have you even considered, just for one teeny-weeny second, that maybe Dan's itching for some alone time too?

I hadn't. He wouldn't – would he? The stinging rebut from my conscience was more than enough to quieten my mind. It freed me up to enjoy the sight of citadel-sized hay bales, swallows dancing on the breeze and bee argy-bargy in the vines. Not to be outdone, our golden path put on a show as it snaked lackadaisically through the landscape, before finally rising up to meet the narrow, chalk-lined road of the NA-7205.

"Slow down pilgrim," I muttered upon seeing a Camino marker.

But it was already too late. The mutiny was well underway, and I could feel myself being dragged, kicking and screaming up towards Sansol.

"Dan, there's something I've been meaning..."

But that was as far as I got before an invisible hand cupped its fingers over my mouth, stifling my voice. Feck! That was my chance and I'd blown it.

My mind seethed with rage. Rage that I poured down onto the road, peppered with small Camino arrows that directed us ever onwards.

"Like, where else would we be feckin' going?" I grumbled.

As we continued upwards, more and more of these tiny arrows started to appear. They seemed to be directing us (with a matter of urgency) to the left-hand side of the road. What was all that about? But instinct told me to move first and ask questions later. Seconds after crossing, a white van came careering round the bend on two wheels. It missed us by inches.

STANDBY five minutes.

This was it. My conscience had lit the fuse.

"You know bud?..." said Dan, casting his eye back along the path. "... I know today's been a whole lot of nothing so far. But the peace and tranquillity out here – it's really starting to work its magic on my soul."

"Welcome to Sansol," I mumbled, trying my best to ignore Dan's comment.

At first glance, Sansol looked like your typical, quintessential hilltop hamlet. It was quiet, with a rustic charm and was filled with higgledy-piggledy streets. Nestled somewhere among this rabbit warren was the 17th century Baroque gem – Church of San Zoilo.

Peppered along the main street was a bar, albergues and a pharmacy. If I'd known about this place sooner, I'd have definitely stayed there as it offered unparalleled views across the vast Navarre plains.

Within minutes of entering Sansol, we were out the other side. There the main road met with its big sister, the NA-1110. At the junction, a quaint, wooden bus shelter became our unsuspecting guide. A small Camino arrow sprayed onto one of its support beams directed us down towards a terracotta-coloured house. Its thick, cream painted window frames gave it the look of a Victorian gent in oval-rimmed spectacles.

As we approached it, we got our first glimpse down at Torres del Rio. It was dug deep into the landscape and surrounded by a thick blanket of forest.

Lording over the town was the 12th century Church of Santo Sepulcro. According to Dan, it was famed for its fusion of Arabic, Gothic and Romanesque architectural styles – not forgetting its octagonal shape. It was considered by many as one of the Holy Grails of must-see churches on the Camino. And another that many experts had suggested had links with the Order of the Knights Templar.

READY...

Our path from the spectacled house turned left, right, then down alongside it. There a thorny, overrun track led us down to a small concrete underpass. This would be our gateway into Torres del Rio. Once through the underpass, all that was left was to cross a small bridge over the River Linares and head on up into town.

...STEADY

Beyond the bridge, my beady eyes spotted a water fountain lurking suspiciously amongst a cluster of trees. Never one to miss an opportunity to top up, we did just that. While doing so, I couldn't help but notice my hands starting to shake. What was that about? Was it the heat? Or just one of the side effects of my digital detox?

...GO! GO! GO!

With my conscience screaming, my body reacted by default. Suddenly, all hell broke loose. My legs took off from under me and – BOOM! Within seconds, I was twenty... forty... sixty feet up the road and charging away on my own. I saw flashes of buildings as I tore up the path. Hostal Rural San Andrés, El Mesón and Casa... something or other. The rest was merely a blur.

That's it, lad! Give it some beans.

Onwards and upwards I went. My head, heart and lungs burned as I passed pilgrims as if they were standing still. It wasn't long before my salt-soaked eyes caught sight of the magnificent Church of Santo Sepulcro.

Nice isn't it, lad? Shame you don't have time to venture inside, as it's right up your street. Seen enough, have we? Right, let's crack on.

Whipped up by my conscience and driven now by guilt, I let rip another huge burst of energy. BOOM! That was enough to fire me up Calle Mayor: passed ochre-coloured apartments and the salmon-fronted Hostal Rural La Pata de Oca. Outside, pilgrims sat gasping like freshly caught fish in the sun. They were all attempting to get their breath back before the short, sharp ascent up to the Hermitage of Our Lady of Poyo (the day's high point at over eighteen hundred feet).

With Calle Mayor cleared, my eyes began darting left and right, anxiously scanning every brick, building or cornerstone to find the next marker and the one beyond that. My mind was in full flight. The reprisals of could I, would I or should I... would have to wait.

All I cared about was carving out my own Camino space and not overcooking it energy wise.

Bizarrely, after eight days, one hundred and forty kilometres, and one dream, I'd somehow stumbled across something that I never I wanted or needed. I just wanted to be alone.

Well, you aren't out of the woods yet!

Suddenly, from behind me, I heard the crunch of boots. The sound startled me. Shit, my conscience was right! It couldn't be... could it? With my focus mainly on the twenty feet of path in front of me, I ploughed on, leaving my two-satellite dish sized ears to fill in the mystery blanks.

Within thirty anxious strides, I concluded it wasn't Dan. It couldn't be. The foot strike, cadence, and breathing pattern were all wrong. Not to mention the fact that I couldn't hear his rucksack's trademark squeak. Whoever or whatever was behind, was clearly in a right old state. I could hear the scuffing sound of an injured foot being dragged, quite literally, along the ground.

Feckin' typical! No sooner had I binned off my Orc hunting mate, I'd found myself being chased out of town by a would-be-leper.

Deep down, I knew I was too quick for the would-be-leper. But he might have better luck with the hapless pilgrims up ahead. All of whom had gathered along the cemetery wall waiting to fill their bottles at the water fountain.

"Should I or shouldn't I warn them?" I pondered.

Nah! Sod it! Plus, why not use the would-be-leper to my advantage? I knew if I could get him closer, his presence would be enough to spark a stampede. In the melee that ensued dirt and dust would get kicked up in all directions, providing me with a blanket of cover to skip away quietly and my would-be-leper friend with a much-needed Pilgrim Meal.

You done daydreaming? I ask, because I've a hot date with some freshly scented towels, soft cotton sheets and a double bed at the hotel later. And I don't want to be late.

With that, I started to creep along the path towards our prey. Seventy feet... fifty feet... twenty-five feet, I was close now – real close. And as yet, no one's ear had pricked up. Better still, no one bolted. Twenty feet... fifteen feet... ten feet. That was as close as I wanted to take the would-be leper. With that, I turned to acknowledge my work was done, then I took off.

I tore down the path, never once looking back. My legs were gunning it around bends, over ridges, passed pilgrims, until BOOM! I was shaken awake by the sight of a monstrous, four-hundred-feet-high-wall. With my lungs burning, I looked up in disbelief.

"Bollocks."

Ahead, I watched as exhausted pilgrims fought for each step on the insane gradient. Slowly but surely, they all began to run out of puff before they started to slide back down the hexagonal, slab-covered path towards me.

"Come on, Midds. You've got this," I said repeatedly.

BOOM!

With my head down, arms pumping and legs firing like pistons – I attacked. Push... push...push. Three-hundred feet... two-hundred feet... come on... one-hundred feet. Keep going, seventy-five... fifty... thirty... almost there.

"Aaaaarrrgh."

At the top I could feel my chest bucking wildly, as my eyes started to roll backwards (never a good sign). And what was my reward for putting myself so deep into the red? A glimpse of my nemesis – the NA-1110.

Once across the road the path aimed itself gently upwards, passed almond groves and towards a curtain of lush, green trees. Behind it was the Hermitage of Our Lady of Poyo.

It was an old, somewhat large and derelict sandstone building. In the centre of the main wall, facing the path was a large, tiled piece of art. It showed Our Lady holding a rather unimpressed looking child, with a terrifying mountain range in the background. One I hoped I would never meet.

Directly opposite the Hermitage was a stone altar, set on a platform of four steps. Behind it was a long stone bench, with bum space going spare. This would provide the perfect spot for a quick pit-stop, so:

➜ I flung my pack down on the altar = 1 Hail Mary

→ Forgot to genuflect = 1 Hail Mary
→ Swore wildly as stinging sweat seeped into my eyes = 2 Hail Marys.
Not that it mattered. I knew I'd be ending my day on my knees anyhow.

Within seconds of opening my pack, I found the offending article I was searching for – my other baguette. I quickly zipped, clipped and donned my pack again, before setting off. I had no time for picnics or pleasantries. Not while there was any possibility of being caught.

Rejuvenated by my pit stop and inspired at the prospect of a bit of downhill, I set off, Franz Klammer-style, slaloming my way down to the NA-1110. There, the Camino came to an impromptu halt – bollocks. I had no time for this nonsense.

"Where the hell do I go from here?"

It was then that I noticed a flicker of colour out the corner of my eye. There was a shape moving off to my right that was traversing the hillside. That would do. With that, I took off after the rucksack and its owner.

By the top of the ridge, I passed the pilgrim I'd been chasing. From there the path directed me down a main road then right, onto a loose gravel path. Ahead I could make out a small group on the go slow. Something was up. What now?

I'll give you:
→ *2/1 someone's hit the deck*
→ *8/1 someone's gone down with heatstroke*
→ *250/1 someone's carked it.*

While I never expected much from my conscience, its ability to turn dark never ceased to amaze me. But maybe it was right. As I approached, I noted that everyone was standing in mournful and respectful silence.

Having edged my way through the group, I came face-to-face with fifty stone mounds of balancing stones. Each one had been lovingly assembled to pay homage to a friend, loved one or lost one.

Suddenly, I could feel my body start to shiver as my mind recalled that fateful night. When the Intrepid Mr. Lynch's text tore a hole in the night. I could see myself reaching over to my phone, grabbing it and unlocking it before staring in disbelief at the message illuminated on it - *I think your mate has been killed in Afghanistan.*

I looked from rock-to-rock at the tributes and pictures. They all turned into images of Mitch: Mitch as a young ATC Cadet, Mitch on DofE expedition,

Mitch at his RAF passing out parade and Mitch in his Bond-like tuxedo. I could feel the emotions starting to well up inside me again. I needed to leave – and fast.

Mitch was still in my thoughts as I came across the sign warning of a 10% descent. But stirred on by my anger at his passing, I drove on. There was little now that could stop my charge. For the next fifteen minutes, I went into full, Ski-Sunday mode. I swished, swayed, ducked and jumped, passing pilgrims with consummate ease.

Finally, things began to flatten out. I liked the flat. Flat was good. Flat was fast. It would also allow me to put even more distance between myself and...

Not now, lad. Not now.

My conscience was right. Not while I still had pilgrims to chase. First up was a lad with a black rucksack. He had an annoying and inconsistent pace. Once caught, he was soon forgotten.

While this process of pass-and-go was great for momentum, it did leave a shitty after taste in my mouth. Especially as on two occasions, I came across broken pilgrims who were having a shocker and secretly begging to pass a kilometre or two with someone – anyone. Sadly, that person wouldn't be me.

It was as the path hit the NA-1110, that I first felt the pangs of the 'hunger knock.' First came the light-headedness. Followed quickly by a narrowing of my depth of field, as white lava bubbles started to appear in my peripheral vision.

Having experienced the 'hunger knock' before, I knew my blood sugar levels were plummeting. If I didn't sort this and soon – it would be goodnight Viana.

With no time to stop, I stopped. For the next ten minutes I threw two bananas, a half pack of TUC biscuits into my mouth while chugging hard on car fumes. Once done, I loaded up and set off, gingerly.

It was during this wobbly, wondrous time when I got treated to yet another mouth-watering sight. This came just as I'd crested the brow of yet another false ridge. Suddenly, the path unfurled like a giant golden carpet before me. On either side of it were magnificent cypress trees, reminding me of Van Gogh's Wheatfield with Cypresses.

"Slow down pilgrim," I muttered... once again, upon seeing another Camino stone marker. This marker was lounging beneath a giant oak tree. Slowing down wasn't something that came naturally. But in this case, it was helped by the sight of a flight of swallows. They dived, swooped and performed aerial acrobatics before me, while in nearby fields, vine groves shook their pom-poms in approval.

A few hundred metres away in the distance I could see a tree line that invariably blocked out the sight of the road on its run-in into Viana. Where it finally broke, I was confronted by the sight of a disused, cream-coloured industrial facility. I'd made it – I was in Viana.

Good effort, lad. Now stop, enjoy the moment. Are you done? I ask, because your loitering is starting to gain unwanted attention from passing truckers. If you know what I mean?

In reality, I'd only stopped for a minute to finish off my water. Once done, I headed towards the mishmash of apartment blocks and into town.

It was as I trudged up Calle el Cristo when I was hit with the unexpected and irrefutable waft of lavender on the breeze. As I looked up, I saw a flotilla of clothes flapping freely from balconies. WTF! Was today National Pantaloons Wash Day?

Earth to space cadet, less gawping – more walking.

I needed to start sparking. It would be easy to get lost in and amongst the rabbit warren of narrow streets and hidden passageways, especially as the Camino markers would have to fight for my attention. I was lost in a world full of signs, road works, diversions, whizzing delivery scooters, screaming kids and old biddies.

"Bollocks."

Suddenly, at the top of Calle el Cristo, I lost sight of the Camino arrows. Righto! Which way? My eyes began to scan left, right, up, down – but with no joy. Then my mind flashed back to a conversation I'd overheard from one of the pilgrim elders, a few days before.

"If you find yourself getting lost, just stop. Stop. Stand still. Then wait for all the noise and distractions to die down. When that happens, the way will show itself," he'd said.

His Jedi wisdom made sense. But I wasn't a Jedi. Nor did I fancy running the risk of getting twatted by a ten-tonne truck while waiting for inspiration to strike. So, I decided to stand on one of the smallest of pavements, while giving it a go.

Nothing.

All I could see was a pharmacy sign, fag butts, a dog curling one out, a wall, a building...

"No feckin' way!"

Suddenly, out of nowhere I spotted a Camino sign. It was embossed onto a stone wall, which formed part of the town's original fortifications.

So... what you waiting for? A royal invitation?

Taking my conscience's advice, I headed up Calle la Pila, towards a stone arch. Above it, hung a banner with the red silhouetted figure of César Borgia.

While I'd be the first to admit I didn't know a great deal about César, I did know he was the son of Pope Alexander VI and a key political figure at the time. I also knew his name appeared in the hallowed pages of Machiavelli's *'The Prince'*.

Once under the arch, I stepped back into the heart of mediaeval times. The cold, narrow, imposing street was lined by stone buildings with rough stonework and decadent iron gratings over the windows (presumably to keep thieves, like me, out). My eyes were drawn to the timeless front doors. Their surfaces had been bleached, burnt and faded by a lifetime of hard summers and harsh winters. Even the air smelt musty and damp, as if refusing to let go of the past.

With a quick left, then right, it was out with the old and in with the new. I traded Calle Algarrada for Plaza del Coso, where my eyes widened at the sight of the exquisite sprawling wonder that was Balcon de Toros (balcony of the bulls).

This baroque building dating back to the 17th century, had recently been reskinned. It was a building where, in times gone by, the well-heeled would flock to sit, salivate, and savour the sight of the bullfight (while avoiding the working class scrotes, like me).

From Plaza del Coso, my path headed down the Jacobean-inspired Calle Rúa Santa María. To my horror, it was filling up with old biddies who were causing havoc by shuffling slowly, stopping abruptly or worse, trying to clothes-line people with their walking sticks.

Little did I know, or was prepared for, what would come next. I was about to become an unwilling participant in a three-hundred-metre-long, impromptu game of Human Pinball, where I'd be bashed, buffeted and bounced up Calle Rúa Santa María, passed supermarkets, bars and the plaque of César Borgia.

I'd eyeballed a water fountain back in the main square, but the rowdy bunch of biddies had other ideas for me. Unable to move or shimmy, I was bounced up Calle Navarro Villoslada, before finally getting turfed out in front of the ruins of the breath-taking Church of San Pedro.

Staring back down the street, I was surprised that my bum had survived without a pinching (like back in Saint Jean). But on the plus side, the ever-growing band of biddies was a good thing. There was no way anyone would be getting passed this lot quickly.

Inspired, I set off down passed the open square before turning left and out through the (time) Portal San Felices arch. Once outside the city walls, the Camino winded its way down Calle Serapio Urra, Calle Fuente Vieja and out onto Calle el Puentecillo. There, a huge Camino arrow, situated above the wooden window frame above the most prominent building, directed me along the ten-foot hedgerows that lined the path of Paraje el Arenal.

It was as I tore down this track that the reality of the day hit me. I had completed a half marathon – thirteen miles. But there was still ten kilometres to go. While the distance was doable, I did have some serious reservations sustenance wise.

All I had left was an apple and a half pack of Haribo.

Which roughly equated to:

→ Food in = 360 calories
→ Energy out = 426 calories per hour
→ Total effort required = 1278 calories (based on three hours' walking).

Therefore, to make it to Logroño, my body would soon begin to consume itself.

OR you could try and find another food source!

"Of course... grapes," I muttered excitedly.

Into the nearby vine groves I went, only to reappear moments later with a punnet of grapes the size of Oompa Loompas. That would do the trick. With that, I set off, buzzing on sugar.

But within minutes, everything in my day would change. It occurred the moment I saw the Hermitage of the Trinidad de Cuevas. Standing in the shade, under the trees was a wounded pilgrim. She looked absolutely broken.

More specifically, her feet were. Even from a distance, I could see her discomfort in her as she swayed uncomfortably from one foot to the other. Both her ankles were strapped with heavy bandages that swelled beneath her white socks and black Teva sandals.

"Buen Camino," she said, as she forced a tired smile through gritted teeth.

"If you're looking for P.T. Barnum's circus, you're out of luck. They skipped town a few years ago. Sorry."

My greeting, though lukewarm, was backed with a mischievous grin. She knew I knew she was in a bad way. Therefore, I saw no point offering tea and sympathy. So, in the absence of that, I poured a big mug of sarcasm.

"Seriously! Are you lost? As what with the fedora, Irish builder's tan and seemingly care-free attitude... well, you look like you're on a come-down after a massive music festival." I said, unable to resist the urge to chuckle.

"And what the feck have you done to your feet? I thought elephantiasis died out centuries ago?" I added, which seemed to soften her face and draw out a smile.

"Hi. I'm Kamila, by the way."

"Shit, sorry! I'm Paul" I said, having forgotten the basic pleasantries of conversation.

"Well... I arrived in Pamplona from the Czech Republic five days ago. My plan had been to buy my boots on arrival. It's just that the ones I got sold, the ones I was advised to buy, are – how do you say it? – too small. How was I to know my feet would expand so much in the heat?

"Well, within hours of starting, my boots started to rub against my big toe and instep. I tried to ignore it at first but couldn't. It was then that I decided to take a knife to my boots, to help my feet breathe. Luckily, I met a guy with duct tape. He helped tape them up to prevent them tearing further." As she explained, her face winced in pain.

"After the first day, my feet were rubbed raw by blisters. But I thought this was just part of the Camino, you know – the suffering. Come the second day though, I could barely walk. So, I threw my boots away and bought these... (pointing at her Teva's). Now my feet are free, hopefully, they will heal," she said, half smiling.

Oi, Casanova! What the hell do you think you're playing at?

I knew where my conscience was headed, but I was fecked. Fecked from the heat, the hunger knock and the constant changing pace. Having already passed two pilgrims without offering any help, I didn't have the heart to leave Kamila out here limping.

It didn't seem to bother you with Dan.

I saw that shot coming. It was a low blow. But Dan, unlike me, still had two to three weeks left on his Camino. I, on the other hand, had only a few days. A few days to try and figure things out. And the only way I could do that was by...

Leggin' it? Leaving him for dead?

I was being goaded into responding. But I wouldn't be baited. I chose instead to return my thoughts to Kamila. There was something about her that was freer than any pilgrim I'd met out here. Was it her age? I wasn't sure, as my guess was, she was early thirties. She just seemed to possess this openness and trust in the world around her. She wasn't fretting or obsessively checking her phone. Nor was she boasting about how far she walked yesterday or how heavy her pack was. I doubt she even knew; she definitely didn't care. She'd come to the Camino to detox from life.

To her, detox meant no phone, no watch, no television and no music. She wanted to be free from it all. And I for one was in awe of her spirit. As the metres turned to kilometres, we discussed everything from life in the Czech Republic, music, food and the Camino, along with the question that everyone seemed to want answering.

"What's the first thing you're going to do when you get in today? Mine's to grab a beer," she said, smiling.

"Honestly? I'm gonna take a shower fully clothed..." came my answer.

Before she'd even had chance to reply, I had dived into the pause in conversation.

"...it saves time and energy."

The look on Kamila's face was one of puzzlement and bemusement.

"Surely a beer comes first, no?" came her reply.

"Not with me. I like to get my gear washed and out on my washing line – which I typically string up on the balcony – as soon as possible. The sooner I get my kit squared away, the sooner I can relax and get my siesta on."

We wandered in this blissful state of nothingness for about an hour, where we both argued the merits of washing or beer first. It was soon after this, that out from the heat haze came a lone figure – a nun.

"Seriously! I'd heard about bandits jackin' pilgrims in mediaeval days. Surely, we aren't going to get turned over by a woman of the cloth, are we?" I said, only half-joking,

Within seconds, I knew we would be. The nun had disarmed us both with her warm smile, kind eyes and open arms.

"Tell you what! This is a textbook jackin' going on right here."

The nun guided us towards a table on the opposite side of the path. It was filled with heavenly treats, including fresh fruit, snacks and an assortment of homemade biscuits. She also had out a blotter and her Camino stamp primed and ready. The only question now was, how much would this cost? Her eyes seemed to suggest – whatever we could spare.

It wasn't until much later, that I found out who the nun was. According to Kamila, the nun was the daughter of Felisa, one of the elders and gatekeepers of the Camino. I knew nothing of Felisa or her daughter's story. But I was itching to find out, so were my twitchy, gunslinger fingers. Sadly, that would have to wait.

Soon after, having left the nun, the outskirts of Logroño appeared. Off to our right as we entered was the enormous AICAPACK factory. In front of it was a sign declaring COMUNIDAD LA RIOJA.

By now, I was done. I couldn't take in any more information. All I wanted was my bed. A bed which waited on the other side of the majestic San Juan de Ortega Bridge.

The sense of relief was almost indescribable as I trudged excitedly across the bridge towards the hotel. Once there, I quickly took a picture of me and Kamila on my camera. She gave me a hug and wandered off smiling.

It was only as I stepped into the cool and relative darkness of the hotel that I noticed a figure in the background of my picture. When I looked again, I knew instantly who it was – Dan. He'd made it too, thank God.

With check-in done and room keys in hand, it was a race against the clock. I knew I had only thirty minutes to dump my bag, string up my washing line, wash my kit, hang it and sort tomorrow's dry kit. If I wasn't in bed within that window, I risked falling asleep wherever I was.

I had to push hard on the heavy-set door as I entered my hotel room. Instantly, I was hit with a sledgehammer of cold air from the air-con unit. I was in ice heaven. With no time, I set to work and made it into bed within twenty-seven minutes and fifty-three seconds.

I woke later feeling nauseous and weak. But still, I had work to do. I needed to find replacement snacks for tomorrow.

In the limitless shops along the side streets, I managed to pick up the usual suspects: Haribo Goldbears, Snickers, a large baguette, nuts, onion rings and two electrolyte drinks.

With the snacks sorted, I somehow managed to stumble onto Calle Portales, a street lined with cafes and bars near the magnificent cathedral. Most of them seemed to offer a version of a Pilgrim Meal for €12. At that point I was too tired to choose between them – any would do. So, I wandered to the nearest cafe and ordered tortilla, patatas bravas, and pork and chips, along with an ice-cold pint of Estrella.

Once done, and still feeling guilty about Dan, I slowly picked my way back through the streets.

I crawled into bed to the sounds of raucous laughter and cheerful voices of half-cut locals. It was this kind of night that had helped to make this adventure so, so special.

But now was my time. I could feel the excitement coursing through my veins as I finally accepted my fate. I was finally ready to go it alone – *it's time*.

~~CHAPTER 12: FIRST DATE~~

7th September, Logroño - Nájera, 30km
Finally.
I woke at 4:06 am into the cool, dark, stillness of my hotel room. I lay punch-drunk and exhausted, cast adrift from my rucksack which seemed to be enjoying shipwrecked life, marooned on its own island and surrounded by a sea of dark, stained laminate floor tiles.

While my rucksack was resting comfortably, my mind was swirling and tumbling after being hit again and again by waves of tiredness. Yet even through the wash, I understood the joy and relief in the word – 'finally'.

"Finally, after nine exhilarating days, I'm alone with her – the Camino."

By then the Camino had taken on the persona of a mysterious, raven-haired beauty with flowing locks and fine features, whose whisperings I'd first heard among the church pews during Mitch's funeral.

The whisperings had started up again on my arrival into Biarritz. But somewhere amongst the noise and excitement of my new world we got separated – *again*. I knew it would be only a matter of time before she came whispering again.

It was somewhere between the excitement of this new dawn and my stomach's first growls of hunger that I drifted off, only to be woken by the first flickers of light as it crept like a policeman's torch from beneath the hotel curtains. It wasn't just the light that had stirred me. It was the disturbing sound of heavy hooves from the floor above.

The undead were waking. Soon they, much like us red-bellied pilgrim piranhas, would need to be fed. I needed to get down to the all-you-can-eat-buffet sharpish, before all hell broke loose.

Within seconds, I was at the lift frantically bashing the 'G' button. What did 'G' stand for? Gluttony? Gorging? Gulping? The lift dropped like a stone. I quickly fired off a prayer silently requesting my breakfast in peace. But I knew full well that thirty seconds was too short notice. But I was always told 'If you don't ask, you don't get'. It was still early. Who the hell would be up at that time anyway? And more importantly, what the hell would there be to talk about?

Lots apparently.

Even before the lift doors opened, I was hit by a wall of sound. Ode to joy, footballers were in town. Their decibel level (at least to my exhausted and irritable mind) was as offensive as their soft touch, baby-blue tracksuits.

Would you look at this shower of arseholes?

For once, I couldn't disagree with my conscience. Ballers were all around me, slumped in chairs, sipping iced drinks, peering over their shades and flicking their over-sized gold watches provocatively in a vain attempt to catch my eye.

And what the fuck's with all the hair oil? These lot look like they've just come off the set of 'Coming to America'.

Why were these chumps up? Had they shit the bed? Or simply had problems getting the midget stripper out and into a taxi? Wait a minute, these were Spanish footballers – not English footballers. My bad.

One thing I knew for certain. If they had come to feed, I was in *big trouble*. I was outnumbered twenty-to-one.

Then suddenly, out of the corner of my eye, I noticed a flicker of colour. As I turned, I was met by a shoal pilgrims swimming towards the buffet – and fast. With no time to waste, I leapt up and latched onto their tail end.

Once inside the buffet area, the shoal split up. Instinctively, we took our positions all along the buffet table. We held our line as we waited for the signal to attack. Each second, marked by the growl of my tummy, felt like an eternity. My body and mind were primed.

Then to my left, came the smallest flicker of movement. Was it intentional? It didn't matter, there was no time to debate. Only react. This one flicker was enough to set off a chain reaction as the attack started.

It descended into a feeding frenzy, as we jostled, bit and tore at anything in plain sight. Such was the ferocity of it all that as I headed back to my table, still lost in a sea of red mist, I was blissfully unaware of what I'd come away with.

It was only as I sat down and took stock that I realised I'd snatched a selection of cold meats, three slices of toast and jam, two small croissants, a selection of cheese slices, two bowls of cereal, a slice of watermelon, a banana, and two yoghurts.

But far from feeling pleased with my haul, I felt anxious and irritable. I felt like I was being watched. I turned and came face-to-face with the mortified faces of the ballers. They were standing dumbstruck, with their mouths aghast. Gone was their earlier swagger, replaced instead with looks of unmitigated fear. I could see their brains working to try and make sense of what they'd just witnessed.

While their mouths daren't speak the words, their eyes were only too eager to ask – *just who were these savages?*

We weren't savages – we were pilgrims.

I turned my attention back to my feast. It was only when my eyes started to roll back in my head twenty minutes later that I realise I was, in fact, full.

I headed back to my room as all thoughts turned to the day. It was a biggie. It would be my first date with the Camino. The thought filled me with a childish sense of excitement.

It would also be the day I broke the thirty-kilometre seal. Thirty kilometres. Fuck. Just saying it aloud sounded ridiculous. On any other given day, thirty kilometres (or eighteen miles, if you prefer) would seem a superhuman effort. But not out there. It was very much like any other day, just an hour or two longer.

Luckily for me, the day would start with a gradual twenty kilometre climb up to the highpoint – Alto de San Antón. On the way up to it, I'd pass through Grajera Park, Navarette and the hamlet of Ventosa.

But first, I needed to get my foot prep sorted. On a lesser day, I'd have it done in a minute, but not for this.

I was all over them. Checking each toe, nail, bit of skin and the space between. This was followed by patting to see if I could feel any hotspots developing. Hotspots were a sure sign that a blister was on the way. But what made locating them harder was the fact that my feet typically ran hot.

I knew I needed to stay switched on. If I didn't, even for a few minutes, that would be me fecked. Blisters, dehydration or hunger didn't need an invite to gatecrash my Camino party. They'd already tried to derail it twice already and with each passing day, I could feel their confidence grow. It was only a matter of time before they really showed up.

With my feet passing the morning inspection, I slowly rolled on my socks, ensuring each toe was comfortable and separated with the sock seam positioned correctly. I finished dressing, laced my boots and headed down to reception to check out.

The immaculately dressed receptionist greeting me thoughtfully with a "Good morning, sir. Sleep well?"

"Like a baby, thank you," came my smiling reply.

With that, I handed over my keys, settled the bill, loaded my pack up and headed towards the exit.

"Sir! One thing before you go. You had a visitor this morning at 7 am. A large gentleman with a beard and a rucksack," said the receptionist, sounding apologetic.

Santa? Gandalf? Hagrid?

"Unfortunately, due to hotel protocol, I couldn't give out any guest information."

Fuck! That must have been Dan.

No shit! Unless you're thinking that Kamila is the original bearded lady.

I thanked the receptionist and headed towards the door, giving it a hefty push.

"Buen Camino!" I bellowed to a cool, empty Spanish street.

Seriously! WTF are you doing? Haven't we got enough on our plate today without you acting like a middle-aged man who's just rediscovered his erection?

"Don't care. Not listening." I knew this would wind my conscience up.

How feckin' old are you? Twelve!

Having scoped out my escape route the day before, I set off towards Calle Ruavieja. It was an old, cobbled street, flagged on either side by dark, freshly cut stones. Inset into one (nearest to the prestigious, glass-fronted, Colegios Profesionales Sanitarios) was a large Camino motif.

It was made up of eight single white lines fanning out from a central point. While there was undoubtedly an official explanation for this, I'd not seen or read one. I interpreted it to mean one of two things:

→ The individual lines represented the coming together of people to a central point – in this case, the Camino.

→ The individual lines represented people heading off from a central point. Forever joined in spirit by the Camino.

The first building I was drawn to as I sauntered along the street was No.44, an aubergine-coloured apartment block. Below, at street level, was a bakery – Panificadora Berceo. What I wouldn't have done for a few slices of sourdough bread, lightly dusted with flour and covered in the marks of Zorro.

Next to the baker's was the salmon fronted Albergue Santiago Apostol. Swinging from the wall opposite was a large, heavy brass plaque emblazoned with a Camino shell. From within the inner bowels of the albergue emerged five sleep-deprived pilgrim stragglers, looking lost in a sea of mind fog as they chuntered wildly to themselves.

Is that...

Even before my conscience had time to finish its sentence, I started whistling.

"Duh, duh, duhduh, duh-duh-duh, duh, duh, duh-duh!"

...Indiana Jones?

Standing directly before me was a five-foot eight middle-aged man, with three-day old stubble wearing a fedora and dressed head-to-toe in khaki. It couldn't be – could it? And if it was, did that mean Marion, Belloq and the Fourth Reich were around here somewhere? I hoped not for Spain's sake. They'd laid out a seven hundred kilometre set of arrows that led straight towards the treasure – the coffin of St. James.

"Good morning," came Indy's opening salvo.

No way! This version of Indy came with plummy, middle-class English accent. He was definitely more Marcus Brody than Indy, which was reinforced by his total inability to blend in.

Of course, he was bloody English. Who else, other than an Englishman, would turn up on pilgrimage in fancy dress? I smiled nervously but was unable to hide the fact that I was utterly crestfallen. I was also mortified that he'd somehow pegged me as English too. What the hell did that say about how I was dressed?

While Indy's anthem was still rattling round in my head, my eyes were drawn to a monstrous, yet magnificent, stone fortress up ahead. This impenetrable beast had three-foot-thick stone walls, with heavily barred porthole windows.

This, I was soon to discover (by way of eavesdropping), was the rear of the Church of Santa María de Palacio, considered by many to be one of Logroño's key buildings. And as such, it was rewarded with the status of an Asset of Cultural Interest.

My eyes couldn't help but notice the discrepancy between the left and right side of the street. It felt like the world had been split in two. On my left was the 12th century gem, Santa María de Palacio. While to my right, was a drab, faceless, unimaginative, grey apartment block. Was that the best we could come up with these days?

As I wandered further up Calle Ruavieja, I was drawn to the shutters that gave the apartments the appearance of being weary and hungover. Which, ironically, wasn't a million miles away from how I was feeling, when I stepped...

BEEEEEEEEEEEEEEEEEEEEEEEEEEEPPPPPPPPP

...straight onto Calle Sagasta and into the oncoming path of a car. A car, whose tyres were now squealing in protest as they skidded towards my milky-white, skittle-thin legs.

Well don't just stand there like a bellend. Move, for feck's sake!

That was the last thing I remembered. The next thing I recall was coming to on the side of the pavement, where I was surrounded by a concerned gaggle of coffee-breathed locals, taking it taking it in turns to paw and prod me.

From my blurred vision, I knew that my head had taken a clout. Luckily for me, my rucksack bore the brunt of the fall. It lay beside me, covered in cuts and abrasions. Overall, I was shaken, stirred and feeling quite relieved at having dodged being hit.

Which was more than could be said for the car driver. He was out of his car, wafting his arms aloft like a master matador as he rattled off supersonic Spanish soundbites.

Seriously, why's he bothering? He'd be better off just calling you a knob.

My conscience made a good point. Slowly, gingerly and with the help of a few locals, I got myself on my feet. My head was throbbing wildly, and the driver's hullabaloo was only making matters worse. In an attempt to de-escalate things, I fired off a few apologies, "Lo siento. Lo siento para todo".

To me, as there had been no damage to either him or his car, therefore sorry was enough. Sadly, Barry Big Bollocks (or whatever the driver's name was) wasn't quite ready to let it go. Not before he had had a chance to assert his authority and masculinity on the situation. He stepped up to me and proceeded to jab me repeatedly in the sternum with his forefinger. *He wanted to make his feelings known.*

Up until that point, I'd been wonderfully apologetic. But things were now headed in a very different direction. Unknowing to the driver, the finger jabs awoke the demons from my junior school playground.

Suddenly, I was nine again and standing in the playground. Around me was an angry mob of Pyrex-bowl-headed council house kids, screaming – *fight, fight, fight!*

Standing opposite was one of my year's finest, knuckle-dragging bullies (of which we had many that had been bred for one single purpose – fighting). He was jabbing me hard in the chest. All in the hope of provoking a reaction. A reaction which would justify his attempted beating.

Why me? Simple. I was a new kid. And worse than that, I was a RAF kid. To them I was an outsider. At best we'd be tolerated. But we would never be accepted – never. I can even recall the explicit instructions I was given before my first day at school.

"Keep your head down and your mouth shut."

Yet being the grey man was easier said than done. Especially as I was the one being shoved, dead-armed, Chinese burned or punched on a regular basis. While my big brother had the maturity and discipline to tow the family line, I flatly refused. It didn't take long for the bullies to learn that I could be pushed to a point. Once reached, all hell would break loose, as I possessed a terrifying temper.

Back in Logroño, the driver had a decision to make. It was in his hands. I'd never walked away from trouble in my life. And with each passing second, I could feel more of my Hulk-like temper start to bubble to the surface.

As I looked on in horror, I could see the driver's big, fat, hairy-knuckled forefinger inching its way towards my chest in slow motion. This was it. This fecker was about to get chinned.

"Fucking move – NOW."

This time the voice that screamed wasn't mine or my conscience. It was Mitch's. He knew if Barry Big Bollocks's forefinger connected with my sternum, slow down pilgrim would become banged up pilgrim.

"SORRY! Fight's off."

With that, I pushed the disheartened crowd aside. As I did, I noticed two pilgrims further up Calle Barriocepo descending a set of steps. Where were they going? I neither knew nor cared. But I needed out of this situation – sharpish. So, I followed them.

The six stone steps descended below street level, to what looked like a stone mausoleum. But as luck would have it, I'd somehow stumbled upon a water fountain. I quickly ran over to it (giving little thought to the two other pilgrims) before shoving my head under the brass taps.

The water that exploded from the tap was ice cold. Such was the shock, that it left me fighting for breath. But still, I kept my head under. I wasn't moving it until everything from the head down was numb.

Once finished, I sat down and began to shake uncontrollably as the adrenaline took hold. I was furious. I was furious with myself for switching off. I was furious that I allowed the driver to get to me. I was also furious at Mitch for intervening, as Barry Big Bollocks really did deserve to be dropped on his arse.

When I'd finally stopped shaking, I made my way slowly back up to street level. The crowds had dispersed, and I was met by the Church of Santiago el Real. A church that had been built in honour of St. James, who preached throughout the region during mediaeval times.

The entrance to the church was made up of one large arch, split between two distinct sculptures. The top sculpture depicted St. James on his trusty steed, leading men into battle against the Moors. In his left hand he held a flag banner, and in his right a sword. All around his feet lay the decapitated heads of Moorish soldiers.

In the second sculpture, St. James was depicted older and wiser, standing in an authoritative pose with one arm out to greet people. In his other hand he held a book, presumably containing his teachings.

The irony of the sculpture wasn't lost on me. I, much like the older St. James, was done with fighting. I'd fought my entire life from junior and secondary school to Shifnal Europeans football, Cubs, Scouts and even university in order to fit in. The reality was that I never really did. I was, and would always be, the aloof grey man. Something that I'd grown to embrace, and even love.

Beyond the church, a long, narrow cobbled street led me towards a light, bright and leafy courtyard. Complete with twenty-five-foot trees, granite benches and aluminium tables and chairs.

These chairs (or snares as we'd jokingly named them since Roncesvalles) had been set to catch stray legs of passing pilgrims. A tactic, which judging from the numbers outside Bar El Parlamento and Odeòn Plaza, had worked a treat.

My eyes quickly scanned the scene for any familiar faces or stray eyes. Those whose eyes met mine, were greeted with a flurry of 'Buen Caminos.' Instinct told me it would be good to have some emergency friends in my back pocket – just in case.

Once the 'Buen Caminos' had been dished out, I turned right at the Parliament of La Rioja building and out through a huge hole punched into a twelve-foot high wall. It was only later that I discovered this was called the Pilgrim's Gate.

From there a few sneaky arrows directed me left, along Calle Once de Junio, then right, across the main square. I was met by brass statues of two trim modern-day pilgrims. What was noticeable was their distinct lack of sizeable rucksack.

"My feckin' lunch wouldn't fit in there."

BEEP! BEEEEEP! BEEEEEEEEEEEEEEEEEEEEEP!

This time my thoughts were interrupted by the cacophony of horns on nearby Plaza de la Diversidad. This five-way roundabout was teeming with life. Why? Where was the world and its wife going at this ungodly hour on a Sunday?

I, just like those stuck in traffic, was itching to get gone. The combination of honking horns, kids screaming, adults bellowing into mobiles and the incessant beeping of crossings and flickering of lights was making me feel queasy. Not helped by the crack to the head I'd received.

Somehow, I managed to keep my head together long enough to spot the arrows set into the cobbles beside Cafeteria Royal. These led me towards the sweeping boulevard of Calle Marqués de Murrieta, which was lined with restaurants.

With my taste buds woken, my mind drifted in and out of consciousness. My eyes started to play tricks on me. In a blink of an eye, all the cars were gone and replaced by a flotilla of supersized plates, which hovered a few inches above the road. Slowly, the dishes were making their way down the boulevard towards me.

The nearer they got, the more I started to salivate. The flotilla was made up of some of my favourite dishes. Yaki udon noodles with chicken, ginger, chilli, prawns and spring onions. Next up was bangers and mash, made with wholegrain mustard and topped with beans. Followed by my all-time favourite – cheese and pickle sandwiches.

To the unknown, I must have looked like a rabid dog. Not that I cared. All I cared about were the udon noodles, dripping with oil as they twirled seductively around an imaginary fork. What I wouldn't do...

Wakey, wakey fatty – we're lost.

"Bollocks!"

It shouldn't have come as a surprise, yet it did.

Well don't just stand there sweating – get Googling!

"You almost had me there for a minute," I mumbled at my conscience.

I'd already reached for my phone. But thankfully, I came to just before firing it up. Bloody hell, that was close. I'd made it to day three of my digital detox and was slowly weaning myself off the tractor-beam style pull of social media – and I felt great. I wasn't about to give up the gains I'd made, no matter what my conscience threw at me.

Gains! You've been lost, mowed down and almost got involved in a ruck. Strong gains them. Real strong.

With the phone out of the equation, I had to rely on 'Old Faithful' and the large bit between my ears.

'Old Faithful' was my SILVA compass. It hung around my neck on a piece of paracord under my base layer top. I'd pre-set it to west, as west was the way. Therefore, to get myself back on track, all I needed to do was follow it.

A fact that was confirmed ten minutes later by the sight of not one, or two, but three pilgrim groups on the road. With my eyes locked on, I followed their every move. Our path weaved between unloved basketball courts, apartment blocks and scary playgrounds full of swings. Then we picked up a paved path offset by freshly manicured lawns that led us towards the main road and a KIA car showroom.

From there I skipped over the pedestrian crossing and followed the arrows as they directed me right, down towards an underpass beneath the A-12.

Like so many underpasses on the Camino, this too was covered in a mural. Except in this instance, the mural was huge. It depicted the silhouetted figures of pilgrims. Their shapes blackened and elongated, reminding me of my shadow at first light with the sun on my back.

Once into the underpass, the true reality of my adventure was laid bare. All along the right-hand wall was a sprayed map of Spain in white and offset against a blood-red sea. The map marked my route, my current position as well as my final destination.

"Fffff..."

What the hell have you signed us up for, fat lad?

"Are you telling me that I've slogged my arse off for seven days and only reached here?" I jabbed my forefinger hard at Logroño on the map.

"Bollocks!"

Well, think of the plus side. Burgos is now only one hundred and twenty kilometres away.

"That's still over five marathons. And as for Santia..."

I stopped short of saying it in full. I still hadn't earned the right to speak its name. It appeared on the far left of the map, like some mythical far-off land.

Within minutes of exiting the tunnel, the path started to level out. With each step my mind started to settle, and I accepted my fate. I was quickly distracted by the sight of early morning joggers pounding the pavement. I also couldn't fail to notice how the old crusties had somehow sneakily bagged all the stone benches. Not that I minded. They'd earned it and as ever, it was great to see them out and about, appreciating the solace and magnificence of yet another magical Spanish sunrise.

With no hope of bagging a seat I ploughed on until I saw the entrance of Parque de la Grajera, where suddenly the world fell deathly silent.

"What's the craic here then, lads?" I muttered.

It was only as I crested the last little incline that I noticed the cause. It was a metre-high, stone reservoir wall. Yet beyond that, there lay a dark, eerie and motionless mirror-like lake. It was mythical and enchanting.

To complete the scene, the lake was framed beautifully by a low-lying hillside of dense forest and set against a flawless powder-blue sky.

I stood there stunned. We were all humbled into submission, unable to find the words in our respective languages to express what we could see. The lake had cast a spell on me and reminded me of the John William Waterhouse painting 'The Lady of Shalott'.

For half an hour I just sat and allowed the stillness of the scene to seep into every pore of my body. With each inhalation, I could feel my energy increase, like a balloon being pumped up. I could have whiled away the day watching nature do its thing.

I set off gingerly in the direction of the pine forest, which I hoped, with it being Sunday, would be tranquil like the lake.

Cheep! Cheep! Cheep!

Overhead in the treetops, chicks fired off the early warning – incoming pilgrims. The next thing I knew, the birds were scrambling to get airborne while a sleepy Korean couple were getting jacked by squirrels on the forest floor. They'd been lured in with the promise of a few close-ups.

With the squirrels preoccupied, I slipped by unnoticed. Or so I thought. That was until my boots started to clatter and vibrate off the wooden slats on a small bridge. Alerted by my presence, and slowly rising from the murky depths, came a stealth school of carp. They, much like every creature out there wanted to extort a payment for safe passage across their waterway.

With no cash to hand, I was begrudgingly forced to offer up my beloved TUC biscuits. Then came the awkward silence, as the carp seemed to debate the suitability of the bounty. In the end they finally agreed on the fee of six biscuits – greedy bastards.

Back on terra firma on the other side of the bridge, I wandered on a bed of soft, fallen ferns, much to the delight of my tired feet. Up ahead, I could see pilgrims starting to break ranks. Some were headed into Cafe Cabaña del Tio Juarvi, presumably for second breakfast. Or perhaps it was to restock in preparation for another jackin'.

Having swerved the squirrels and pleaded poverty with the carp, I was still ok for 'G' (grub). I certainly had enough to blag or barter my way out of any tricky situation. Providing I didn't run into anything bigger or fearsome than a squirrel.

"Now what kind of a lunatic builds a wood cabin out here?"

I chuckled as I was reminded of one of my favourite scenes from '*Blazing Saddles*'. In it, the dastardly Mayor Hedley Lamar builds an impromptu toll booth in the middle of the tundra in the hope of extorting money from petty criminals, Mexican bandits and Indian agents – which incredibly, worked.

Surely someone wouldn't be brazen enough to try that old trick. Well, good luck to them if they did. There would be no way anybody was going to get a copper coin out of me, that was for certain.

Well, except maybe this fella!'

From behind the wooden cabin counter came what looked like the largest human to ever walk the Earth. He was enormous. About six foot five with hands like shovels and shoulders that blocked out the sun. Not only was he large, but at first glance he almost looked feral, with his grey unkempt hair, wild eyebrows and bushy beard. Yet oddly he seemed at home in his monk's robes. Robes which made him, at least in my eyes, look like a pleasant mix of Obi-Wan Kenobi and Captain Caveman.

Whatever the big fella wants, he gets. Got it?

I wasn't going to argue with my conscience.

It was only as I came within striking distance, when I caught and read the white banner strung across the front of his cabin.

"Hola, Marcelino."

Euw, O-la, Marcelinooooo.

Not only was my Spanish unremarkable, but it also came across as very camp. Not that that seemed to scare the big fella. He simply thundered towards me and offered his giant-sized man paws in friendship.

While we were shaking hands, I tried to establish the link between Marcelino and the Camino. Then I recalled an article I'd read a few months before. In it, it revealed Marcelino's full name – Marcelino Lobato Castrillo. He was... no, he is, one of the most well-known and respected Camino elders, having walked it many, many times.

So NOT your typical Brixton-based mugger?

Marcelino's role was part-historian, part cheerleader and in charge of promoting forest harmony. His cabin was a veritable larder, stocked with enough snacks to bring the weariest of pilgrims back from the dead.

While I was overjoyed to see my hand return from his, it was tinged with an unbreakable sadness, because I knew my hablar wasn't as fluent as I'd wanted it to be.

Yes, I could speak basic Spanish, but not enough for the really important questions like:

→ What called Marcelino to the Camino?
→ What had he learnt from doing it?
→ What was the one piece of advice he held sacred?

This information would be gold. But I'd never be able to ask, let alone understand. With that resigned thought and the ever-growing thud of pilgrim hooves getting louder behind me, I set off again.

"Hasta luego, Marcelino. Buen Camino."

After leaving Marcelino, the path rocketed skywards. But my efforts were rewarded with a spell-binding view. The hillside was awash with vine groves, with old, white-washed outhouses peppered amongst them, their doors flung open. Behind me, I could see the path I'd taken as it snaked down the road.

Just peeking through the tree line was a sliver of blue water that flickered and shimmied provocatively, brought to life by the sun's rays dancing on its surface. This was why I'd come to Spain. This was what I needed to see and feel to make my spirit sing again along...

BEEP! BEEP! BEEP!

My thought was interpreted by the blasts from a tractor horn (a tractor with an engine that seemed to have died or had purposefully been killed). As I turned, I saw Mr. Farmer sitting on high in his air-conditioned cab. He was looking towards the lake, lost in the beauty and craftsmanship of God's creation – just as I was.

"Venga, venga, venga!" came the shout from his cab.

Next thing I knew, the smiling farmer flung open his door and directed me towards the back of his trailer, where he climbed onto it to forage amongst the grapes. He emerged moments later with a huge punnet and offered it to me.

Hang on a minute. I'd seen the Korean couple stitched up by squirrels not more than ten minutes before. Now this fella was offering me *free* grapes. What was the catch? Was this a genuine act of kindness? Or was he merely safeguarding his own interests by ensuring I got off his land before I carked it? Luckily for me, the kindness in his eyes and warmth in his smile said he was just cheering me on.

At the top of Alto Grajera, the two worlds, old and new, collided once again. This time, the only thing to separate them was a thin wire fence covered in makeshift reed crosses. Were these here to protect us from the mayhem of modern life? Or perhaps to acknowledge the suffering Jesus endured for the freedoms we enjoy every day?

The gravel path slowly fell away, passing grey storage facilities, haulage yards and the aubergine-coloured La Asomante building as it went. It was just after the haulage yard when I caught sight of a huge silhouetted black bull made of flat steel. This was the infamous Osborne bull. A symbol used by the Osborne Sherry company to promote their brandy from Jerez.

Soon after the bull sighting, the two worlds, devoid of the wire fence merged. Sprayed onto the road in yellow were the words: 100M CAMINO. Reluctantly, I joined the N-120 road, ever conscious of the white line that marked the tightrope wire of the hard shoulder.

I held my breath as the road headed towards a blind bend. Luckily for me, I was directed right, down onto a loose gravel path. It seemed to trickle down, like silver poured into a blacksmith's mould, between a huge vine grove and into town.

Along the way were two key features of the landscape – the San Juan de Acre monastery, the Don Jacobo Bodegas Corral winery, and the Church of the Assumption.

Little remained of the monastery, but it seemed to have lost none of its magic, judging by the excitement on the faces of sweat-soaked pilgrims who'd found a water fountain they'd looked long and hard for.

From the monastery, the road dropped down to the Don Jacobo vineyard, before kicking up once again as I hit Pasada de la Orden. Halfway up, I was met with a large rectangular map of Navarette, complete with everything I'd need to know and more.

There, arrows directed me left, up a steep staircase lined with railway sleepers into town. On Calle la Cruz – I hit the wall. Within seconds my blood sugar plummeted, my mouth ran dry, and spots started to appear in my vision. That wasn't good.

Out of nowhere, I saw a pilgrim wandering towards me, clutching a freshly made ham and cheese bocadillo.

There's your answer. Rob the fat lad?

WTF? I couldn't do that.

Why not? You're hungry. He won't be, not until 2050.

Seriously, was that the best solution my conscience could come up with?

Well, if you grab it, he's hardly going to give chase.

Having dodged one rumble already, I wasn't about to start another with my pilgrim brother. I also knew if I tried and got caught, all it would take was one Big Daddy splash from him and it would be game over.

Your loss.

Minutes later, having bought and not fought for my bocadillo, I joined the fat lad and seven other pilgrims on the benches along Calle la Cruz.

Silence fell upon the shoal for a few minutes. The first, second and third bites were heavenly. By bite four I felt the whoosh as blood was marshalled towards my stomach. While the bocadillo quietened the rumblings, it did little to quieten the thoughts of having bitten off more than I could chew.

With the last morsel of food despatched and my doubts starting to grow, I set off. But not before firing off a few 'Buen Caminos', along with an apology to the fat lad who, quite rightly, looked utterly perplexed by it all.

I made my way along Calle Mayor Baja. It was small and claustrophobic with barely more than an arm's length separating opposing houses. I imagined that families in days gone by would offer food from the second-floor kitchen out and across to their neighbours.

My route from here crawled ever upwards, passing a much-needed water fountain before dropping me at the doors of the colossal Church of the Assumption. Beyond the church, the street slowly started to widen. This was undoubtedly in preparation for jettisoning me out into the wild and back alongside – you guessed it – the N-120.

I spent five hundred metres woefully outnumbered by cars speeding by as I headed towards the cemetery. Beyond that would be a 12th century gateway and salvation. Time to wave goodbye to the hard shoulder and hello to a wide gravel path, protected nicely by a thicket of grass.

Ahead in the heat haze, I noticed a once tightly knit walking group start to shatter. Its effect was slow at first. A few feet here and there. Then there was a regrouping. Then those feet extended into yards. Until finally, the cracks started to shatter, severing the elastic between them all.

Not long after, the whole energy dynamic of the group had changed. Those who were strong started to churn up dust, leaving the weaker ones shell-shocked and confused. They'd spend the remainder of the day being baked alive in their own, very real version of pilgrim purgatory.

While it was torturous to see, it did at least give me something to focus on. For the next hour my mind drifted into a catatonic state. All I could see were pilgrims, pilgrims and more pilgrims.

Such was my numbness to the surroundings that I almost missed the turn towards Vitivinicola de Sotes, a large, cream-coloured building, most noted for having a glass observation deck.

It was just as the path returned once again to the A-12, when my day turned dark. As I looked up, all I could see was a grey, soul-sucking straight path. It was made up of loose gravel/quicksand as it sucked my boots down into it.

With each step I could feel my thighs growing heavier and leaden. With each step I could feel the extra effort it took to extract my boot from the hungry gravel. And with each step, I could feel the sun drawing nearer as it turned the heat lamp up to the max. It was a perfect storm. The combination of a eighteen miler, intense heat, sleep deprivation and loss of bodily salts caused my head to erupt. I stopped dead in my tracks.

"That's it! This here. This here is me done," I said, finally admitting defeat.

As way of acceptance, the gravel seemed to swallow my whole foot in an attempt to drag me under.

"Oh, for the love of God."

Gone were all the happy thoughts. Like an Etch-a-Sketch drawing, they'd been erased. Replaced by my darkened thoughts of being mowed down, mugged, scorched and terrorised by cars. The final nail in the coffin had been this firewalk through quicksand.

"Yeah, but it's great viewing."

The sniggering sound of Mitch's voice returned. I could almost see him now – sitting with his trotters up in God's Bar, poised on a white stool with a Guinness in hand, half cheering me on, half enjoying the spectacle of me about to have a full-on meltdown.

"Fuck's sake! Why is everything such fuckin' hard work? Need a train? *Sorry, zee train's broken.* Need a shop? *Sorry, we're shut.* Need breakfast? *Zee shops open at 7:30 am.* Need a bed? *Try the next town.* Need a poo? *Have you brought loo roll?* Need solitude? *What do you mean you can't find peace when wandering beside a main road, with articulated lorries tearing down the road honking their horns?"* All this was just the warmup act.

And what's with the lack of butter and potatoes? For feck's sake, I'm half Irish. I was nineteen years old before I had my first meal without spuds. I feel like I've gone back in time to the Famine. I just want them boiled with a little bit of salt. Is that too much to ask? Oh yeah, and some bacon and cabbage too.

The tirade bounced around the inside my head for the next hour. What were the laundrette opening times? Were pilgrim meals anti-veg? Was St. James really buried in Santia... or was it all a cunning plan cooked up by the Catholics (of which I was one) to open up new pilgrim routes throughout the world during mediaeval times and get the cash rolling in?

Thankfully, I saw my misguided rant for what it was. It was my body screaming out that it was starting to really struggle with the heat, sleep deprivation and new routine. It felt like the Camino was handing me my arse. After kicking it up every hill and around every bend.

Luckily, my rant let up just long enough for me to notice a sign directing me left, away from the A-12 and its gravel graveyard.

"Halle-fuckin'-lujah!"

But surely this was just a test? Wasn't it God's plan to just pour on the misery until I quit or burst into flames? Apparently not.

My feet may have been relieved to be back on shin-cracking concrete, but the rest of me wasn't. I was in a right sulk and walking like a scolded kid: head down, shoulders hunched and bottom lip out. I remained in this state as I scuffed my feet all the way up and into Ventosa.

We're here, tubby lad!

"Don't care, not interested. I don't want to play anymore. I want to go home."

From my position on the road, I could see pilgrims at a nearby bar drinking beer, laughing and screaming at me to come and join them.

"Fuuu-" I couldn't even swear. No sooner had an expletive left my mouth than a car would roar by, stifling my words. Soon after the bar I spotted another sign emblazoned with 'Santiago'.

"Oh, why don't you just shag off?" I threatened it. All this petulant goading was really starting to get right on my tits.

Soon after the sign, the surface underfoot changed again. By then my feet arches were nervous wrecks and exhausted by the ever-changing conditions. But I ploughed on regardless, trying to appreciate at least a little of these magnificent surroundings. That lasted all of five minutes, until the savagery of the gradient went up. The climbing I thought I was done with was biting back.

By the time I reached the white, stone barn (which I marked as the summit of Alto de San Antón) I was done, spent and utterly broken. Not even the '94 London Marathon had put me in the gutter like this. I had to fight even to remain upright.

"Jesus H Christ. There are still eight kilometres to go. How the feck am I going to do that?" I said, despondently.

I was flat out of luck, energy and ideas. And for the first time since arriving, I felt myself admitting that I'd fallen out of love with the Camino. What was the point? I'd had enough. I knew that I'd let Mitch, Help for Heroes and all my friends and family down by quitting. But feck it. All I wanted was someone to come along and take me away from it all.

"Bloody hot, isn't it?"

I could feel myself starting to cry. I didn't even need to turn to see who it was – it was Indy.

For a few moments I stood broken in the silence. I tried to take in the extraordinary beauty of the flatlands before me through a sea of salt tears.

Every part of me ached. Ached with a raw emptiness I hadn't felt since Mitch's passing.

Thankfully, my train of thought was interrupted.

"Hi, I'm Neil."

So definitely not Indy.

"What's wrong with your foot?" I replied exhaustedly.

"Turned my bloody ankle on those ruddy large rocks back there. Vicious buggers they are," he replied.

I chuckled at the calm, measured, newsreader-like manner of his response.

"Mind if I hobble down the road with you? As you seem in as much disrepair as me – possibly worse?' said Indy, half-smiling.

"Please do," I replied, feeling half excited.

In fact, I couldn't think of a more comical way to end the day. What with Indy hobbling down the path favouring his right leg, exclaiming crikey every fifty metres, and me shuffling along favouring my left leg, exclaiming *oh, for feck's sake!* And while Neil retained a certain level class and decorum, I really couldn't have given two shits.

In keeping of two lads on their last legs (feeling like we were at the gallows) the gloves came off and the piss-taking began. Indy took the mickey out of my banged-up pack, ridiculously long shorts, pot belly and limp, while I ripped into him about his last two movies and his fear of snakes.

When we finally slithered our way to the outskirts of Nájera, Indy's phone started to blow up with a flurry of messages.

"Don't mind me. It's just the ladies asking me if I want to join them for dinner. You should come! They're a lovely bunch, all early-forties and great fun," he said, unable to contain his grin.

So, he was Indy after all! How else could I explain how a middle-aged man in fancy dress had attracted a bevvy of lovely ladies?

While I appreciated his offer, the only thing I wanted was to rest. It was 6:30 pm at that point, which left me fewer than twelve hours to find my hotel, forage, wash my kit and prep for tomorrow.

We said our goodbyes and Indy tootled off, limp-free to enjoy his evening, leaving me to try and remember what feckin' side of the River Najerilla my hotel was – left or right?

Sod it, I'd ask someone at Bar Navarra, the hotel would have to wait. Thankfully, within seconds of sitting down the pub owner brought me a beer.

Had I ordered it? Or had he taken pity on me? Whatever the reason, I was, as ever, eternally grateful.

Within two sips of my ice-cold beer the pain of the day started to melt away. This gave the pub owner just long enough to point out the local sights. The best place to eat in Nájera was there. The best place to drink with views over the river, it seemed, was there. And the best place to enjoy happy locals and a warm evening was there. Not that I'd be seeing much after 8 pm. But I did tend to agree with what the pub owner said.

After sinking my beer, I went off to forage for tomorrow. Better to do it then, stopping at whatever shops there were en route to my hotel, as there wouldn't be any later.

When I finally arrived at the hotel, the owner ushered me inside. She took one look at me and decided to give me my room key. There was none of the usual palaver about checking and photocopying passports. Why did they do that anyhow? She quickly pointed out the emergency exit, but my mind was shot. If I didn't get to my room sharpish, I'd be happily found on the stairs dribbling, snoring and in my underpants.

Within seconds of entering my room, I collapsed. The room was ice cold, just how I liked it. But my heart was bucking wildly in my chest and the sweat was pouring out of me.

One look in the mirror confirmed that I looked like a sack of shit. The day had pushed me hard. Way harder than I had even imagined. I came into town with an empty tank, flashing warning lights and flat tyres.

My very last thoughts as I slipped in and out of my daze were that I needed to eat, I needed to drink, I needed to wash my kit and I needed to wash my body. None of that happened. Instead, the sound of John Williams' orchestra pumping out Indy's theme tune started playing in my head.

Duh, duh, duhduh, duh-duh-duh, duh, dun, duh-duh, duh-duh-duh-duh-duh.

Then sleep took me.

~~CHAPTER 13: BIG TOE 'TONE'~~

8th September, Nájera - Santo Domingo de la Calzada, 23km

"G8289042, Middleton – Paul. You have been brought before this court to answer charges brought against you by Big Toe 'Tone'. These charges relate to an incident that occurred on the afternoon of September 6th.

"The charges include:

1. Assault, causing actual bodily harm
2. Dereliction of duty
3. Failing to provide adequate leadership

In regard to these offences, how do you plead?"

I was shaken awake at 3:15 am by yet another ayahuasca-type dream in which I was standing inside a kangaroo court being cross-examined by a wide-eyed tawny owl. Yet, bizarrely, the first question my mind wanted to ask was – how did I plead?

Exhausted. Insanity. Numb. Take your pick.

All I wanted, well, needed, was a decent night's nip. And preferably one free from the bed beaters, night terrors and troubled inmates who wandered the corridors of my mind.

Ping... ping... ping

Oh FFS, what now? My arm automatically started to sweep the duvet in a semi-circular motion, hunting presumably for my phone. Except in that instance, it wasn't. It was sleeping soundly on the wooden dresser.

So, if the pinging sound wasn't my phone – then what was it?

Slowly, I dragged my half-beaten carcass upright. There I sat motionless, wiping the eye bogies from my face. Poised and ready to ambush the ping when it resurfaced.

Ping... ping...

I could feel that it was close. I gently reached over to the wall to turn on the light. All I needed was one more ping and I'd have it.

Ping... ping...

"Gotcha, you bastard."

I threw back the covers and to my horror were five gnarly-looking blisters staring back at me. The leader was a pumped up, puss-filled brute with a blood-red face.

"Fuuuuuccccccckkkkk."

Where the fuck had they come from? They sure as shit weren't there the night before. I had checked – hadn't I? But with my mind fog, I couldn't say for sure. Not that it mattered. At least it explained why Big Toe 'Tone' had a face like thunder as he surveyed the trench line of my toes. Where the enemy was dug-in deep.

"'TENTION!" Tone's voice boomed and all my toes straightened up as he launched into his speech.

"Righto, lads, I'm not going to piss about! Numbnuts here..."

Was he talking about me?

"... has dropped us all in the shit. And it's my job to get us out of it. I'm not gonna lie, today is going to boil your piss. You're gonna be taken, hooded and plunged, into a world of darkness, where you'll be expected to operate in cramped, dusty and airless conditions – within millimetres of the enemy. Now, I know many of you are itching for a scrap. But you MUST NOT, and I repeat, you MUST NOT – under any circumstances, engage the enemy. Is that understood?"

The hotel room floor fell deathly silent. My only hope was that it would remain that way. But Tone was far from done.

"Righto, lads, we need to crack on. I want to see everyone ready to go in fifteen minutes. So, drop your sad-ons, wrap your tits in and start sparking. Any questions? No? Well, don't just fuckin' stand there – move it."

The guilt I felt as I looked down at my ravaged feet was indescribable. I'd dropped a bollock. I'd gone too hard, too fast and too deep. Now I – we – would have to pay the price for it.

The best I could hope was that Tone and the lads would help me hobble to Santo Domingo de la Calzada. Assuming I was going to get that far. Which was by no means a foregone conclusion.

But my feet weren't my only problem. I was also on my chin straps energy wise. I woke shivering, my head banging and my back still stiff from my run-in with 'Barry Big Bollocks.'

In an attempt to deflect attention away from my impending doom, I began to pat my feet dry before carefully applying blister plasters. Within seconds, everything fell silent. I could no longer hear the violent, antagonistic and ear-splitting screams of the enemy – my blisters. Their voices were now muffled by a thick, impenetrable wall of sound-proof plaster.

"Now for the moment of truth."

I raised my right foot up tentatively, before taking aim at the dark abyss that was the inside of my boot. Then slowly, I lowered it, allowing the darkness to consume it.

"Jeeeeeeeeeeeeezzzzzzzz..."

Instantly, every cell in my body went rigid. I'd somehow forgotten how swollen my feet were, now they were wedged in tight. There was only one thing for it – keep pushing. I could feel the threat of bile creeping up as I wiggled my feet further into my boot. It felt like my feet were being rubbed raw with coarse sandpaper. Once in, my feet would be staying put. At least until I'd got the visual of sandpapering out of my head.

With my feet sorted, all thoughts turned to food. Even though I was ravaged by hunger, I felt too lethargic to eat. Which was just as well, as that morning's meagre offering would only have made Mr. Bumble proud. I was faced with another semi-stale French baton, the only thing I'd managed to salvage from my forage the day before.

"Well, you can feck right off."

I tossed the baton into the bin. That was it, I was done. I was tired of eating bland, tasteless shit for breakfast (or at least, so I thought). Minutes later the reality of my situation hit home. There weren't many places open at this hour. So back to the bin I went. I reached inside and grabbed the baton, now caked in bin juice.

"Well... beggars can't be choosers."

Slowly, holding back gags, I began to chew. While it tasted rank, it did at least take my mind off the dark thoughts that had started to gather. They'd come to remind me:

→ How bad things were with my feet – *like I needed reminding*

→ How low my energy was – *like I needed reminding*

→ That my day of reckoning was fast-approaching – *like I didn't know that.*

I got halfway through the baton before admitting defeat. I needed to change focus and fast. The quickest way to do that was to run through my morning ritual of checks. Once satisfied, I headed outside, where I was met by yet another flawless, blue Spanish sky.

I set off slowly, trudging my way along Calle San Fernando, towards the river Najerilla, where I spotted a small yellow arrow on a low wall that directed me across the bridge.

Once over and with no waymarkers for guidance, I took a punt on Calle Mayor. Halfway down, my eyes were drawn to a flashing digital screen attached to a pharmacy. On it, in big, bold, green numerals was the temperature – 22C. Ouch! Already 22C at 8 am. It really was gearing up to be a boil-in-my-boots kind of day. F-a-n-t-a-s-t-i-c.

Soon after the pharmacy, Calle Mayor became Plaza de España where off to my right, stood the 11th-century monastery of Santa María La Real. I continued up onto Calle San Marcial. I passed Carnicería Sofi, Café Bar Metal and Albergue Sancho III, until I hit Calle Hórreo, a ramshackle of a street that led me back towards the monastery.

Well, if having two run-ins with a monastery in a matter of minutes wasn't a sign, what was? Heeding the warning, I unclipped my pack and set it down beside me. It was time to call in a few favours.

Like many a failed Catholic, I wasn't shy on leveraging my previous convictions to gain personal advantage. After all, that was why I'd attended Sunday school, choir and become an altar boy. I'd done my time. Now I wanted my kickbacks.

In fairness, it wasn't God I was after – it was Mary. She had always been my go-to girl. But I knew in order to get to her, I first had to go through God's switchboard. Once I got patched through, I closed my eyes, calmed my thoughts and began to pray.

"Hey, Mary. I need your help. I'm really beginning to struggle out here. My body is slowly starting to break down and my mind is coming undone. I feel like the Camino tide is starting to turn against me. I know I have no right to ask you, but can you watch over me today?"

I finished my prayer with a soft amen and stood in stunned silence. I'd unknowingly let the pressure of the Camino's must walk, must carry, must keep up mindset get to me. I knew I had. What made me furious was that I'd seen it. But I couldn't resist its pull.

I knew something had to change. If I didn't, I risked wrecking everything.

With this sobering thought in mind, I set off along Calle Costanilla, a street lined with modern apartments, broken up by a cluster of trees and a small area of grass. Halfway up to the right of the path was a large sandstone boulder. Sprayed onto it was a crude, single, golden arrow which directed me off the concrete and onto a sun-baked dirt track.

"Righto, lads. Look lively," came the encouraging shout from Tone.

In a matter of metres, both the gradient and my pulse skyrocketed. This was what I needed. Less time for thinking, more time for doing. The effort required to pull up the hill instantly silenced the dark thoughts which had now taken up position on my left shoulder, well within whispering range.

The higher I climbed, the more desolate it got, and the calmer I became. Until finally, I crested the summit and was met by the sight of an enormous field of vine groves to my left and enormous sandstone boulders to my right.

But wow – what a view. In the distance, through the early morning haze, I could see two features. One, a deep scar gouged deep into the Earth's surface – my path. The other, a solitary Y-shaped telegraph pole sitting alone in the featureless landscape.

For the next hour, that telegraph pole became my focus, as the path slithered and swayed passed breeze block-built barns, abandoned farm machinery, fallow fields and across a small stream.

With each passing step, I could feel the loving calm of my Camino 'bubble' wrap its arms around me. In this other-worldly state, colours were brighter, sounds softer and my thoughts freer. In fact, the only sound I heard was the steady, rhythmic thump of my heart.

"Yooooo rrrr riigght ad?"

Suddenly, I was stirred awake from a mumbling on the wind. Had someone spoken or had I imagined it? Such was the state of my dazed mind, I could no longer tell. Nor did I trust the answers it gave me.

"Yooooo rrrr riigght ad?" The sound came again.

The words sounded slurred, like I'd heard them while my head was being submerged in bath water. Whoever it was probably wasn't talking to me anyhow. In an attempt to block them out, I focused even harder on the path.

"You alright, lad?"

That time the question came through with Dolby surround sound clarity. And better still, the voice was a) English and b) a northerner. Most likely from the People's Republic of South Yorkshire.

As I turned to answer, I was met by two wide smiles, along with a thunderous clap across my shoulder blades.

"Nah! I'm fecked," came my somewhat jaded response.

"Well, fecked! I'm Kev, and this is June," he said, chuckling. "Mind if we tag along with you for a while. Or at least until you find your parrot?"

Cheeky bastard! We'd only met and already he was likening me to Long John Silver.

"If you must," came my equally unenthusiastic and sarcastic response.

Within seconds of our agreement the strangest thing occurred. They both spilt up and positioned themselves on either side of me. What was that about? Had they really come to help me? Or had they plans to relieve me of all my worldly goods? If so, they could start with my feckin' rucksack. They could have had that no bother.

The one comfort I had (if they hadn't come to jack my pack), was that I had company. Assuming that I'd be able to hang onto their coattails for the remaining three kilometres into Azofra. Thankfully, June, being a true Yorkshire lass, was both friendly and chatty. Something I cunningly seized upon as a way to slow our pace even further.

"You remind me of our lad," came June's opening gambit.

In that instant, everything about her changed. Her face lit up, her voice softened and lowered, and her body relaxed.

"He's off in the Philippines..."

I could tell by her set-up that she had a tale to tell, so I drew nearer.

"He originally went over there a few year back, to learn to surf. Ain't it funny how different generations see the world? Back in my day, surfing was all about Fistral Beach, Newquay and hanging outside Fat Willy's Surf Shack. I doubt I could have even told you back then where the Philippines were," she said, chuckling.

"Isn't it a few miles north of Blackpool, further up the M6?" I replied, smiling.

"Within weeks of arriving he'd fallen in love. Then out of the blue he calls to tell me he's going to open a hotel. A hotel – I ask you! He had trouble building a Lego tower as a lad. Now all of a sudden, he was Bob the Builder."

I had to admit, I admired her lad's 'feck it, let's do it' attitude.

"Within twelve month, the hotel was up-and-running. Then, on its third anniversary, a storm hit. And when I say storm, I mean a biblical storm. It ripped through the island, pulling down power lines, uprooting trees and homes. It took a large chunk of the hotel with it, too."

The tone in June's voice suddenly changed. She became anxious. I watched as she started to scratch her arm erratically. I could see her mind searching for the next words. Whatever was coming, was something deeply personal.

"Those first forty-eight hours after the storm hit were the worst of my life. There was nothing. Only silence. With the power out, there was no way I could contact my lad. So, I spent those hours glued to the box, anxiously waiting for any updates..."

She started to trail off again. This time Kev drew near.

"I just didn't know. I just didn't know whether my lad was dead or alive! And every time I tried to call, all I got was static, or the dead man's click."

I could feel my body run cold. I used to call static the 'dead man's click' too. I'd received that many times while waiting to be patched through to Mitch during his time overseas.

All three of us were starting to well up. It was about to get a whole lot worse, as June recounted the moment she heard the precious words – "Mum, I'm okay."

She continued on, but my eyes were welling up with tears. All I could think was how lucky she was. What I wouldn't have given to have had one last call with Mitch. Just to hear him scream out, "Alright, student boy!" before he'd start to cackle down the phone at me. What typically followed was a flurry of Mitch one-liners. Or a summary of one of his mad-cap adventures.

My favourite was when he asked me if I fancied going to Paris by Eurostar – for a cuppa. Who does that? Well, Mitch did. His plan was simple. Get on the first train he could to Paris, followed by the next available train back. Mitch wasn't fussed about the arts, nor did he give a monkey's about any *je ne sais quoi* bollocks. He did it because, as a foreign contractor, he could only do so many days in the country before HMRC started to crawl all over his arse. So, Paris was the easiest option.

"Well, I guess this is it – Azofra," said Kev.

Having lost track of time, my eyes were drawn to a small cluster of white flecks in the landscape, about four hundred metres from us. To the left of the path was a large, concrete irrigation ditch on stilts which led us down to the foot of town. And what a town. The place looked like a sixties Spaghetti Western film set. All I could see was one street – Calle Mayor. On it was a bar, a shop, a mangy looking dog and a few places for a pilgrim to get their head down.

Further along Calle Mayor, I could just about make out the infamous red of a Coca-Cola sign. Below it, a woman was busying herself setting up snares – green plastic tables and chairs. The sight was enough for my body to initiate its own shut down sequence.

"Lads, I'm going to have to leave you here, I'm afraid," I said, reluctantly.

And that was that. Within a matter of minutes, Kev and June were up the road. But with a table bagged, a drink ordered and the sun warming my bones, I was more than happy to melt into the plastic seating.

It was a good ten minutes before I braved looking at my feet. Slowly, I began to extract them from my boots. Once out, I seductively started to peel off my socks and was greeted by the sight of my pair of clammy, anaemic milk-bottle-coloured feet. They looked like they'd been stolen off a corpse (at least when compared to the rest of my dusty, wind-burnt exterior).

But colour aside, it felt great to free Tone and the lads from the heat and pressure of the day. It also gave me a chance to dust off the fine layer of crud choking my sock.

"Righto, lads. Seems like Numbnuts has decided to take a break. Don't waste it. Grab yourself some shade. Stretch yourselves out or get your heads down. We go again in fifteen minutes. For fuck's sake, whatever you do, don't go winding up the enemy."

Tone made a good point. I needed to double check on the enemy's position. At first glance, all seemed well. My first line of defence, my blister plasters, were holding firm. But as I lightly tapped them, I could hear the blood-curdling screams of my blisters, desperate to get out.

"Lads, gather round. Our next checkpoint is Cirueña. A small hilltop town, nine kilometres west of here. We've two main road features to watch out for – the N-120 and A-12. We need to keep these to the right at all times. Or at least Numbnuts does.

"Secondary features to watch out for include: a river, a Roman pillar and a canal. Now the canal is key. If Numbnuts is switched on and notices it, happy days. All then that's left, is a seven-kilometre bimble into Cirueña. On the other hand, if he misses it, we'll be doing laps of farmers tracks 'til we drop," said Tone.

"What's with the sad-ons, lads? Yes, we've got another bloody climb ahead of us. But what would you rather? A seven hundred metre climb over seven kilometres? Or a four thousand feet ball-bagger getting ragged over the Pyrenees again?" This abrupt point brought Big Tone's briefing to a close.

Geed up and reinvigorated by Tone's no-nonsense approach, I set off. At the bottom of Calle Mayor, the Camino markers directed me right, then left and across the LR-206 road. From there I was redirected back into the wilds, where the only other thing I had for company for the next hour was regimented lines of vines, farm storage huts and discarded wooden pallets – oh! And not forgetting the Spanish heat.

Occasionally, as I walked, I would hear the hum of a bird, the whistle of the wind or the whir of cars in the distance.

Suddenly, a huge scream tore the day in two. Before I had time to react, two mountain bikers tore passed me, the lead rider frantically pinging his bell.

"WTF! You can do the Camino on bike? Is this a joke? Who knew?"

I certainly didn't. But how did that work? Just as I was coming to terms with biking the Camino, my mind was disturbed by the rhythmic clippity-clop of hooves. As I turned, I was blinded by shafts of morning light. Out from the light came a grey steed with black speckle markings.

Sitting astride it, dressed in a neon green jacket with a matching sleeping bag strewn across her lap, was a white-haired old lady. Beside her, on another trusty steed, was her partner who was decked out in a black beret, thick blue jacket and jeans. They both wore packs on their backs that were covered in Camino patches.

"WTF! You can do this on horse too?"

Things were starting to get silly. What next? Camino by car? Camino via mouse clicks? Camino by horse seemed almost as absurd as the tales I'd heard about mediaeval times, when the rich would send their minions to walk it while they stayed at home rogering the servants, their cousins or anything with a pulse. While I admired their energy efficient approach to the Camino, it did miss the mark – massively.

And how did Camino by horse even work? I chuckled as my mind started to serve up some comical end-of-day scenarios. Like who'd get the top bunk? Surely the horse should get first dibs. After all, it had done all the work.

And what about the pilgrim meal? Who'd get that? Surely the horse's nosebag deserved to be filled first. And what about the Compostela? Who'd receive that, the rider or the horse? Surely the rider couldn't claim it.

But there was one thing I knew for sure. I didn't want to be anywhere within earshot when this was being decided.

Back in the real world, I could see toy-sized cars hurtling down a road. That meant, assuming Tone's briefing was correct, that the canal was around there somewhere. And sure enough it was. Granted, it didn't resemble any canal I'd ever seen (having grown up a stone's throw from the Grand Union in Birmingham). But I'd spotted it, which meant I/we had to turn left.

Underfoot, things were starting to heat up along with the soaring temperature. But this was offset by the pleasure of the rich, terracotta-coloured path I hobbled over. It was covered with the lightest dusting of stones, many of which had fallen into the deep groves and gullies left by tractor tyres.

It was just after the turn when things started to open up. My path cut its way through a barren and featureless Riojan wasteland. The only splashes of colour came from the slivers of grass that lined the path verge and low hedges that divided football-sized fields.

In the distance, black silhouetted figures were strung out in ones and twos. It was a joy to watch as pilgrims appeared then disappeared. In the vastness, I could feel my mind start to slow and I slipped once again into my trance-like, 'bubble' state.

In this space, all that existed was the next step, the next breath and the next heartbeat. Occasionally, I'd hear the crackle of static on a power line or the cooing of a bird. Or I'd be distracted by the battleship-sized hay bales that lined the path side, where someone would invariably be having a dump.

Not long after the hay bales the path started to crawl upwards. In the distance on my left, I could see a thicket of lush, freshly watered forest. Such was the intensity of the green that I half expected it to be a mirage. Off to my right, on the brow of the hill were clumps of buildings. One of which was the Cirueña golf course.

Whose bright idea was it to put a golf course there? I edged towards it, passing hawkers selling drinks from blue ice coolers and pilgrims strewn out in a picnic area, contemplating their fate.

At the top of the climb, I was spat out onto Avenue La Rioja. It was an eerily quiet street made up of a mishmash of red brick apartments, grey brutalist architecture and family homes with fake Tudor beams. The place was stonily quiet. The only thing that moved was a riderless swing, that rocked menacingly back and forth in a nearby playgrounds.

The playgrounds gave me the willies. So much so, that even when I was a few streets away, I could still hear the rusty creak-creak of ungreased swing hinges. Luckily, within ten minutes I was out of earshot and out onto the other side of town, stomping down the hot concrete of the LR-204, towards the roundabout.

Once I hit that, I turned left. My destination was back into the wilds from which I'd come. With the climbing done for the day, all that was left was an arrow-straight calf-pounding path downhill to Santo Domingo.

"Push on now, lads," came the rallying call from Tone.

He was right, too. We were about ninety minutes from victory. More importantly though, we were ninety minutes away from cotton sheets, a cool shower and the 16th century ex-convent, now the fabulous Bernardo de Fresneda Parador.

Unknowingly to Tone and the lads I'd decided that tomorrow would be a rest day. We'd covered one hundred and forty kilometres since Pamplona. I needed to rest, as every cell in my body was screaming to stop.

The dusty path hit the LR-204 road. Not long after turning left, the sanctuary of silence was shattered by the piercing sound of car horns, drivers screaming and kids shouting. While my ears tried to adjust to the shrieks, my eyes had to battle with the wealth of street furniture.

Once into the heart of Santo Domingo, my first mission was to find a pharmacy. I needed a resupply of blister plasters. Sure enough, no sooner had I hit Calle San Rogue, then a pharmacy appeared.

With my feet sorted, I looked down the tree-lined path. To my right were all the bars, restaurants and shops, with locals sitting out under parasols, hiding from the heat of the day. Straight ahead, cutting through the skyline, were the beige colossal stone walls of the Parador.

Suddenly from beneath my moobs, I heard a growl. Stomachs number one and two were empty. Such had been my focus on my feet, I'd forgotten to feed. But they'd have to wait. First, I needed to check-in and dump my kit. After that, it would be all about the food – nothing else.

As soon as I walked into the Parador reception, the day melted away. While it was menacingly hot outside, the Parador was perfectly cool.

My body adjusted to the temperature after a few minutes as a gentle breeze came in from the courtyard doors. I stood for a while and I watched the eagle-eyed grounds people clip hedges like master craftsmen, their secateurs click-

click-clicking. My nose drew in the heavenly freshness of a newly-watered garden, which contrasted greatly from the other, less desirable, scents I was picking up – *Eau de Moi.*

I smelt like I'd just been released from the morgue. Thankfully, the receptionist neither flickered nor flinched as my undertones of caked-in sweat drifted around on the breeze. Once I got my keys, I quickly retreated towards the staircase.

"Paauuuul!"

Though my eyes hadn't adjusted to the darkened interior, I knew instantly whose voice was calling me.

"Indy!" I replied.

He'd somehow managed to find another harem of women to join him. Or were they the same group? I didn't know. But it did make me wonder – who was this man? How did he do it? Having both seen and smelt me, he quite rightly passed on the idea of a hug.

But he did suggest meeting the next morning for breakfast, as he too was taking a rest. As I headed to my room, I briefly looked back to see Indy's arms draped around three women, who were laughing wildly at his tale.

"What have we here then?" I said, as I turned the key and stepped inside.

The coolness of my room hit me instantly. I quickly dumped my pack and collapsed onto the bed. The sheets were folded back invitingly. The wooden headboard was sculpted to look like three tiers on a viaduct. On either side of the bed were blue, heavy-set silk curtains. While underfoot were clean terracotta tiles. If this was what heaven was like, I really wouldn't want to leave – ever.

My initial plan was to lie down for fifteen minutes, or at least until the world stopped spinning, then eat. The reality of the situation was that if I put my head down for forty winks and woke up two hours later, I'd be desperately hungry and absolutely honking.

Knowing I'd be arrested on smell if I ventured out reeking this bad, I grabbed a shower then headed out. I decided there would be no trawling the streets looking for the perfect spot to eat. I'd simply find the nearest pub or bar serving food and that would be it – job done.

My feet hit the street and I began following my nose. It seemed to know where to go. It led me left, right, and down an alley, where all of a sudden, I could pick up the chitter chatter of Spanish and the occasional English word.

I'd already decided that whatever was around the corner would have to do. But as I turned, I saw a flash of grey hair – it was Dan. He was sitting at a white plastic table with his nose buried in a book.

"Fuck, what do I do now? Bollocks."

I could feel my guilt starting to overwhelm me. I'd behaved like a proper chopper towards Dan. A guy who was undoubtedly one of the kindest, funniest and most sincere blokes I'd met here. What should I do?

"What do you mean, what should you do? There's only one thing for it, silly bollocks," came the reassuring honest assessment of Mitch's voice.

"Dos cervesa, por favor. One for me and one for hop-a-long here," I said sheepishly, smirking at the barmaid.

Upon hearing my voice Dan lifted his head up from his book. Then there was the pause. Shit! Which way would this go?

"Paauul, my brother. Great to see you, my man! How's it going?"

He got up gingerly, as his feet were in bits. Within seconds he'd thrown his arms around me, giving me one of his giant bear hugs. Suddenly all the stress and nonsense of the previous day started to ebb away. All was good again in the world.

"Mind if I join you?" It was a rhetorical question, but one I felt needed to be asked.

"Of course, bud! Take a seat," came his somewhat nervous reply.

We sat smiling knowingly at each other while we waited for our beers to arrive. Now felt like the perfect time to get the awkwardness out of the way, at least on my behalf.

"Look, about the other day..." I started.

"It's okay my brother – I understand," came his smiling response.

"... I know you do. But here's the thing. I'm not sure I do. You see, over the last few days it's felt like the walls have been closing in on me. I've properly got the fear. On the one hand, my tired mind and battered body are so ready to call it a day. But on the other hand, each step nearer Burgos, brings me one step nearer to the gallows. The gallows being – modern life.

"I can feel it, modern life wants me back. It wants me back in my old clothes, back in my old routine with my same mindset and outlook, as if nothing has changed. But everything has changed – I've changed. I'm not sure I'm ready to go back. Or if I even want to. There is something about this place that's stirred something deep within my soul. Something that I've lost...

"...The day I took off, something just went off inside my mind. It wasn't about the day, you or anyone else. It was purely me. I was drowning in unanswered questions and my plan for dealing with them was to try and outrun them – to wear them out. But this failed spectacularly, as instead of freeing my head, all I felt was guilt, shame and sadness for being an arsehole and leggin' it from you. That's fucking awful behaviour. For that, I'm truly horrified and deeply ashamed – sorry," I said, quietly.

"As I said, I know, I get it. Your days out here are short, and mine are many. I've so many thinking days ahead of me. Which could be a good thing. It could well be a bad thing. But it's all good my brother. Now, are we going to drink these beers or wait 'til they get warm? I know you Brits love your warm beer," said Dan, chuckling.

We chinked glasses and drank. I felt relieved that Dan understood. His eyes said he did. Now with the heaviness of the day taken care of. We settled back into our old comedy double act routine.

"Now check these bad boys out," said Dan excitedly. He began to gingerly open his boots and extract his foot, before removing his socks.

"For the love of God! Tell me, you haven't been walking on those feet, have you? Jesus, those feet are minging," I said in horror, as my eyes stared down at his battlefield of blistered toes.

Unable to resist, I slowly extracted my feet from my boots. The slowness seemed to help dramatize the tension, as Dan looked on eagerly.

"Righto, check these fuckers out." With that I peeled off my socks, then gingerly teased the edge away from one corner of my blister plaster to reveal my worst blister.

"Jesus! That's just nasty," said Dan wincing as he looked on.

"Reckon I can top that though," said Dan eagerly, as he folded back a plaster near the trench line of his little toe.

"What do you make of this, then?" he said, proudly.

"Honestly, is there nothing you can't beat me at? First you can handle beer better than me. Then you whoop my ass in Poohsticks. Though I'm convinced there was something suss going on. I can't prove it, but I know. And if that isn't bad enough, now your bloody blisters are bigger, gnarlier and more painful than mine. Not that I'm complaining," though clearly, I was.

But that was enough to set us both off laughing. It also set the tone for the next three hours, where we just sat in the sun drinking beer, reminiscing about meeting in Bayonne train station, his herculean effort to reach Roncesvalles, along with his blatant cheating at Poohsticks and death by bocadillo.

All the while we nattered, a table nearby of Brits led by Mr. Yorkshire and three stooges was slowly getting louder and rowdier, as one of them pulled out a guitar. Peppered in between their sing-along, a local radio station seemed to be serenading us with Camino-related hits:

- → 'Livin' on a Prayer' by Bon Jovi (wasn't that the truth)
- → 'Wind of Change' by Scorpion (I hope the wind didn't)
- → 'Sympathy for the Devil' by The Stones (one of Mitch's favourite tunes)
- → 'Going Under' by Evanescence (the last time I'd heard that was in Jo's flat).

The evening had been the perfect way to sign off our Camino. Yes, I still felt unbelievably guilty about legging it from Dan. Especially when a quiet word about the walls closing in would have done the trick. I also felt guilty that it was this that had fucked up both our feet. But I felt proud and immensely grateful to the Camino for bringing us together for one last time.

But he definitely did cheat in Poohsticks – *no question.*

~~CHAPTER 14: EYE SPY~~

10th September, Santo Domingo de la Calzada – Belorado, 23km
I spy with my little eye, something beginning with... beige.
- → **Beige** hanging drapes
- → **Beige** throw
- → **Beige** stonework
- → **Beige** mirror frame
- → **Beige** covered chairs
- → **Beige** menu
- → **Beige** food
- → **Beige** pilgrim statue
- → **Beige** path
- → **Beige** farmers' fields
- → **Beige** dog
- → **Beige** crops
- → **Beige** hedgerows
- → **Beige** roof tiles
- → **Beige** church
- → **Beige** snacks
- → **Beige** featureless landscape
- → **Beige** gravel stones
- → **Beige** hay bales
- → **Beige** farm buildings
- → **Beige** plaques
- → **Beige** leafless trees
- → **Beige** stone arch
- → **Beige** cup of tea
- → **Beige** thoughts.

Blue pool.

~~CHAPTER 15: 72 BEDS~~*

11th September, Belorado – San Juan de Ortega, 24.5km
"Seventy-two beds," I mumbled into the darkness.
I woke up at 4:27 am to the chattering of teeth and the involuntary shaking of my limbs. Though still clothed and wrapped tightly in blankets, it still wasn't enough to ward off the chill that had set up camp deep within my aching bones.
"How did I get here?"
The last thing I recalled was stumbling numb through a dry, dusty and featureless landscape. Yet there I lay on a blue, paper thin, rubber mattress being crucified at every turn by wire bed springs. Packed like a sardine into an albergue dorm that reeked of stale breath, lingering farts and the putrid stench of rotting and dying flesh.
Outside, on tungsten-lit streets, a battle was raging hard between the forces of light and dark. It would be there on those whispering windswept streets, where light would make its final stand. Its only chance of survival lay in its ability to fend off the night until reinforcements, or the first flickers of morning, came.
While light battled darkness, I battled exhaustion. I hadn't slept more than forty winks in eight hours. And now my patience was being tested by what sounded like the scratching of a burrowing hamster on the bunk opposite. Whatever me laddo was searching for was yet to be found. But that would only be a matter of time.
BOOM.
Suddenly, the darkness was cut in two by a single, piercing shaft of white light. It seemed as though the 'Horror of Roncesvalles' had returned with a vengeance.
"You've got to be fuckin' kidding me?" A growly, sweary voice spoke out from the void, which for once wasn't mine. What was this clown up to? Had

he messed his pants? Misplaced his porn stash? Or suddenly remembered he'd left the oven on back home? Either way, he was making himself as popular as a haemorrhoid on a fresh arsehole as he began to dress. Where the hell was he off to anyhow?

"Seventy-two beds," I mumbled again.

That represented the sum total of mattresses available at San Juan de Ortega. Which for many, would be the day's final destination. Through my mind fog and sleep haze, seventy-two beds sounded plenty. After all, all I'd need was one of them. But as my mind slowly whirred to life, it began to draw a rather different conclusion.

"Wait a minute... there's like, thirty-odd pilgrims in this albergue alone," I whispered into the darkness.

That was without taking into account all the other pilgrims dotted around the village in the various albergues, hotels, municipals and pensiones. To make matters worse, my mind dredged an even more terrifying figure from its depths.

"Thirty-five thousand pilgrims." I breathed.

I'd read that upwards of thirty-five thousand pilgrims would walk the French Way in September. But why had my brain served this up pre-breakfast?

→ 35,000 pilgrims ÷ 30 days = 1,166 pilgrims.

→ Therefore, 1,166 new pilgrims would be joining the French Way – each day.

Had it been this horror statistic that had sent 'Nervous Nigel' spinning like a top off into the dead of night? And if he'd worked this out, how many others had he told? Out there, secrets had a way of spreading faster than bed bugs.

Not that it mattered. It was too late. 'Nervous Nigel' had sounded the alarm, and that nervous energy was spreading like a contagion to all four corners of the dorm.

It was time for me to face both the reality and uncertainty of the day.

→ The reality – seventy-two beds.

→ The uncertainty – would I be getting one?

One thing that was for certain was the lack of time today for dilly-dallying, making daisy chains or blowing kisses Mitch-style at cattle. If I did, I ran the serious risk of ending the day blistered, broken and without a bed. And being told by a unsmiling albergue owner – "*Completo*". Which, roughly translated, was Spanish for "jog on, fatty – we're full".

If that didn't sound bad enough, I'd also be scraping against young whippersnappers, twenty years my junior, on half power and on one good leg. Not too dissimilar from the luckless Black Knight in *Monty Python and the Holy Grail*.

"But were all this lot headed to San Juan? How could I be so sure?" I muttered.

Simple. The first flurry of villages: Tosantos, Villambistia, Espinosa del Camino and Villafranca Montes De Oca, all came within thirteen kilometres of Belorado. Logic told me that 'Nervous Nigel' hadn't tipped out his scratcher at insane o'clock to do a walk which he could have easily done by 9 am.

What was more likely was that he'd target the next village, San Juan de Ortega, twelve kilometres further along. In my mind, twenty-five kilometres represented a fair schlep. Especially as it included two big climbs – Alto Mojapán and Alto de la Pedraja – which both stood at over three thousand feet.

Undoubtedly, there would be a select few on stellar form who'd push passed San Juan. Their final destination would either be Agés at twenty-seven kilometres or Atapuerca at thirty kilometres. But this would require a super-human effort, something my body was no longer capable of.

Outside, the night air bit hard at my fingertips as I rummaged through the waist pocket of my rucksack, on the hunt for my Petzl head torch. I slipped it on and felt the excitement of my first pre-dawn yomp beginning to build. All I had to do was hit the 'ON' button.

"No. No. No. This can't be happening."

My path did not illuminate before me. Instead, I stood, looking like a right plum, shivering in the darkness. Even the streetlights seemed to shake their heads in shame at me.

Why wasn't the friggin' thing working? If the batteries were dead, I might as well have sacked off the day and gone back to bed. Finding the Camino arrows in broad daylight was often challenging. So, trying to find them in the dead of night, while they hid like master snipers amongst the street furniture, well, let's just say, I didn't fancy my chances.

"Think, damn it!"

There was no way my batteries could have been dead. I was taught, on my first ever expedition, to turn batteries backwards whenever they weren't in use. It had been drilled into me. All I needed was to wait for my brain to catch up and remember this.

"Of course."

Quickly, I fumbled with my head torch's back plate. Which was tricky when my hands were shaking like a meth junkie. Then POP! I was in.

Instantly, the darkness transformed into a ghostly, swirling mass of tumbling light. I stood transfixed by the dream-like abyss before my eyes. Its hypnotic swirls seemed to be calling, 'Go back to bed. Go back to bed.' My body softened at the very thought. What I wouldn't have done for one or two hours of solid sleep.

Thankfully, my mind pulled me back from the brink. Spurred on, no doubt, by the thud of boots from behind. The undead were starting to gather, which meant the race was on.

Up ahead, I could see the anxious looks of head torch beams. Pilgrims were already struggling to see the arrows. This was a red flag. I needed to be extra cautious. All I wanted to do was follow the herd. But I'd fallen into that trap before. The last time it happened, it cost me and Dan four kilometres and a whole world of energy we didn't have.

Today I couldn't afford to waste a yard – not one. So, as I set off, my eyes scanned every streetlight, cobble stone, drainage cover, kerb and half-built breeze block wall. The popular hiding places of Camino arrows.

As I picked my way down Calle Mayor, Calle Raimundo de Miguel and Calle Hipólito López Bernal, my eyes were drawn to the graffiti that proclaimed its love for the Camino, its pride for Castile-Leon, along with the support for an independent Basque state.

After clearing the houses, I saw the demonic eyes of articulated lorries' headlights. They looked like food-ravaged prehistoric beasts as they tore down the N-120 highway, hunting their next meal.

While I waited for a gap in the traffic to appear, I could see two small groups of pilgrims form behind me. I counted three... four... five pilgrims. Five pilgrims. Shit! They alone would take up nearly ten per cent of the beds at San Juan de Ortega.

Once across the N-120, I turned right onto a path that ran adjacent to it. To my left, I could see a dimly-lit grassy area with wooden benches – presumably a park. I could also hear the faint trickle of water from the River Tirón.

"Morning!" I exclaimed nervously, as I came face-to-face with a Camino marker, positioned precariously in the middle of the path. There was something about these silent cheerleaders that always brought a smile to my face.

My next checkpoint lay five hundred metres away and took the form of a ghostly-looking Repsol petrol station. Its pale exterior, empty forecourt and thin white roof stretched out, like a spindly finger into the night, trying to tempt drivers in.

Feck the drivers, I wanted in. I was starving. But I knew if I stopped, I'd get dropped. And bagging a bed, trumped bagging a baguette. Plus, I had snacks to spare.

Once I passed the garage, the darkness slowly returned. Up ahead, sporadic holes were being punched in the night's curtain by bobbing head torches. One of them must have belonged to the day's chief protagonist – Nervous Nigel.

Further on from the garage, I came to the mini, or mini-est, roundabout and some hedgerows. Perfect. Camouflage was exactly what I needed. Once I was among the hedgerows, I knocked back the intensity of my torch beam.

People wouldn't chase what they couldn't see. In my head, this restored my advantage and gave me the edge. It was this thought that drove me into the darkness's arms for the next few minutes.

"Buen Camino!" An unsuspecting shout from a female voice rang out from somewhere within the abyss. I tried to hone in on where I thought it was coming from, then BOOM. The night was lit up by a torch from within a picnic area. My initial thought was that it was a little early for finger sandwiches, bubbles and smoked salmon tartine. But if it was on offer, it would be rude to say no (it wasn't).

Instead, I was treated to a surgical theatre scene straight from an episode of M*A*S*H. On the operating table was a pilgrim's foot illuminated by a white light. The foot was in a horrendous state. She had a large, weeping flap of skin that peeled away from her sole.

"Need anything?" I asked reluctantly, praying she didn't need a hand.

"New feet," came her blunt response.

Sadly, I didn't have any in stock, and if I had – I would have replaced mine. While the lighter side of my mind sympathised with her plight, the darker side was silently celebrating. I'd just leaped up one place on the bed leader board. Once I'd passed her, she wouldn't be catching up to me anytime soon.

As I wasn't needed, I wished her well and continued along the hardened path until, finally, my boots struck the shin-shattering concrete of Calle Real – and Tosantos.

For those first few brief seconds, I stood and admired the ghostly line of houses with tufts of scruffy grass outside their front doors. Then out of nowhere, my whole body started to shiver and shake. Instantly, my mind transported me back to the horrors of my '94 London Marathon.

"Uh oh!"

Black ghostly patches started to appear in my vision, followed quite quickly by a blurring and narrowing of my peripheral vision. I knew my 'oh shit' moment wasn't far off. And this time, there would be no crash barrier or kind-hearted St. John's Ambulance volunteer to catch me.

Anxiously, I grabbed the first sturdy thing I saw. This just happened to be the sign welcoming me to Tosantos. Some feckin' welcome, that! I was desperate to make a move. But where? And how? My hands refused to budge, and my legs shook like an abandoned dog. Come on, Midds. Think, damn it. What's your next move?

I was spinning out by the fact that I'd been utterly blindsided. It had come out of nowhere, without any of the usual indicators of trouble:

→ No light-headedness
→ No trouble making decisions
→ No slurred speech.

"Fuck."

For the first time since '94, I was scared – really scared. I was no longer in control of my body. As if to prove this, my legs buckled and I hit the deck, which actually came as a blessed relief. At least I couldn't have fallen any further.

I knew I needed food – and fast. Not that fast was an option. In fact, life seemed to be moving in slow motion. I watched, google-eyed, as my arm glided passed my face, on its way to my stash of snacks at the top of my rucksack.

My eyes were drawn to the shiny Haribo Goldbears wrapper that flickered in the light. I picked a handful from the packet. Had the bears always been so small – and so, so squidgy?

In an effort to restore calm, I closed my eyes and tried to focus on breathing. I-n-h-a-l-e, e-x-h-a-l-e, - i-n-h-a-l-e, e-x-h-a-l-e. But it was hopeless. My attention was constantly being broken by the thud of boots and shouts of 'Buen Camino'.

"Fan-feckin'-tastic, five more beds gone. Only sixty left to go."

But there was nothing I could have done. I felt fucked. End of. What I needed was a number for 24/7 emergency Camino breakdown service. What I wouldn't have given for some roadside assistance – or a tow. But that wasn't forthcoming. It would be down to me to carry out the repairs on my withering body.

My biggest fear was whether I'd make it to San Juan de Ortega. And if not, what then? And if I did make it, what would it cost me to get there? I didn't stand a chance in the state I was in, so I resisted every physical urge to move. Instead, I cracked into my emergency rations and like a hungry hippo I scoffed the lot.

When I finally did set off, I did so gingerly. I knew by going slower, I'd be inviting every bed-hungry pilgrim to attack me, but it was the only card I had left to play. My usual attacking pace of 4.5-5km per hour was binned. From then on, I'd have to trundle along at 3km per hour – max.

"This pace is desperate stuff. Pensioners shuffle around Sainsbury's quicker than this" I muttered, ashamedly.

But if that was the difference between getting somewhere and getting nowhere, I'd take it every time. The challenge was keeping a lid on my effort and my bruised, ageing ego.

But I knew the dangers that lay ahead. If I came crashing to a halt at Villambistia or Espinosa del Camino, that would be me finished. The next day would be the last of the Camino, so there would be no way that I'd be able to make the thirty-eight kilometres from there to Burgos.

If I was foolish enough to attempt it, I knew there would only be one winner. And I could feel the Grim Reaper already rubbing his hands with glee.

At the top of the road, I spotted a water fountain. Much like after my run in with 'Barry Big Bollocks' in Logroño, I needed to shake things up. With that, I placed my shivering head under the tap in preparation for what would come next.

The water that gushed out was bitingly cold. But much like smelling salts under a weary boxer's nose, its effect brought me back round.

Suddenly, Tosantos sprung to life. I began to notice large, whitewashed stone houses, scratches of lawn outside the front doors, an old steel bench and a rose bush. The accompanying soundtrack for the day came from a chorus of swallows who had been woken by my heavy breathing and thuds.

Undeterred, I shuffled down Calle Real, a leafy lane offset by hedgerows. At the bottom I noticed a blue rectangular sign in front of an electrical pylon that directed me left. Once I turned, my cover was blown. There would be no more camouflage support from the nearby hedgerows. I was now alone, wounded and out on open ground.

Ahead, the path shimmied like a silver stream in the moonlight. With the hedgerows gone, the wind tore at me. I was forced into tortoise mode, as I pulled my shoulders to my ears and buried my hands deep into my pockets. Through the howls of the wind, I could hear the nearby news fizzing down a powerline. Off to my left, trees huddled together for comfort, in an attempt to keep warm.

For the next few minutes, I just kept my eyes down and my thoughts imprisoned. All that mattered was the next step, the next yard, the next metre. Every step was progress, no matter how slow. Every step was another one closer to my goal – and bed.

It was this thought that was buzzing through my head as I reached Villambistia. It was a little after 7 am when my eyes were drawn to the large silhouette off to my right, the Church of San Esteban.

"Two down. Only seventeen to go."

This thought was met by a wall of numbed silence. I knew on a good day; seventeen kilometres could be covered in little over four hours. But at the day's rate, it would take six brutal hours – possibly more. My thoughts were broken, as ever, by the chuckling sound of Mitch's voice inside my head.

"Come on, fat lad. Only seventeen kilometres to go."

I wished I could've seen his face again. But I knew if he was there, he'd have wasted no time in ripping into me about my skater boy look, my gammy leg. Or the fact I was the only pilgrim out there gaining weight. In return, I'd undoubtedly clap back at him about my disappointment in God, who for whatever reason, was now allowing Villa fans into heaven. I was desperate to find out how Mitch had smeagoled his way past God's bouncers.

"Morning," came a call from behind.

"For feck's sake," I replied.

Still lost in thoughts of Mitch, I turned straight into the gaze of a torch beam.

"Sorry! Sorry, sorry," came the apologetic sound of a soft, nervous female voice. She was clearly as spooked as I was.

"I'm so, so sorry," I replied. "It's just that..."

I could feel my voice begin to crack as I tried, and failed, to finish my sentence. I could feel a warm, salty tear roll down my face and motioned at the dust swirling in her torch beam. It was that that had caused my eyes to stream – honest. The next thing I felt was a warm, comforting hand across my shoulder.

"Are you okay?" She asked, concerned.

"I will... I mean... no. I'm just having a real shit day," I blubbed.

"Well, take it easy. Remember, the Camino isn't here to break you. It's here to help you," came her thoughtful response.

Those words were the mysterious woman's parting gift. When I looked up again, she'd set off down Calle la Fuenta, across the bridge and up the road. I stood alone in the darkness, gulping in air like a fish out of water.

Jesus, what had brought all this on? I knew the last few days had been rough. Made worse, no doubt, by my body's Judas-style betrayal. But was there more to it? I had felt the pressure of the Camino slowly starting to build over the week. Was it this, along with my exhausted state, that was causing my mind to short circuit?

Or was it the fact that I was still pissed off at God? As well as the realisation that I hadn't come to terms with Mitch's passing. But how could I? How was I meant to deal with his death? Culturally, talking about death was frowned upon. But why? We're all destined to be worm food. Why not accept and acknowledge it? Instead, we avoid all talk of it, leaving those left behind to walk around in numbed silence, too scared to talk – and unable to heal. It had left me feeling like a ticking time bomb, just waiting to explode. How the fuck could that be deemed healthy?

"Easy now, fatty. We've still got a job to do."

Unsurprisingly, it was the distant sound of Mitch's voice, that brought me round. He was right. I still had a job to do. And me standing around blubbing like an out of work circus clown wasn't getting it done.

So, I set off, blowing hard into my cheeks as I tried to muster some enthusiasm into my weary legs. I headed down Calle la Fuenta, passing a water fountain and a sheltered area, complete with water trough. These troughs were used by locals in days gone by to wash their smalls and pantaloons.

Further along, a Camino sign next to an eerie children's play area directed me onwards and down a rough gravel path, towards Espinosa del Camino.

I spotted a large cream building, Espinosa del Camino ALBERGUE. Eight pilgrims tipped out from it, looking fired up and ready to attack the day.

"Thiiiiinnnngs, can only get better," I sang sarcastically.

I knew this was bollocks. A theory that was being supported wholeheartedly by Big Toe 'Tone', five blisters and my ever-tightening psoas. Within metres of setting off, the racing snakes had passed me as they tore down Calle Villafranca.

"Bye then, ta-ra! Thanks for coming!" My sarcasm was in full flow.

Then suddenly, one young upstart cruised past me at high speed and close proximity, which he thought was hilarious. He wouldn't have found it as funny if this had happened ten minutes earlier, as I'd have more than likely clotheslined him or stuck my leg out. That would've learned him.

At the bottom of Calle Villafranca, I came across a monstrous farmhouse-cum-albergue. This was the final gateway for what lay beyond – nothing. The blankness of the landscape mirrored the emptiness and rawness I felt inside.

In an attempt to claw back some control over my deteriorating mental state, I tried counting steps. It was a basic technique from back in the day – used to judge distance and help focus. But I gave up within metres. My brain simply couldn't hold the thought. So, I wandered onwards, lost in a haze of anger, tiredness and frustration. But somehow this blackness helped tick off the kilometres.

I was pulled from my daze by the sound of a backfiring car exhaust. It was as I pulled back the branches from the undergrowth of the path, that I came across a large car park. Miraculously, I'd somehow made it to Villafranca Montes de Oca.

The car park was bustling with the beeps of articulated lorries, slamming doors of delivery vans and noise of the locals. The air was filled with the intoxicating and heavenly scent of petrol.

At the opposite end of the car park was the aubergine-coloured powerhouse, the Restaurante El Pajaro. This doubled up as a bar/restaurant and hotel/hostel. The plastic chairs and parasols outside were all occupied by pilgrims. It seemed as though everyone had had the same idea. Fuel up there before tackling Alto Mojapán and Alto de la Pedraja.

The effect of the air con as I entered the restaurant froze the sweat to my skin, causing me to shiver uncontrollably. I wasted no time with pleasantries. There was no buen caminos, holas or any of that bollocks. Instead, I got on with the business in hand and ordered a ham and cheese bocadillo, two Snickers bars, a can of Aquarius and a nuclear strength coffee.

While the food provided the fuel and comfort I needed, it did little to calm my whirring mind. Once outside, all I could do was look on in quiet disgust as a steady stream of pilgrims passed me by. Bed-thieving wankers, every last one of them.

"What if, just for once, you could just let things go?" I mumbled to myself.

Let things go. WTF. I had five agonising blisters, lead legs, a twisted pelvis and twelve kilometres still to go. Plus, with every passing minute, another bed-thieving wanker disappeared up the road.

"Righto, let's get this shitshow on the road," I muttered.

Fifty metres on from the restaurant, along the N-120, I spotted a water fountain. Knowing I had two big battles ahead, I topped up. Directly after the water fountain was the Church of Santiago Apostle. In front of it was a blue and yellow Camino sign, attached to a wooden stake that directed me up the cobbled Calle Hospital, passed another water fountain, two tourist information boards and the three-star Hotel San Antón Abad.

The path rose savagely as I made my way up to the stone walls of the restaurant and the adjacent albergue. At the top of Calle Hospital, the cobbles gave way to a dirt path. It would be there under the savage gaze of the sun, where the battle for my Camino would be won – or lost.

"Right, you fecker. Let's see what you're made of," I muttered.

I wasn't sure that laying down the gauntlet to the Camino was a good idea. But feck it, I'd had my arse kicked for days. Yes, I was still very much on the ropes. And yes, it wouldn't take much to put me back on my arse – again. But there was strength in my chippiness – there always was. There was no way that I wouldn't be ending the day in San Juan de Ortega – even if it killed me.

Therefore, any thoughts I had that didn't support this outcome should ship out. Otherwise, I'd have to cut them out of own head with my pink spork.

I trudged onwards, up through the forest where sharp stones, like thorns, lay in wait to pierce my boot and rile my temper. Neither worked. I was already at boiling point.

Though I was conscious of my self-imposed three-kilometre-per-hour limit, it was impossible to maintain. My mind was in full on attack mode and Big Toe 'Tone' and the lads were right with me. How long my fury would last was anyone's guess. But if it got me up the Alto Mojapán – great. If it helped me collect pilgrim scalps on the way – even better.

Up ahead, I could see two pilgrims stumbling and stalling on the savage gradient. Their scalps would do for starters. As would the three scalps beyond them. With each scalp taken, I could feel the power shift once again from them back to me. The feeling of power was intoxicating.

The higher I climbed, the more the forest threw its protective branches around me. It too felt the sun's fury, as it fired down ray after ray into the deep canopy. All in the vain hope of penetrating it and punishing me.

It finally got its chance minutes later, as the path widened, and the forest retreated. There dirt gave way to scorching hot concrete.

I could see pilgrims starting to dismount their bikes. They had all parked up and gathered alongside a stone obelisk, their heads down in silent prayer.

The obelisk was around seven foot high and was surrounded by a low, stone wall topped with a metal barrier that was wrapped with ribbons left by passing pilgrims.

The monument had been built in memory of the three hundred people who were executed by supporters of General Francisco Franco during the Civil War.

I stopped briefly to contemplate the inhumanity of war. After all, it was war and the remnants of it that had taken Mitch. What was eating me, was the fact that Mitch hadn't gone to Afghanistan to hurt people. He'd gone to help rebuild Afghanistan. His role in clearing munitions was to help ensure that future generations got the chance to grow up in safety. Where they would be free to play and prosper – I was proud of him for that.

After ten minutes of quiet contemplation, I looked up. Ahead, an arrow-straight path stretched downwards as far as my eyes could see, cutting the forest in two. Somewhere out their lay San Juan de Ortega.

"Is this day EVER going to feckin' end?"

By then I was shattered from the emotional rollercoaster of the day. But I was at least grateful for the downhill, even if it caused my stride to shorten even further, which now resembled that of a high-wire tightrope walker.

Thankfully, the downhill only lasted for ten minutes before I hit the rickety bridge over the River Peroja. From there I began the final climb of Alto de la Pedraja, a short savage climb, littered once again with hungry ankle-biting rocks.

I'd battled my way to the top in a haze of exhaustion. Until finally, the three-metre-wide path extended ten-fold and the forest retreated. I was on an open plateau under the melting gaze of the sun.

In front of me, a long line of pilgrims stretched off into the distance. While behind, I could see pilgrims gaining on me fast – they wanted their scalps back. Flustered, I reached for my guide. I needed to know how long I was expected to hold them off for.

"Six kilometres!" I shouted in disgust.

Two happy-clappy pilgrims breezed past me as my scream carried into the wind. Both looked shiny and new, hardly a bead of sweat out of them. While I, on the other hand, looked like I'd been fished out from the sea.

"You know what? Fuck this and fuck the Camino. I'm sick of it. I came here to escape the bullshit of modern life, not bathe in it. Can someone, anyone, tell me what's remotely spiritual about tipping out of bed at 5 am to spend the day scrapping against my fellow pilgrims – just to bag a bed? I'll tell you, shall I? Nothing." My rant was in full swing.

"How's this any different than my life now? Where I have to be at the New Park Road bus stop by 7:43 am on the dot if I want to stand any chance of getting on the 137 bus down Brixton Hill? It isn't! Well, that's me done." And with that, I launched my pack, then broke down.

For the next twenty minutes I was utterly inconsolable. A few pilgrims stopped to check on me, but my head was hung low in shame. What the fuck was I even doing here? What was this even achieving? Other than crushing my hardened spirit into the dirt. I could hear waves of questions coming at me. Whys, what ifs and if onlys. They'd all go unanswered, and they could all feck off. My head was in freefall, all I needed was to cry it out.

When I finally did stop crying, I simply felt empty and numb. Maybe it was time to revisit that thought from earlier, the one about letting go of things. What if I decided to be more like Ryan, Dan or Kamila? They all seemed to have had the Camino spirit nailed. They were all happy, optimistic and just content living in the now. They weren't snarling at pilgrims. They weren't getting caught up in the Camino Wacky Bed Races. Nor were they breaking down and having hissy fits.

From now on, any pilgrims I'd see, I'd wish them well, not kick the legs from under them. And if I passed one, I'd check to see if they were okay or needed anything. Rather than my current mindset, which was always trying to think of ways to slow other people down (a sly boulder slid into their packs would work a treat).

It wasn't much, but what I'd learned most from the Camino was that it was the little things that made the difference. It could be a smile, a hi, the offering of some sweets or asking if someone was okay. After all, wasn't this what the Camino was all about – love, family and being helpful? Not squabbling over seventy-two beds.

With my mind starting to calm and clear, I went and dusted off my rucksack and threw it over my shoulders. I took a giant deep breath and started off again. There was no denying that every ounce of me felt beaten to a pulp. But I'd just focus on the next step and the step beyond that. And if I got to San Juan de Ortega and all the beds had gone – that was that.

I'd just sleep outside, kip in a barn or book a taxi. I was done fighting my fellow pilgrims. Just like I was done fighting my Judas body. It wasn't its fault it had broken down. I'd put it through hell for days, all it ever asked for was love.

When San Juan de Ortega finally came into view, it was like a mirage. So much so, that I didn't quite believe it. One minute I was stumbling along a path, the next I'd passed the church and the sight of a stone albergue, where a long line of rucksacks were lined up against the door.

To my amazement it wasn't yet open. This could mean only one thing; I'd bagged a bed. I put my rucksack down in line and collapsed on the stone floor, my heart bucking in my chest. I'd made it – somehow.

I didn't move a muscle for half an hour, not for lack of trying. My body just refused to budge. It had done what I'd asked of it, and it wasn't going to do anything more.

When the albergue finally opened I got my Credencial stamped and hobbled up the beautiful wooden staircase where I was led through one room of bunkbeds and into another. Due to the fact I didn't plan to move for the foreseeable future, I took a bunk bed nearest the bathroom. This would keep any energy expenditure to an absolute minimum.

In my head I'd planned to drop my kit, strip and head to the showers. When in reality I didn't have the strength to make up my bed, take off my shorts or wash. I simply collapsed in a sweaty heap on my bed and dutifully feel asleep.

I was woken several hours later by excited chatter of fellow pilgrims. It was time for the communal pilgrim meal. While everyone else sprang into action and headed eagerly down the stairs, I sat up in bed, numb. The thought of having to move, blink or even smile seemed exhausting. Not only would I have to try and navigate conversation at the meal, when I could hardly hold a thought, I now faced the horrifying reality of how to navigate the wooden staircase, as I could barely stand.

Somehow, I'm not sure how, but I managed to get myself upright and to the topflight of the stairs. From there, I looked down at its steepness with the trepidation of a downhill skier. Shit, it looked steep. To make matters worse, I no longer trusted my ankles or legs to support me. So, what was I going to do? I did the only thing I could think of. I plonked my bum down on the top step, then thumped my bum down every other step of the staircase like a petulant five-year-old, much to the horror of the pilgrims who were lining up ready for a feed.

'The Camino isn't here to break you,' was the thought rattling round my head during the pilgrim meal. But in all honesty – it had. It had lured me in, shown me some breath-taking sights, introduced me to an extraordinary country and culture, then it had picked me up and battered me into the dirt.

I was now at the point that every cell in my body was pleading for me to stop, which left me feeling utterly vulnerable. I was alone, I was exhausted, and I was still the best part of twenty-seven kilometres away from Burgos.

But there was a part of my brain that understood that was part of the role of the Camino. Its role wasn't to make me, or anyone suffer. What point would that serve? Its role was to slowly peel me like an onion. To peel away the dead layers (and years) of bad behaviours, bad thoughts and self-limiting beliefs and to hopefully replace them with a more positive and optimistic outlook, like that of my buck-toothed, bowl-headed, quirky younger self. It felt like I was just on the cusp of something.

Z-z-z-z-z-z-z-z-z-z.

* Seventy-two beds, approximately the number of beds available at the time. More may have been added since this publication.

CHAPTER 16: SEVEN CAMINOS

12th September, San Juan de Ortega – Burgos, 27km
"SEVEN TIMES."

I stirred early, remembering last night's chat from the racing snake in the orange cape on the bunk opposite.

"This is my seventh Camino," was Tex's opening gambit for the day.

I didn't reply. I had no words. I just stared back at this man in his mid-fifties through glazed and exhausted eyes, while all around my bunk lay the shattered remains of my broken body and battered ego.

"If things go well, it'll be my quickest Camino to date – twenty-nine days." I could sense that his words were now starting to gain momentum.

"How many days do you think it'll take you?" he probed inquisitively.

I didn't reply. I really wanted to. But I genuinely feared what my answer would be, as the very thought of trying to formulate words was too exhausting. So, in the interest of pilgrim harmony, I let him continue.

"My first Camino back in the day took me thirty-six days. Imagine that? *Thirty-six* days, that is so, so slow," he said.

While I knew Tex meant no harm, and he was merely looking for a bit of late-night banter before lights out at 10 pm, he was clearly having trouble reading the room or gauging my body language. Did he not see I'd been utterly KO'd by the Camino? Did he not hear my ass thump down the thirteen steps of the wooden staircase on my way to the evening Pilgrim meal?

But more importantly, had he not seen the mournful looks that fellow pilgrims had cast in my direction? Their looks said, in no uncertain terms, that was it – GAME OVER. They'd officially cast me adrift as an ex-pilgrim, as surely there was no way I could have continued.

As I slowly descended back into sleep, my mind couldn't shake his words. Seven times.

Beep beep! Beep beep!

I was cruelly ejected from slumber at 5 am by the sound of a disgruntled watch going ape shit. Surely it wasn't time to go again. Jesus, no it couldn't be. I couldn't have had more than one hour's kip all night. What with all the twenty-one bum salutes, leg cramps, and snore shells ricocheting off the white-washed albergue walls.

All that was topped by m'laddo on the bunk above, who sounded like he'd spent the night mud wrestling an anaconda in a Peruvian swamp. How else could he have explained the violent thrashing that was going on above my head?

I looked right from my bunk, through a haze of eye bogies, drawn towards the source of the beeps. I should have known – Tex. His impressive, pearly-white, tombstone-sized teeth went a long way to explain his impressive night vision. What the feck was he doing? Packing.

Surely to God, after six Caminos, he'd learnt *how not* to be the albergue wanker? A title reserved for the most selfish of scrotes, who hadn't learned the principle of pre-packing ahead of an insane o'clock departure. It left us all cruelly exposed to what sounded like a Run-DMC scratch session as he zipped, unzipped and re-zipped his gear.

"Seven times," I mumbled, shaking my head.

Well, good luck and tatty bye. There was no way I'd be moving from my scratcher anytime soon. The place could have burned down around my ears and all I'd have been capable of doing was turning over. But Tex had inadvertently shattered the peace and kickstarted everyone's day.

I lay back in quiet anticipation, ready to enjoy one of my favourite scenes of life on Camino – the stampede.

It reminded me of the classic scene from *The Lion King,* when a young Simba falls into the gorge and into the path of rampaging wildebeest. The only difference was that the charge today would be led by the pilgrim undead, as they fought for their position at the most prominent of watering holes, the loos and showers.

With my bunk nearest the bathroom, I had reserved the best (though not necessarily the safest) seat in the house. As the seconds ticked by, I could feel the tension build. All it would take was one cough, a twitch or sudden movement and the whole place would erupt. Fantastic.

Suddenly, out of the blackness they came. Five ghostly figures with their heads down, eyes glazed over and elbows out. They glided across the chilly, tiled floor towards the door, with no sign of slowing. It had disaster written all over it.

The next thing I heard was a crunch of bone on wood as one of the undead thumped hard against the door frame, shaking the supporting wall like an earthquake tremor.

For a second the whole dorm froze. Then slowly, the injured party began to pick himself off the deck, before gathering his thoughts, towel and wash kit. He walked gingerly through the door, into the piercing white light of the bathroom. With him gone, the charged nervous atmosphere within the dorm started to settle down.

In fact, it calmed so dramatically, that I didn't notice my mind beginning to drift as my eyes grew steadily heavier. Soon I was sparked out, cradled in the safety and comfort of my scratcher – snoring wildly.

I woke up ninety minutes later, shivering into a New World. Where the hell was everyone? The once dark and musty-smelling dorm was semi-deserted and bathed in light with its main window thrust open. All that remained of Tex was the imprint of his body on his blue rubber mattress. Well, that, plus a pair of his trainers, his phone charger and a pair of socks. All victims of his early morning madness.

"What's the bloody time anyhow?" I mumbled, to no one at all.

6:30 am.

I wondered if Tex had made it to Burgos yet. After all, he'd had a ninety-minute head start. Surely that was more than enough time to *arriba arriba* his way twenty-seven kilometres:

→ Through the forest to Agés

→ Wave to our ancestors' million-year-old bones at the UNESCO Heritage site in Atapuerca

→ Bounce through Orbaneja.

All before the long, lonely, run in through the sprawling suburban jungle that was Burgos. There, he'd undoubtedly stop for tea and scones at the many cafes that lined the cathedral, before telling anyone who dared to approach him that this was gearing up to be his fastest Camino ever – twenty-nine days.

While his aim seemed to be speed before spirituality, mine was much simpler – could I stand? How tricky could that be? Well, judging from the previous night's humiliation where I was forced to descend the wooden staircase on my arse, I'd say *very tricky*.

The look of horror in the eyes of fellow pilgrims as I thumped down each step would forever be etched in my mind. I couldn't unsee them now, and I used my anger at my own demise to hoist myself up to a sitting position. That was the easy part. Then for the moment of truth. I picked up one leg and placed it on the floor, then picked up the other. I grabbed firmly on the metal frame of the bunk and heaved upwards.

I did it. I was upright. But the effort required to stand was excruciating. My whole body felt as fragile as a stack of Jenga blocks. All it would take was one flick or a gust of wind and my world would come crumbling down around my knees. What I wouldn't have given to have gone back to sleep then somehow be magically transported to the outskirts of Burgos.

Now I was up, it was time to loosen things up. Thankfully, I only had a few steps to shuffle to the showers. Once in the cubicle, I stripped and waited for the warm jets of water to wash over me.

"Aaargh! It's f-f-feckin' freezing!"

The shock of the near baltic temperature sent me crashing against the white plastic cubicle.

"Argh, come on now," I stuttered, shivering violently.

With no sign of the cold water letting up, I grabbed for the protection of the shower curtain. I pulled it taut in front of me before directing it at the shower head. The effect sent ice-cold water spraying up the walls, against the windows and into the other cubicles, much to the frustration of the few remaining pilgrim stragglers. But why were they bitching? It wasn't as if they were faring any better than me. Or were they?

While I'd been quick to sneer at Tex's lack of pre-planning. I had to tip my Stetson to the lad, as I could guarantee he hadn't started the day with a Wim Hoff ice shower.

Once I escaped the shower, I dried myself and started my prep for my big day. It would be my last on this Camino. But would it be my last, period? I couldn't say.

"Morning, lads!" I said, staring down at my dishevelled feet.

What had I done to them? Not even the blister plasters could hide the crimes I'd committed. While I patted them dry, I could feel the rising tension between the two warring factions – healthy versus unhealthy toes.

In an attempt to bolster some sort of peace process, I grabbed the zinc oxide tape from my bag. Then I set about separating each toe as if boxing opponents. Hopefully this small act of kindness would be enough to alleviate any further friction or animosity. But as ever, I'd leave riot control down to Big Toe 'Tone'.

"Hang in there, lads. Only one more schlep to Burgos. Once we get there it's going to be boots off, pack down and feet up. Then Numbnuts here is taking us all out on the lash. How's that sound?" came Tone's rallying cry.

While his speech was hardly Churchillian in tone, he did make a valid point. Every cell in my being was screaming at me to stop. And when I did, Tone and the lads would be suitably rewarded. But first, we needed to get to Burgos. I needed one last, big push – from everyone.

I slowly got dressed before checking my bed area. With my gear on, I shuffled towards the stairs. I stopped momentarily as I came to the banister.

Who'd have thought that I'd be standing there? Ready for one final dance with the Camino. I certainly didn't. Not based on the previous twelve hours.

Outside, it was blacker than Darth Vader's mood. Up the road I could see pilgrims' head torches bouncing in the moonlight, then stopping suddenly to debate. It was clear they were torn on where to go next. They certainly weren't helped with the sign offering *alternative routes*. At that time in the morning, no pilgrim wanted to think, all we wanted was to follow.

"Come on, lads. Make a decision!" I mumbled as I edged closer to them. "If in doubt, ask yourselves what Scooby and Shaggy would do?" I chuckled.

To my surprise, and going against Scooby and Shaggy logic, they opted to stick to the safety of the road (which didn't have streetlights – so hardly safer), rather than taking on the enchanted forest.

"Well, I didn't see that coming," I said, shaking my head in disgust.

With their lights and plight now fast disappearing up the road, it was time for me to strap on my head torch, pull up my big boy pants, and take on the forest alone. *Yikes.*

All I could see before me was the menacing, darkened silhouettes of thirty-foot high trees. As I edged near, I could hear the sound of shuffling on the wind. Was it my imagination, or had the trees taken five giant steps back, as if to welcome me?

Cautiously, I moved forwards. I'd taken less than twenty or thirty steps, when the shuffling started again. As I turned, I noticed that the trees had closed in behind me. There was no going back now, they'd cut off my escape.

With no daylight to ease my overactive mind, my ears were alive with the rustling sounds of every branch and live creature in the undergrowth. The forest was waking. No doubt stirred from slumber by the heavy thud of my lead legs and piercing gaze of my torch beam.

"Co-co-co," came the frustrated call of a bird on the wind, its wings flashing before my eyes.

"Did that bird just call me a forest waking wanker?" I wondered out loud.

I knocked back the intensity of my torch beam. But it was all a little too late. I knew somewhere on a leaf was a millipede making the wanker gesture at me.

As I struggled to adjust to the low light, my senses became increasingly aware of thuds just a metre or two into the ferns. The sound was subtle at first, but slowly started to build. Whatever it was, it was large.

"Well, two can play that game."

With that, I turned off my head torch, plunging myself into a world of darkness.

Righto Midds, explain your thinking. There's a large, yet unidentified, creature within mauling distance of you. Yet in your infinite wisdom, you believe that your best form of defence is blindness. How does that work?

The only way I could explain it to myself was that if I was now blind, then maybe the creature was too. With the tables turned, I stood deathly still, waiting for its next move. Whatever it was – a Yeti looking for a late-night Aldi, or an alien wandering about pissed with a bottle of Thunderbirds in hand – it was close and getting closer. I readied myself for flight and fright. Then, off to my right, the ferns began to shake violently. This was it! It was coming.

Neeeeeiiiggghhhh.

Suddenly, an ear-splitting shriek rang out through the forest, sending startled birds to the heavens. Next came a violent rustling of the ferns, before finally, out popped the head of a magnificent white horse.

"You gotta be kidding me," I said, startled.

I'd been outwitted by a horse. And not just your regular horse, a pantomime horse at that. It knew how to play 'it's behind you' to perfection.

With the ghost of the forest exorcised, my blood pressure slowly started to ease. As a show of respect, I knelt down and found a giant wodge of grass, still with morning dew on it. I tore it from the ground and offered it up as reward. With the peace offering made, I doffed my invisible cap in a show of respect and set off again.

About ten minutes after Horsegate, the forest slowly started to shuffle backwards in retreat. I'd made it. It was then that it hit me. This was it. This would be my last walk in a forest until Galicia (assuming I would make it that far).

I turned slowly to imprint the memory of the forest in my head forever. But it was too late. The trees had already closed behind me, slamming that door shut forever.

With the forest gone, the first signs of morning light started to flicker through the low-lying mist that clung, like a comfort blanket, over the rooftops of Agés. There was something magical in this scene that stopped me dead in my tracks.

Was it the cobalt-blue sky? Was it the romanticism of a hamlet lit by candlelight? Or so it seemed. Or was it the gut-wrenching reality that I was four hours away from being ripped from this place of sanctuary and thrust back into the mayhem of mainstream society?

I wondered if this was what had brought Tex back to the Camino so many times. Maybe he craved the silence between heartbeats? Maybe he lived for the moments of profound beauty? Or maybe he had a pact with the Camino that each trip would reveal more of its secrets to him?

The one thing I couldn't get my head around was the emotional rollercoaster that was the Camino. One minute it was kicking dirt in my face and driving my spirit into the floor. The next, it offered up views over the Pyrenees or Alto del Perdón that were so breath-taking, it shamed me to silence and brought me to tears. It left me with this constant craving of more and anticipation for its next move. How did it do that?

As I walked into Agés, along Calle San Juan de Ortega, my thought was broken by the sight of four happy, but weary, pilgrims crashed out on green plastic chairs outside a albergue.

But wait a minute. Where had this lot come from? I hadn't seen any torch lights ahead of me. Not since the group who'd bottled the enchanted forest.

"Chick-chick-chicken," I muttered, enthusiastically.

Suddenly, I felt the childish urge to dump my pack and start strutting around, flapping my arms like a chicken. One look into their eyes told me it was true. While my eyes were still wild from my run-in with the pantomime horse, theirs appeared dull and lifeless, as if the road had sucked the life out of them.

Agés, as a hamlet, reminded me a bit of Ludlow with its rickety, oak-beamed houses, daubed in cream and terracotta. Outside, their hanging baskets collected smiles from passers-by. There was a charm and stillness to this place that I instantly fell for.

As I wandered through, I couldn't help but be drawn to a sign for Agés in brittle, twig-like letters. Underneath it, written on a wooden plaque in white, capital letters was SANTIAGO – 518km.

"Five hundred and eighteen kilometres, shit the bed," I muttered in disbelief.

The distance seemed laughable. Why would anyone in their right mind walk that? An even bigger mystery to me was how the Camino idea had caught on in the first place. Imagine being the priest trying to sell this to his congregation. How would he have gone about it?

"I bring before you, my flock, a new way to appease your life of sin and debauchery. It's called the Camino. A Camino is in essence – a spiritual pilgrimage. One which you must walk alone, unless of course you're filthy rich. In which case – send a minion.

"It is to be walked without help from servants, hookers or horses (or horses who are hookers). For many it will start in the foothills of the Pyrenees and end at the Cathedral in Santi-" (still wasn't saying its full name – not yet).

"Along the way you will face fierce heat, horse bandits, biting winds, mental anguish, hunger, sleep deprivation and physical hardship. Righto! Who fancies a bit of that then?"

Back in reality, I had reached the edges of Agés. From there, the world just seemed to fall away. Replaced by a single lane, soul-sucking stretch of road into oblivion.

In the distance I could make out the odd blob of colour, undoubtedly pilgrims. Other than that, all I could see were barren fields and a flat freshly laid road, offset against a watercolour painted, opaque sky. All was good in the world and better still, all was quiet.

"Buen Camino, mate," came the silence-shattering sound from behind me.

"Oh, fuck!" I sighed.

I didn't even have to turn to know who was. It was Mr. Yorkshire and his three stooges. I was, of course, right. Dan and I had run into this lot during our impromptu reunion at a small bar in Santo Domingo de la Calzada.

At the time, Mr. Yorkshire and crew were sitting, half-cut, on a table near us. They'd been at the bar a few hours and were getting more and more boisterous, much to the annoyance of the local old boys who'd obviously snuck out of their homes in the hope of grabbing a cheeky beer and some peace and quiet.

My lasting memory was leaving the bar three hours later, halfway through one of Mr. Yorkshire's murderous renditions, in that case 'Paint it Black' by the Stones. As I left my eyes apologised to the old boys, who sat there picking their noses and tutting in disgust (oh, the irony). I prayed then that I'd never have the misfortune of bumping into them again. Yet there they were.

In fairness to Mr. Yorkshire, a lot had occurred since our first meeting. Most notably, to both our feet. I couldn't help but wince as I looked down at his Percy Pig coloured legs and his two heavily bandaged and swollen ankles that were lashed with electrical tape into a pair of open toed Teva sandals.

"*Jesus*. You look like Mr. Bump," I said, alarmed.

"Aye, lad. Me feet are jiggered."

"Ours too," added the three stooges.

I must admit I was a little bit taken aback by these fellas. What were they doing? Just one look at their hobbling, wincing and leaning on makeshift walking sticks told me they were fecked. Why were they putting themselves through it? If that was the state of them on day twelve, how ruined would their bodies be by the time they reached the finish? Providing they didn't spontaneously combust in the meantime. And all this effort for what? A Compostela – a certificate.

I knew, having pre-judged Mr. Yorkshire previously, that I needed to wipe the slate clean (at least in my mind). So, I reached into my pack and pulled out my favourites – Wine Gums. I'd carried them since Saint-Jean-Pied-de-Port, and they were going to be my celebration treat upon reaching Burgos. But sod it! Everyone needs a lift once in a while. And nothing quite hits the spot like Wine Gums, or Haribo Goldbears.

Luckily for me, my silent apology was accepted with open palms. With their fists now full, Mr. Yorkshire and his three stooges smiled then hobbled on ahead. Not long after, I came across a three-metre high, cream-coloured banner on the side of the road.

On it, was a blue ink illustration of a young man who was clearly an early adopter, and possibly the originator, of the modern-day mullet hairstyle. Above him, in large blue letters was the word Atapuerca.

Atapuerca had been given a UNESCO World Heritage status a few years before, after explorers had discovered remains of our ancestors dating back over a million years ago. While impressive, I couldn't help but wonder what the hell our ancestors had been doing out there, in the arse-end of nowhere?

According to Tex, there was an exhibition a kilometre off the Camino track that explained it all.

"It's well worth a visit," he'd said.

But a kilometre there and a kilometre back equalled two kilometres. Those two kilometres could be the difference between me arriving in Burgos on my feet versus me arriving in a wooden box – no thanks.

"If you're pushed for time. There's always next time?" had been Tex's next shot.

"Next time. Good luck with that," I uttered defiantly.

For me, it was a one-time trip. There would be no Camino re-runs. No best of sevens. No Caminos for the fastest time, or silliest walks. Once I got to Burgos, it would be tools down and trotters up. Then I was going to seek comfort in several pints of Guinness. For which I hoped Mitch would, at least in spirit, join me.

Towards the bottom of Calle Camino de Santiago, the only road in and out of Atapuerca, I noticed a triangle of gravel to the left of the road. Sitting on it beside a tree was a small, rectangular Camino sign that directed me left, onto a path that passed some recently restored farmhouses.

"This is it, Mitch. One last climb up the Cruz de Matagrande."

Though not technically correct, it did make me chuckle. But first, I needed to conquer the three-thousand-foot beast. It was there for the first time that I thought of the magic moment. The moment when I reached Burgos. The moment I peeled my sweat-stained pack off my back for the last time, found a chair beside the cathedral – and dissolved into it.

But I was torn. That moment would also represent the end of my Camino. Yes, my body was broken and pleading with me to stop. But my spirit, my true spirit, felt a deep and raw emptiness from the pit of my stomach. It wasn't ready to go back. It wasn't ready to leave the sanctuary of this sacred space. There was still so much to see and unlearn from the Camino.

I wasn't ready to leave behind my Camino family of Dan, Hwan, Ryan, Joyous Joy. Or all the faces I'd seen, met and said 'Buen Camino' to along the way.

"Get a grip lad, and start sparking," came the shout from Tone.

He was right. The finish was within sniffing distance. But I knew from my expedition days, that most injuries occurred within sight of home when people switched off, relaxed, and went into party mode.

So, I quickly parked all other thoughts and focused on the job at hand. The bottom half of the climb was along a sun-baked path that had been forged as much by footsteps as by rainwater gullies. The higher I climbed, the rougher the ground became, with shale becoming fist-size stones. Each step was uncertain, unplanned and upon uneven ground which caused my feet to remain tense and cramp.

"Feckin' stones. Will ya just feck off!" I screamed.

It was only down as a short and sharp two-kilometre climb. But my feet felt every bloody stone of it. Onwards and upwards I went, with my heart thumping like a jackhammer. I could feel Mitch's invisible hand on my back, helping to lighten the load.

Soon I was skirting beside a barbed wire fence that lined a military facility (my guess was that it was some sort of radar base). It was as I pulled back the branches from a tree that I saw it.

A ten-foot high, twig-like cross sitting on a mound of stones and framed by a line of wispy white clouds. As I wandered towards it, my stomach started to churn wildly. I so wanted to cry out: Mitch, I've made it, Bear I've made it, G I've made it. *Spirit – I've made it.*

What came out instead were tears. Floods and floods of tears. I was inconsolable and I couldn't figure out why. Was it relief, sadness, exhaustion, happiness or pride? But as I wandered on, my eyes were drawn to huge concentric circles of stones to my right. Just after I saw a large rusty iron sign that translated to:

'Since the pilgrim dominated the mountains of Navarre in Burgete and saw the extensive fields of Spain, you have not enjoyed a more beautiful view than this.'

I looked out across the wide-open, low-lying patchwork plains. I could see the path zigzagging before me, cutting into the Earth. To my right, I could see the glistening white pillars of what looked like a castle. On second viewing, it was a factory – more's the pity.

In the distance, almost lost in the low-lying fog, was a large settlement that must have been Burgos. And beyond Burgos, was the place that I'd heard whisperings of over the last few days. It was a place spoken of with fear and dread – the Meseta.

But the Meseta would have to wait. The descent of the Cruz de Matagrande was shin-aching and calf-busting. It certainly was on a par with the descent into Roncesvalles.

Luckily, within twenty-five minutes, things started to settle down. I couldn't recall ever being so happy to see tarmac as I was that day. Such was the wealth of emotions that flooded through my mind that I couldn't recall Villaval, and only remembered Cardenuela Riopico for the cafe in the albergue.

As soon as I swung the doors open, a wall of noise hit me. Yet instead of running from it, like I would have done in Brixton, I embraced it. Inside, there was a mass celebration going on, as pilgrims separated by the road were reunited. Everyone was hugging, kissing, laughing wildly and checking each other like chimpanzee families.

Once I'd got my coffee I went and joined a small group of pilgrims at the far table nearest the window. I'd run into a few of them before, and recalled how they too were finishing in Burgos.

"So, we've done it!" I said, hardly able to contain myself.

All around me I could see their huge relief and happiness. Though we were all strangers, we'd all been broken and remade by the road. I could feel a deep-seated sense of peace and contentment amongst my adopted Camino family. I also felt a sense of connectedness to others that I hadn't felt, but had yearned for, for years.

For the next hour we all sat laughing, joking and swapping stories. I congratulated those who, like me, were finishing in Burgos. I also wished 'Buen Camino' to those going onto Santia- (I still daren't utter it).

Gone forever were the ankle-breaking paths of the Navarre. All that was left was a simple run in towards Orbaneja, passed the airfield. Followed by a mind-numbing walk through the suburban jungle to Burgos.

But what then?

That was the thought that was circling as I headed off. Each step represented one nearer the gallows. The gallows being real life. It was ridiculous. For days I'd been praying and visualising the moment when I'd finally come to a stop. And now that this moment was fast approaching, I wasn't sure I was ready to go back. How will my body and mind react to the noise, speed, mayhem and pollution of mainstream society? What if I couldn't cope?

By the time I'd reached the airfield fence, I'd decided. I didn't want to go back. I really didn't. I didn't want to return to life among the lemmings. Nor did I want to go back to a life controlled by pings, beeps or digital distractions. Not ever. Not after all this. I'd finally found a part of me, the explorer, that had been missing since the DofE expedition days.

Beep beep. Beep beep.

Suddenly, a phone went off behind me. I could feel my anxiety levels starting to rise instantly. But I was happy knowing at least that it wasn't mine. While I'm sure they'd be forever grateful for who had texted. I was happy to keep my phone where it belonged, in my pocket and sleeping soundly.

Once past the airfield, the noise of modern life started to ramp up. I was in the industrial wasteland of car showrooms, outlet stores and factories.

Somewhere in and amongst it all, I spotted two fellow pilgrims. They too seemed to be in a state of shock. Saddened by a world that had grown too loud, too fast – too quickly. In an effort to preserve our sanity, we (me, Kim and Lynn) huddled together and walked as one.

The chatter was nervy at first, as all of us were fighting our demons. Driven mostly by our anxiety about restarting our lives. But as we passed the green fence that protected the Bridgestone tyre factory, our minds turned to what we had seen, felt, learned and experienced. The effect of which calmed my mind as I re-ran bumping into Dan, Ryan, beers on the balcony, staring on in awe at the sunset, smiles from strangers, grape punnets from farmers and warm hugs from stray dogs.

Then, out of nowhere, Kim pointed to a large brown and white sign containing a silhouetted cityscape illustration. Below it, in large, white capital letters was the word – BURGOS.

"We made it, Mitch. We did it."

Yet somehow, it didn't feel real. I just stopped by the roadside in shock as cars, buses and people whizzed by. Was this it? Were we done?

To commemorate the occasion, I asked Lynn to take a picture of me by the blue Burgos clock by the roadside that read – 12:27 pm.

We slowly made our way into town in silence. I had no words; I was in shock. Shock that I'd made it. But also, in shock as I'd now been turfed from the pilgrim path and put back among the noise and mayhem of the great unwashed. Okay, what would I do now? The hallowed silence that followed this question hung in the air indefinitely.

I genuinely didn't know what to do for the best, but with some bands striking up on a nearby street and traffic in full flow, I opted to seek the sanctuary of my hotel room. I was greeted by the warmest of smiles from the receptionist and a 'Buen Camino.'

It had been a Camino of many faces. Yet overall, it had been a good one. I headed up to my room. Finally! I slowly peeled off my rucksack and planted it on a nearby chair. The sense of lightness and relief was overwhelming.

While it felt good to be free of my pack, I knew within a day that I'd miss the sense of the protection it provided. It had protected me from life's winds and so much more. But that was as far as I got thought-wise, before I collapsed and fell into a deep sleep.

I woke up confused three hours later. Where was I? Who was I? How did I get there? It took a few minutes for me to come back down to earth.

"Righto lads, time to keep that promise."

With that, I headed to the shower praying that it had hot water. I grabbed the shower curtain and gingerly turned the tap. YES! It was warm. The relief I felt as the soothing water poured over me was instant.

I knew it would take more than one shower to remove all the engrained layers of pilgrim pong that had built up over my body. But one would definitely take the edge off it all. Plus, it was Guinness time.

I stepped out into the street a freer and lighter man. But a man that was now suddenly lost. What would I do now that I didn't have to follow my beloved yellow arrows? And how would any other pilgrims distinguish me from anyone else – except by smell?

I hobbled my way down towards the Cathedral, finally having traded in walking boots for my trainers. The effect was heavenly, I was hobbling on air. I spotted a bar directly opposite the Cathedral table in the sunshine and ordered a Guinness.

"Cheers, Mitch! Go easy on God, bud. She's doing the best she can."

I took a giant swig. It felt velvety and light and so, so good. I could feel a small part of my brain starting to bubble with questions about what happens next. The reality of which I didn't know, nor did I care. I was still too tired, too numb and too weary to answer. And what was the rush for an answer anyway – just chill.

For two hours I sat motionless, shell-shocked. My eyes stared into the abyss and for reasons unknown to me I simply just couldn't stop smiling.

There was undoubtedly something special, no, sacred, about the Camino space. In itself it was so many things: a life affirmer, an emotional reset, solace to contemplate life, a space to grieve, a space to reconnect with Mother Nature or in my case – Spirit. On a good day it opened me up to the simplicity and beauty of life. While on the bad days it had viciously attacked my character, insecurities, place in this world and the person I had become.

Was this the reason why Tex kept coming back? Was this place his sacred space – his spiritual home? A place where he would come to check in on himself. A place where his thoughts and dreams were set free to fly, like Spirit, on high.

I still remember Tex's parting shot that morning as he headed for the door.

"You'll come back; I know it. I can see it in your eyes. You need this place as much as I do."

I feared Tex might well have been right.

Printed in Dunstable, United Kingdom